Love in Contemporary Cinema

This book looks at social representations of romantic love as portrayed in films and interpreted by their audiences, using cinema as a means for analysing the state of romantic love today, and the touchpoints and disconnects between its representation on screen and the lived experiences of film audiences.

Through a media sociology lens, the book draws on analysis of five contemporary romantic films and the meanings brought to and made from them by socially and economically diverse audiences. Employing both textual analysis and primary interviews, the book contests overly pessimistic perspectives on modern intimacy while acknowledging and exploring some of the challenges, woes and changes that romantic love is experiencing in late capitalism. Concerns and debates over monogamy, the teleology romantic love and the division of labour in relationships percolate in this book's examination of how audiences' responses to these films reflect their attitudes and expectations regarding romantic love.

This book will have great resonance for scholars and students of not just film studies and media studies, but also audience studies, media sociology, philosophy, gender and sexuality.

Benjamín de la Pava Vélez is a sociologist with a PhD in Media and Communication from the London School of Economics with a keen interest in the sociology of emotions, mediatisation, representations and critical theory.

Routledge Advances in Film Studies

Re-reading the Monstrous-Feminine
Edited by Nicholas Chare, Jeanette Hoorn and Audrey Yue

Ethics of Cinematic Experience
Screens of Alterity
Orna Raviv

Why We Remake
The Politics, Economics and Emotions of Remaking
Lauren Rosewarne

Hollywood Remembrance and American War
Edited by Andrew Rayment and Paul Nadasdy

Film Noir and Los Angeles
Urban history and the Dark Imaginary
Sean W.Maher

Australian Genre Film
Edited by Kelly McWilliam and Mark David Ryan

Flashbacks in Film
A Cognitive and Multimodal Analysis
Adriana Gordejuela

Trans New Wave Cinema
Akkadia Ford

Love in Contemporary Cinema
Audiences and Representations of Romance
Benjamín de la Pava Vélez

Love in Contemporary Cinema

Audiences and Representations of Romance

Benjamín de la Pava Vélez

First published 2022
by Routledge
2 Park Square, Milton Park, Abingdon, Oxon OX14 4RN

and by Routledge
605 Third Avenue, New York, NY 10158

Routledge is an imprint of the Taylor & Francis Group, an informa business

© 2022 Benjamín de la Pava Vélez

The right of Benjamín de la Pava Vélez to be identified as author of this work has been asserted by him in accordance with sections 77 and 78 of the Copyright, Designs and Patents Act 1988.

All rights reserved. No part of this book may be reprinted or reproduced or utilised in any form or by any electronic, mechanical, or other means, now known or hereafter invented, including photocopying and recording, or in any information storage or retrieval system, without permission in writing from the publishers.

Trademark notice: Product or corporate names may be trademarks or registered trademarks, and are used only for identification and explanation without intent to infringe.

British Library Cataloguing in Publication Data
A catalogue record for this book is available from the British Library

Library of Congress Cataloging-in-Publication Data
A catalog record has been requested for this book

ISBN: 978-0-367-75852-3 (hbk)
ISBN: 978-0-367-75853-0 (pbk)
ISBN: 978-1-003-16428-9 (ebk)

DOI: 10.4324/9781003164289

Typeset in Bembo
by Taylor & Francis Books

Contents

Acknowledgements viii

Introduction 1

   Paddling at the edges of the philosophy of love 2
   The process 4
   Analytical premises 6
   Gender, class and films 7
   Romantic love in film and audiences 7
   Identity and film audiences 8

1   Celluloid love: Romance, ideology and self-commodification 16

   Psychoanalytic theory and eros 18
      Eros and Plato 19
      Narcissism, identification and difference 22
   Feminist and queer theories on love 25
   Historical and sociological approaches to love 30
      Denis de Rougemont and the foundational myth of romantic love 30
      Intimacy in contemporary sociological approaches to love 32
      Self-commoditised love 34
   Romantic identity 35
      Projective identification 36
   Ideology 37
      Gramsci and counter-hegemony 39
      Liminality and ideology 40
   Conclusion 44

vi Contents

2 Audience research, audiences of romance   53

The incorporation/resistance paradigm and the ethnographic turn 57
From the women's films and melodrama to the bromance 59
Romantic audiences 64
    New orientations in audience research 68
    New (studies of) romance 69
    Today's audiences 72
Conclusion 73

3 Love and technology: Control, affordances and prejudice   81

Introduction 81
Commodified love, commodified subject 83
    Intimate subject 87
Romantic affordances 90
641 91
    Numbers and female purity 96
Conclusion 99

4 A class apart: Love, expectation, and the middle-class construction of self   104

Introduction 104
Production and characteristics of Blue Valentine *and* Once *105*
Of realism and 'not-meant-to-work' romances 106
On characters of a romance and discourses of romance 109
Platonic love in the era of globalisation 114
A studio for love 118
A motel or the classed rules of the game 120

5 Of happy endings and new men   127

Introduction 127
'How many times can you fall in love before you can't anymore?' 129
And then it ends 130
Beyond the happily ever after 136
    Anxiety and masculinity 140

6 Conclusion   150

Introduction 150
Affordances, expectations and commodified reality 153
    Commoditisation of love and self 154

Classed love 155
Teleology of romance? 156
Masculinities 157
Achievements and ways forward 158

Index 162

Acknowledgements

It is only fitting that in a book dealing with love, I recognise the love of my family who've supported me through it all. Pilar, your undying belief in me is what's got me to where I am today. Alonso, I can't wait to race you. Hilda, your emails have always put a grin on my face. Nubia, you spoil me to no end.

I love you Valentina. Your warmth, kindness, patience, empathy, embraces and brown, gleaming, tender eyes illuminate my life every day. I believe in us. Thank you, Doda!

Shakuntala Banaji: I've yet to meet a more inspiring human being. Your courage, passion, empathy, support, feedback and care have helped this project and me more than I can ever repay you for.

Camilo, Camilo and Manuel, my brothers from another mother.

Throughout this journey, I've met a few people who I cherish dearly: César, Daniel, Fabien, Felix, Nauris, Rafal, Yanning, Valeriy and Xiaoxi. The jokes, the booze, the hugs, the talks, the rants, the tears, the laughter, the films, the walks, the music, the games. The love.

Thank you for the academic and professional support and opportunities: Myria Georgiou, Sonia Livingstone, Leslie Haddon, James Deeley, Cath Bennett, Nicole Garnier, Michael Etheridge, Mary Morgan, Jane Hindle and Paul Sullivan.

To those who collaborated with me, to those who opened their doors to a guy who wanted to screen some films and talk to people, thank you.

My former lovers, thank you as well.

Introduction

In 2006, Colombia joined the nation-branding bandwagon with the motto: 'Colombia is passion.'[1] The logo was a white heart on a red background. This exemplified a private sector effort to promote the 'hard-working' nature of Colombians and Colombian private companies in order to boost exports. While marketing experts aimed to highlight what we call '*berraquera*', which can be roughly understood as an entrepreneurial attitude to overcome unfavourable odds and situations, they forgot the sociopolitical and cultural aspects of what Colombian passion is: a country with the dubious record of the longest-lasting civil conflict in the world;[2] a country, that before that conflict began, lived through one of its bloodiest times, aptly called '*La Violencia*';[3] a country where gender violence is rife;[4] a country that lived through the bloody times of Pablo Escobar; a country where the president at that time and its military killed over 3,000 innocent farmers, students and union leaders, and dubbed them as guerrilla members.[5] Many of us in the academic community were beyond sickened. Thinking back on these events, it is clear that my formation and sensibility as an anthropologist in Colombia played a crucial role in developing an interest in this 'passion' that the branding spoke of. This is in great part because a large body of Colombian anthropology deals with the many facets of the conflict, including one which, no matter the time, is hard to stomach: massacres.[6] In the 'anthropology of conflict', with an emphasis on massacres, we learned that the perpetrator tends to de-humanise his/her victim. Further, when massacres are such a common occurrence and an effective way to terrorise the population (adding the centralist governmental ineptitude to do anything about them), the perpetrators, at some point, learn to enjoy this (Guzmán, Fals Borda & Umaña, 2005; Suárez, 2008; Uribe, 1990, 2004; Uribe & Vásquez, 1995). Some become passionate about it.

Against this national historical background, I also experienced – and continue to experience – a deep personal struggle with regards to forms of masculinity and my own romantic life. I once had a girlfriend who enjoyed dancing. 'Me vas a extrañar' by the Binomio de Oro[7] plays during a party at a friend of ours. The song's theme? A man has had an affair with another woman and impregnated her. Fearing God's wrath, he wants to have the baby. The catch? Most of the song deals with how the first woman will *definitely* miss the guy if she decides to leave him; affair, baby, other woman and all.[8] I – uncomfortable with the patriarchal discourses embedded –

DOI: 10.4324/9781003164289-1

refuse to dance or even sing along to this song. My girlfriend, however, has no problem doing both. Born to a generation of parents and into a culture that extolled the roles of 'women-as-carers', as belonging to the kitchen and emotional, and 'fathers-as-providers' who do not cry,[9] in a very *machista* country, how exactly should a man that does not wish to love in the same manner as his forefathers, biological and putative, love? How should he 'be' inside a relationship in a way that will foster love, in a nation that seems addicted to violent conflict?[10]

As a cinephile, I became increasingly intrigued by films' romantic plots and subplots. Fuelled first by discussions with close friends on my favourite films, and then reading Roland Barthes' *A Lover's Discourse* (1990), Jacques Derrida's *Politics of Friendship* (1997) and Emmanuel Levinas' *Totality and Infinity* (1969), I became obsessed – or if you prefer the irony – *passionate* about romantic love, intimacy, relationships and the beloved/other. Perhaps in future, I will delve further into Storgic love. In any case, it is fair to say that, at the time when the idea for this book was conceived, I was as in love with the idea of *what it means to be in love* as I was with a particular someone: my then girlfriend. This is how I came to write a book about romantic love in cinema and audiences' responses to it.

Paddling at the edges of the philosophy of love

In the West, there are three main ways in which romantic love in film has been studied. First, as an ideological construct that serves to reify and reinforce capitalist consumer society, commoditisation and alienation, patriarchal sociocultural values and mandates, nationalistic values, naturalisation of colonial history and colonialism and the maintenance of the status quo (Illouz, 1997; McKee, 2009; Sharot, 2010; Shary, 2011; Smith Jr., 2009). Second, as a satire, a critique of bourgeois values and capitalist culture, as ideological critique; particularly focused on the works of Douglas Sirk and Woody Allen (Gledhill, 1987; Wartenberg, 1999). The third route has taken a formal and/or historical approach, detailing the technical, aesthetic and narrative devices of melodrama and women's films and how these have changed depending on broader social and cultural historical processes (Elsaesser, 1987; Nowell-Smith, 1987; Vincendeau, 1989).

The works within these three proposed divisions have focused primarily on the cultural product itself and not on the production conditions or the reception of texts. There was a general disregard for the audiences' romantic experiences and their engagements with romantic films coming from film studies, philosophy and psychoanalytic approaches. This shortfall began to be addressed by researchers of international cinema and literary traditions in the 1980s and beyond, and as part of the British cultural studies tradition (Ang, 1985; Banaji, 2002, 2006; Iglesias Prieto, 2004; Livingstone, 1989; Radway, 1984). In the last couple of years, however, rather than *talking* to audiences about romantic films, audience research on romantic films has become increasingly circumscribed to analysing online comments from platforms like IMDb or returned 'back' to textual approaches (Alberti, 2013; Deleyto, 2003; Gibson & Wolske, 2011; Kalviknes Bore, 2011; Modleski, 2014). It would seem that there is a belief that, theoretically, nothing more useful can be ascertained via audience discussion. However, at least in the context of London, at a time when traditional British masculinity has been argued to be in crisis, when buying a house is almost impossible for young couples,[11] with the proliferation of zero-hour contracts and the casualisation of much young labour,[12] with technology through dating apps becoming increasingly important for how a certain sector of the population meets their romantic partners,[13] what, if anything, has changed in both the representations of romantic love and the audiences who interpret them? In other words, in the current romantic panorama,[14] with its possibilities, its constraints and its challenges, this book explores potential shifts as well as some continuities both on- and off-screen.

This book focuses on film for several reasons: First, the argument that films act as a primary vehicle for carrying, producing and experiencing the cultural symbols and practices of romantic love, partly because cinema grants love and romance an audiovisual life and narrative reach that it lacked when depicted in painting, print, theatre or music (Dowd & Pallotta, 2000; Evans & Deleyto, 1998; Illouz, 1997; Shary, 2011; Shumway, 2003). Arguably, TV provides this as well, but it does so by spreading out the romantic narrative over several episodes, seasons even. In contrast, the film formats permit the condensed in-depth exploration of specific romantic themes that do not ask of the audience previous knowledge of the characters or their relationship. Further, some of these themes, like sex, polyamory and same-sex relationships have had marginal to no exploration in *popular* TV shows.[15] Hence, for my research, by focusing on film there's a wider and richer pool of romantic narratives and audiences to choose from.

Further, David Shumway (2003) argues that romantic films speak not only of romantic love on screen, but are also a commentary on romantic practices and ideals in society. He argues that films do more than just reflect the changing ideals and practices of romantic love in the West, they also contribute to shaping them. This book takes a similar starting point as Shumway's but is crucially different. Whereas Shumway assumes that a purely textual approach to romantic films is sufficient for disentangling all aspects of their purpose, meaning and resonance, I argue that it is necessary to also analyse audiences and their different relationships to romantic films because it is in the interaction between audiences and texts, *and beyond* as Nakassis (2016) argues, that it is possible to understand the shifting patterns of emphasis in meaning-making and the ways in which individuals, groups, contexts and circumstances play a role in filmic meaning.

This book is also interested in interrogating claims made about intimacy, romantic love and relationships. The main historical shifts identified, and the logics behind these changes, are: intimacy's growing importance, the increased focus on the 'self' before the 'us', greater periods of sensual and sexual exploration, a shift from the social to the individual promise of happiness, and romantic love's intertwinement with consumerism and capitalism. These are the elements that this book seeks to support, nuance, critique and elaborate on based on the fieldwork and in the context of London (Bauman, 2003, 2007; Beck & Beck-Gernsheim, 1995; Giddens, 1992; Illouz, 1997, 2007; Sennett, 1996). The book also contributes to debates on the processes, shifts and continuities of representations of romantic love. Thus, the films which form the backbone of this account loosely adhere to the idea of the 'event' film as proposed by Thomas Austin (2002). That is, the films were highly successful economically, critically and/or popularly, bringing narrative innovations to their genre, and some have endured past their screening time.

The process

When choosing the films, I set several criteria, including box office, critical acclaim, English as the main language of the film and date released. I also prioritised choosing at least three films that clearly dealt in the themes of class, gender and race. Finally, I decided to focus on the heterosexual romance as I was aware that LGBTQ romances would not attract the same ordinary cross-section of the population of East London that I hoped, and to an extent managed to, attract (cf. Javaid, 2019). Thus, via an extensive process of accretion and elimination of films and narrative elements, I purposefully chose the first three films that I used for fieldwork: *Once, Blue Valentine* and *(500) Days of Summer*. This was due, in part, to the themes explored in the films: contingency and fragility of relationships in *Blue Valentine* and *(500) Days of Summer*, female agency and masculinity in *(500) Days of Summer* and platonic, impossible love in *Once*. The themes and topics these films deal with are those mentioned before. I chose these films not only because they were economically and critically successful, but also because they received wider cultural interest. During the group discussions of these three films the topics of technology and gender roles were overwhelmingly prominent in the general discussions about romantic love, intimacy and relationships that usually followed from the one focused on the film. I decided to include *Don Jon* (Gordon-Levitt, 2013), and *Her* (Jonze, 2013) in my sample of films to further sharpen the data I was gathering on these two topics. I chose these two films as they had been released months prior to the beginning of my fieldwork and I considered that they would provide a gateway to rich discussions about not just technology and gender roles, but also about intimacy, class and masculinity.

In line with what I have argued for in the previous pages, I complemented the textual analysis of the films with both group and individual interviews of audiences. The interviews were carried in London but the respondents were not drawn exclusively from England. In London, I decided to recruit participants through the help of Hackney Council and its many community centres (like the Afro-Caribbean Women's Development Centre, the African and Caribbean Consultative Forum, Asian Women's Forum, Over 55s Focus Group and DayMer Turkish and Kurdish community centre), off-licence owners and snowballing of early participants. With the help of the C.L.R James Library in Dalston, Hackney, I secured at least a permanent venue to screen films. However, plenty of times I used venues of the community centres to screen the films.

I screened the aforementioned films a total of 36 times to groups of three to six people, most of whom had not seen the films before. This followed the logic of creating compatible discussion groups, easing the need for participants to explain themselves to each other and focus on the questions and subjects posed by the moderator (Montell, 1999; Morgan, 1997, 1998). I did this in community centres or in the library, depending on the times and availability of those interested. Through flyers, chain e-mailing, snowballing and help from merchants of the area, I managed to diversify the socioeconomic, racial and age groups of the participants as much as possible; this in view of the fact that these films' intended audiences are relatively young, white, low-middle to middle-class women (Bauman, 2003; Sharot, 2010; Shary, 2011). Further, because the advertised topic skewed the sample towards female participants, only 30 per cent of all unique participants (25/87 total) were male. Of the participating men, most of them came as partners of their significant other. I did semi-structured group interviews first, following up with individual interviews with some of the participants. A group interview is, in much of the literature on qualitative methods, usually referred and/or conflated with a focus group interview (Alasuutari et al., 2008; Barbour, 2007; Deacon et al., 2007; Flick, 2014; Fontana & Frey, 2008; Holstein & Gubrium, 1995; Kitzinger, 1995; Krueger, 1998; Kvale, 1996; Marková, 2007; Millward, 2012; Morgan, 1997; Silverman, 2013, 2014; Wilkinson, 1999). Suffice to say, those who do make a difference, argue the focus groups are more structured both in terms of questions and type of participants; as well as having either a far more authoritative moderator or an almost completely 'invisible' one, both of which were far removed from my interests. The interview excerpts found in this book come from this extensive fieldwork and are the basis, jointly with the films, of the thematic and discursive analysis of romantic love, film and its audiences herein presented.

An initial group interview provided several limitations and advantages. On the one hand, a group setting can suppress the 'voice' of dissenting minorities and fall into an interaction led by a particular unchallenged perspective (Gibbs, 1997; Krueger, 1994, 1998; Morgan, 1996). Further, it can somewhat inhibit more intimate topics for discussion, like sexuality and polyamory, depending on the overall make-up of the group being interviewed. Yet, as Kathryn Roulston (2008) suggests, this type of conversational interview has the potential of having participants sharing things they normally wouldn't in a more structured interview. However, she also points out that there's always a risk of manipulation of what and how something is shared by the participants. At the same time, it is an opportunity to understand how concepts, themes and opinions are socially negotiated and constructed and articulated individually and through peer interaction (Millward, 2012; Silverman, 2014). Further, as Madriz and others suggest, a feminist perspective on focus groups and/or group interviews can be beneficial to allow women to empower themselves and bond (Hyams, 2004; Montell, 1999; Morin, 2005; Pini, 2002; Wahab, 2003; Wilkinson, 1998). While many feminists advocate same-gender focus group interviewing, particularly when it comes to oppressed minorities, others have pointed out that gender is not necessarily enough to warrant cooperation, and empowerment in feminist research; class, race, sexual orientation, education level and other factors cross-cut the possible interactions, frictions, questioning and collaborations between researcher and participants (Beoku-Betts, 1994; Garg, 2005; Gatrell, 2006; McDermott, 2004; Riessman, 1987; Temple & Edwards, 2002; Zavella, 1993, 1997). In addition to this, as Janet

Finch (1984) questioned, when does collaboration stop and exploitation begin in research with women? I addressed this issue by offering my time, resources and help beyond the interview time in a sort of quid pro quo exchange with any participant who wanted to take me up on the offer, based on the anthropological tradition of Orlando Fals Borda (1973, 1979), known more widely as Participatory Action Research and the recognition that almost all qualitative work involves some sort of 'trade-off' (Skeggs, 1994, 1997). These tasks included handy work for the spaces and community centres that hosted me, speaking with those who wanted to have an informal, non-recorded chat, baby-sitting, and so on.

It is important to acknowledge these methodological biases and other elements that may have intervened in the collection of the data, so as to understand better three things. On the one hand, I have tried as much as possible to minimise the asymmetry in power between myself and those who collaborated with me, given the topic studied. On the other hand, the arguments put forward here consider love to be as much of a social phenomenon as an individual feeling; therefore, the ideas, practices and emotions it produces and reproduces constitute a discourse (in a Foucauldian sense), the analysis of which in relation to its cinematic representations and several specific topics is the focus of this book. Finally, it also helps to clarify to whom it is aimed at and relevant for, mainly heterosexual, Western(ised) women, men and the films they consume.

Analytical premises

The book is based around two axes. First, it seeks to understand how the competing discourses surrounding love, intimacy and relationships are valued and adopted by people and films for certain discursive effects. Second, it looks at what boundaries, oppositions and juxtapositions are employed by films and audiences in their beliefs, practices and interpretations of romantic love on- and off-screen (cf. Bauman, 2003; Beck & Beck-Gernsheim, 1995; Dromm, 2002; Gornick, 1997; Gould, 1963; Hendrick, 1992; Luhmann, 1986; Martin, 1993; Ortega y Gasset, 1957). It is in the tensions, the disruptive moments where cultural phenomena must be positioned. It is via an analysis of these disruptions, with their myriad contexts and connotations, that it becomes possible to suggest how this contested field unfolds, to ascertain if it is changing, or simply has the appearance of change, and to establish the 'strategies' and the 'tactics' of its 'users' (Certeau, 1984). Thus, in order to enquire about this 'self' before the 'us' of romance, I explored how it is being represented in cinema and through figure(s) of love, borrowing from Roland Barthes' concept. I explore one of these tensions through an analysis of the ambiguous/unhappy ending in several contemporary romantic films, like *Blue Valentine* (Cianfrance, 2010) and *Once* (Carney, 2007), the new emotional demands and educations for men in *(500) Days of Summer* (Webb, 2009) and *Don Jon* (Gordon-Levitt, 2013), and the role of technology in our romantic engagements in *Her* (Jonze, 2013). To connect this to the two axes, I will analyse these endings through three analytical intertwined elements and their genealogy.

Gender, class and films

United through music, the platonic couple in *Once* (Carney, 2007) have their relationship put to the test time and time again because of the financial instability of an aspiring musician and the reduced means of the flower seller who helps him. In a similar situation are the characters in *Something Borrowed* (Greenfield, 2011) but, as upper-middle-class individuals, financial worries do not get in the way of their love affairs. *Once* is a film where the couple cannot partake in dates or other contemporary romantic practices because of their class position, *Something Borrowed* is a film devoted entirely to the changes wrought in the couple's relationship through contemporary romantic practices like dating and going out. Eva Illouz (1997) argues in her book *Consuming the Romantic Utopia* that media, film included, play a central role in changes to romantic love as a concept and a practice. She traces the history of romantic love from the beginning of the twentieth century and its shift from Victorian 'private' ideals and utilitarian customs to a more 'public' and hedonistic consumer/leisure-oriented *practice* of love. Based on this shift, she argues, both how we talk about love (and connected to this, how we conceive it) and our romantic practices are informed by our class positions. Furthermore, there is an existing tension about cultural competences – borrowing the term from Bourdieu (1984) – and a self-perceived lack of them, the 'ironic distance' of the middle and upper classes clashing continuously with the apparent 'over-identification' of the working class. This tension is not unique to film or to romantic love, but rather it traverses both. Illouz's work, however, focuses on print media; film is only dealt with marginally, while I foreground films and their 'intended' audiences in the reproduction and contestation of ideologies of romance and constructions of love.

Films feed on and reflect on contemporary romantic practices while also proposing a set of subject positions which the audiences, in an 'ideal' case, would take on completely. This, however, is hardly the case most of the time. Antonio Gramsci (1971) did not believe that human subjects were entirely docile and ever ready to comply with ideologically hegemonic demands. Hence, he articulates the notion of what has since come to be named as *counter-hegemony* to account for those moments, movements, groups, those sparks and bursts that challenged the status quo. What's at stake is to broaden scholarly perspectives on a 'politics of love': to discuss how it is the relationship between moment, film, audience, socioeconomic and cultural factors that influences and creates spaces for counter-hegemonic discourses or identities, and to explore the afterlife of these discourses once the final credits have rolled.

Romantic love in film and audiences

Alongside this concern for a 'politics of love', I argue that the affective experience of romance on screen provides far more than escapism inscribed within a hegemonic script of romance. It allows the audience to imagine new alternatives of romance and to experience different modes of catharsis and pleasure. This is because melodrama is a popular genre for it has a unique appeal and method of delivering its message based on displaying and evoking emotions, invoking the audience's emotional and affective participation. Romance films demand from the audience a complete 'suspension of disbelief', a great degree of identification and an emotional commitment to the story. Thomas Elsaesser (1987) argues that in melodrama, the construction of pathos is used to deal with psychological problems and sexual repression. He understands pathos as a crucial element to melodrama as it allows melodrama to go beyond empirical realism, to elaborate plots and make twists and exaggerations. Affects are thus part of the text, they inform its reading; and as such their meaning is not fixed. What is at stake is the 'reality effect' (Aumont, 1992; Barthes, 1977) of the scene, the ability of the text to convince and of the audience to be convinced. Here logos and pathos are not necessarily opposed. The verisimilitude of a scene can be coupled with an affect (and often is) to provide a reader/viewer with a lasting identification with one or more of the elements of the scene, or with the scene itself. Thus, I treat *affect*, and the *affective*, as a way to experience social reality and a pivotal element in the construction of audiences' conceptions of love and self.

Identity and film audiences

Why is the background blurred in a scene where A and B are about to kiss for the first time? Is there a reason behind the fact that the female lead is seldom taller than the male lead? Is it random happenstance that intimate moments on screen are lighted with a warm, yellow side light? This list of questions might have very different answers, pertaining to contexts of both production and reception. Few elements in commercial cinema are left to chance; a controlled environment is after all one of the key differences between cinema and 'real life'. Then, the hundreds of choices behind a full commercial feature that begins with a script and ends with its release can be seen as a unity of conscious decisions of what to show and, ergo, of what to hide, exclude or ignore. Film scholars who focus on melodrama have pointed out several prominent elements in these films: thematic music, close-up shots, triangular desire-based plots, internalisation of conflict and an ambivalent relation to realism (Doane, 1988; Gledhill, 1987; Vincendeau, 1989; Williams, 1998). However, the popularity of melodrama as a genre has partly paved the way for other (sub-)genres like chick-flicks, rom-coms and indie films that adapt, follow and borrow these elements without using them prescriptively. Further, as Neale and Krutnik (1990) argue, the resilience of the romantic film, drama, comedy and comedy-drama is due to the adaptability the subject of romantic love has to historic changes (see also Kaklamanidou, 2013). It is necessary to look how historic changes affect representations of love on-screen and how people, who experience these changes in and out of the film, negotiate, and articulate these representations through their own life-worlds. Thus, the single most significant element that I emphasise are the processes of audiences' interpretation, appropriation and negotiation of representations of romantic love for their own romantic behaviours and aspirations.

Borrowing from Martin Barker's (2006) concept of 'viewing strategy', the questions above also indicate that film viewing involves a range of aesthetic, sensuous, emotional, cognitive and imaginative processes all converging to form the experience of watching. These 'viewing strategies' are considered here not only for their relevance of speaking about the filmic experience but also about the ideas, practices and personal experiences that inform them.

This book is organised around these three elements. In particular, I'm interested in looking at the intersection of emotions, class and gender in the audience reception of contemporary romantic films. Chapter 1 will discuss the key and overarching theoretical concepts and discussions of the book. I trace how different disciplines have conceptualised romantic love, from evolutionary biology to queer theory, and elucidate the main discussions these disciplines have about love. From this, I also outline my use of the main concepts of identity, ideology and hegemony. and how this relates to film spectatorship. In Chapter 2 I connect the concepts examined in Chapter 1 to the history of reception studies and its different schools of thought and methods, ranging from the 'effects' tradition, Screen theory and British cultural studies to contemporary approaches. In this chapter, I privilege audience studies that have dealt with romantic love and its representations.

Chapter 3 addresses issues of episodic sexuality, monogamy, online dating and technology based on discussions of two films: *Her* (Jonze, 2013) and *Don Jon* (Gordon-Levitt, 2013). It introduces the concept of 'romantic affordances' to highlight how emotions, fantasy, past romantic experiences and the everyday are intermeshed in audiences' articulations of their romantic identities through representations of romantic love. This entails considering the possible ideological contradictions and the relationship with audiences' own positioning as subjects. At the same time, it contests the idea that technology and late-stage capitalism are seen as reducing romantic love to a simple series of economic decisions by showcasing how different audiences navigate these new affordances and develop tactics of their own. Chapter 4 focuses on how class affects the position audiences take vis-à-vis two working-class romances, *Blue Valentine* (Cianfrance, 2010) and *Once* (Carney, 2007). I analyse how the different discourses of love present in the films (romanticism, intimacy and Platonism), as embodied by the characters and their situation, operate to bring class as an enabler and a hurdle for relationships to work while at the same time reproducing problematic ideologies of gender roles. To do this, I also explore how ideas of realism in *Blue Valentine* and of fantasy in *Once* (in the form of an impossible love) work in opposite ways to highlight or 'naturalise' the adoption of either perspective.

Chapter 5 further elaborates how gender roles in films are received, contested and negotiated by audiences. In this chapter, I go back to *Blue Valentine* while also including *(500) Days of Summer* (Webb, 2009). In doing so, I make use of the literature and history of melodrama and women's films to understand audiences' reactions to differences and continuities between these two genres and the elements the two films borrow from or innovate on. Further, as part of the analysis of gender roles, I explore audiences' reactions to the new type of 'feminised masculinity' exemplified by the character of Tom in *(500) Days of Summer*. I contend that Tom's masculinity is competing for hegemony with a classic masculinity. Finally, I gauge how the 'unhappy' endings of these films are received and articulated by audiences, highlighting how fragility and contingency are increasingly normative aspects of our contemporary romantic identities. In Chapter 6, I bring together the main subjects of the book and the results of the investigation. Thus, I revisit the link between affordances and hegemonic discourses of romantic love such as the hetero-marital couple, while also pinpointing the complications that the commodification of love bring to the equation. In conclusion, I also highlight the role that social class continues to play in representation of romantic love and for its audience, to suggest that far from being a perfunctory backdrop, it shapes, symbolically and materially, the conditions on which contemporary relationship are built or founder. Finally, while class endogamy might continue to provide a somewhat solid foundation for romantic liaisons, this practice does not guarantee the lasting success of such relationships. Far from it. Thus, not only are films catching up on this uncertainty, the uncertainty is usually coupled with a larger concern over the contestation of masculinity. The book closes with some final remarks on future research agendas in this arena.

Notes

1 See http://www.semana.com/especiales/articulo/colombia-pasion/79583-3
2 https://es.wikipedia.org/wiki/Conflicto_armado_interno_en_Colombia and http://www.centrodememoriahistorica.gov.co/micrositios/informeGeneral/ This report, published in 2013 by the CNMH (National Centre for Historic Memory), estimates 5.7 million Colombians have been internally displaced, with over 220,000 dead, over 25,000 disappeared and around 30,000 kidnappings during the conflict. The 220,000 number, however, does not include the number of victims of non-lethal violence in the conflict involving landmines, car bombs, torture, child-recruiting, sexual and gender violence, to name a handful. If one accounts for this, the number jumps to almost 6 million people.
3 https://en.wikipedia.org/wiki/La_Violencia
4 http://www.eltiempo.com/politica/justicia/cifras-de-violencia-contra-las-mujeres-en-colombia/16758400. http://www.semana.com/nacion/articulo/la-muerte-rosa-elvira-cely-crimen-abominable/258867-3 This is the case of a woman raped, beaten and impaled in a park. https://mundo.sputniknews.com/americalatina/201511241054029806-colombia-violencia-genero-cifras/. In Colombia, it is impossible to know the full extent of gender and sexual violence given not just under-reporting, but also because this type of violence within guerrilla groups and by them is almost never reported.
5 https://en.wikipedia.org/wiki/%22False_positives%22_scandal
6 https://en.wikipedia.org/wiki/Bojay%C3%A1_massacre, https://es.wikipedia.org/wiki/Masacre_de_El_Saladohttps://en.wikipedia.org/wiki/Mapirip%C3%A1n_Massacre.
These are just three out of almost 2,000 massacres. http://www.verdadabierta.com/desde-regiones/5996-veinte-anos-de-una-guerra-sin-limites-en-uraba In Urabá alone, there have been at least 100 massacres.
7 https://www.youtube.com/watch?v=q_51Ero8Vc4
8 This woman, according to the latest 'science' on relationships and competition, should be thankful the man cheated on her, as this is an 'evolutionary adaptive' lesson she can use to spot prime males next time. (See Morris et al., 2016.)
9 Laura King (2015), in her history of family men in Britain from 1914 to 1960 eloquently points out that the idea of 'men-as-provider' is a comfortable myth that undermines the different modes in which men engaged in masculinity and fatherhood. These different modes have continuously paved the way for 'new men' as

well as new 'crisis of masculinity'. There is no such history in Colombia, so I can't say how cross-culturally applicable it would be, considering the historical and present influence of 'machismo' in Latin America. Nonetheless, it is intriguing.
10 For a thoughtful, evoking and painful work on the relationship between violence and our search for love and intimacy, see Bonino (2019).
11 https://www.theguardian.com/business/2015/may/04/first-time-buyers-need-to-earn-77000-a-year-to-live-in-london and https://www.theatlantic.com/business/archive/2016/08/millennials-the-mobile-and-the-stuck/497255/
12 http://theconversation.com/is-job-insecurity-becoming-the-norm-for-young-people-22311 and Courtois & O'Keefe (2015); Hudson (2014); Standing (2008).
13 See https://www.oii.ox.ac.uk/archive/downloads/publications/Me-MySpouse_GlobalReport.pdfhttp://www.pewresearch.org/fact-tank/2016/02/29/5-facts-about-online-dating/ and Rosenfeld & Thomas (2012).
14 This is not to say that there haven't been and aren't other economic crises, natural and social events, wars, cultural debates and revolutions that have constrained and inflected gender relations, and *greatly* coloured the possibilities for romantic love and intimacy across the globe. Indeed, the work of Cherry Potter (2002) highlights this in the case in Hollywood. Rather, I merely wish to highlight some of the socioeconomic conditions that impinge on the pursuit of love, particularly for young adults.
15 A notable exception was the TV show *The L Word*.

References

Alasuutari, P., Bickman, L., & Brannen, J. (2008). *The SAGE handbook of social research methods*. SAGE.
Alberti, J. (2013). "I love you, man": bromances, the construction of masculinity, and the continuing evolution of the romantic comedy. *Quarterly Review of Film and Video*, 30, 159–172.
Ang, I. (1985). *Watching Dallas: soap opera and the melodramatic imagination*. Methuen.
Aumont, J. (1992). *Aesthetics of film*. University of Texas Press.
Austin, T. (2002). *Hollywood, hype and audiences: selling and watching popular film in the 1990s*. Manchester University Press.
Banaji, S. (2002). Private lives and public spaces: the precarious pleasures of gender discourse in Raja Hindustani. *Women: A Cultural Review*, 13(2), 179–194. https://doi.org/10.1080/09574040210148988.
Banaji, S. (2006). *Reading "Bollywood": the young audience and Hindi films*. Palgrave Macmillan.
Barbour, R. S. (2007). *Doing focus groups*. SAGE.
Barker, M. (2006). I have seen the future and it is not here yet …; or, on being ambitious for audience research. *The Communication Review*, 9(2), 123–141. https://doi.org/10.1080/10714420600663310.
Barthes, R. (1977). Introduction to the structural analysis of narratives. In *Image Music Text* (trans. S. Heath) (pp. 79–125). Fontana.
Barthes, R. (1990). *A lover's discourse: fragments*. Penguin.
Bauman, Z. (2003). *Liquid love: on the frailty of human bonds*. Polity Press.
Bauman, Z. (2007). *Consuming life*. Polity Press.
Beck, U., & Beck-Gernsheim, E. (1995). *The normal chaos of love*. Polity Press; Blackwell.
Beoku-Betts, J. (1994). When black is not enough: Doing field research among Gullah women. *NWSA Journal*, 6, 413–433.
Bonino, S. (2019). *Nature and culture in intimate partner violence: sex, love and equality*. Routledge.

Bourdieu, P. (1984). *Distinction: a social critique of the judgement of taste*. Routledge & Kegan Paul.

Carney, J. (2007). *Once*. Icon Film Distribution.

Certeau, M. de. (1984). *The practice of everyday life*. University of California Press.

Cianfrance, D. (2010). *Blue Valentine*. The Weinstein Company.

Courtois, A., & O'Keefe, T. (2015). Precarity in the ivory cage: neoliberalism and casualisation of work in the Irish higher education sector. *Journal for Critical Education Policy Studies*, 13(1), 43–66.

Deacon, D., Pickering, M., Golding, P., & Murdock, G. (2007). *Researching communications: a practical guide to methods in media and cultural analysis*. Hodder Arnold.

Deleyto, C. (2003). Between friends: love and friendship in contemporary romantic comedy. *Screen*, 44(2), 167–182.

Derrida, J. (1997). *Politics of friendship*. Verso.

Doane, M. A. (1988). *The desire to desire: the woman's film of the 1940s*. Macmillan.

Dowd, J. J., & Pallotta, N. R. (2000). The end of romance: the demystification of love in the postmodern age. *Sociological Perspectives*, 43(4), 549–580. https://doi.org/10.2307/1389548.

Dromm, K. (2002). Love and Privacy. *Journal of Applied Philosophy*, 19(2), 155–167. https://doi.org/10.1111/1468-5930.00212.

Elsaesser, T. (1987). Tales of sound and fury: observations on the family melodrama. In C. Gledhill (ed.), *Home is where the heart is: studies in melodrama and the woman's film* (pp. 43–69). BFI Publishing.

Evans, P., & Deleyto, C. (eds) (1998). *Terms of endearment: Hollywood romantic comedy of the 1980s and 1990s*. Edinburgh University Press.

Fals Borda, O. (1973). Reflexiones sobre la aplicación del método de Estudio-Acción en Colombia. *Revista Mexicana de Sociología*, 35(1), 49–62. https://doi.org/10.2307/3539564.

Fals Borda, O. (1979). *El problema de cómo investigar la realidad para transformarla*. Tercer Mundo.

Finch, J. (1984). It's great to have someone to talk to: the ethics and politics of interviewing women. In C. Bell & H. Roberts (eds), *Social researching: politics, problems and practice* (pp. 70–87). Routledge & Kegan Paul.

Flick, U. (2014). *An introduction to qualitative research* (5th edn). SAGE.

Fontana, A., & Frey, J. H. (2008). The interview: from a neutral stance to political involvement. In N. K. Denzin & Y. S. Lincoln (eds), *The Sage Handbook of Qualitative Research* (3rd en) (pp. 695–727). SAGE.

Garg, A. (2005). Interview reflections: a first generation migrant indian woman researcher interviewing a first generation migrant indian man. *Journal of Gender Studies*, 14(2), 147–152.

Gatrell, C. J. (2006). Interviewing fathers: feminist dilemmas in fieldwork. *Journal of Gender Studies*, 15(3), 237–251. https://doi.org/10.1080/09589230600862059.

Gibbs, A. (1997). Focus groups. *Social Research Update*, Winter(19), 6–11. http://sru.soc.surrey.ac.uk/SRU19.html%5CnAccessed:26/06/2012.

Gibson, K., & Wolske, M. (2011). Disciplining sex in Hollywood: a critical comparison of *Blue Valentine* and *Black Swan*. *Women & Language*, 34(2), 79–96.

Giddens, A. (1992). *The transformation of intimacy: sexuality, love and eroticism in modern societies*. Polity Press.

Gledhill, C. (1987). *Home is where the heart is: studies in melodrama and the woman's film*. BFI Publishing.

Gordon-Levitt, J. (2013). Don Jon. Relativity Media.
Gornick, V. (1997). *The end of the novel of love*. Beacon Press.
Gould, T. (1963). *Platonic love*. The Free Press.
Gramsci, A. (1971). *Selections from the prison notebooks of Antonio Gramsci* (ed. Q. Hoare & G. Nowell-Smith). Lawrence & Wishart.
Greenfield, L. (2011). Something Borrowed. Alcon Entertainment.
Guzmán, G., Fals Borda, O., & Umaña, E. (2005). *La Violencia en Colombia*. Taurus.
Hendrick, S., & Hendrick, C. (1992). *Romantic love*. SAGE.
Holstein, J. A., & Gubrium, J. F. (1995). *The active interview*. SAGE.
Hudson, M. (2014). Casualisation and low pay. https://www.tuc.org.uk/sites/default/files/Casualisationandlowpay.docx%0A.
Hyams, M. (2004). Hearing girls' silences: thoughts on the politics and practices of a feminist method of group discussion. *Gender, Place and Culture: A Journal of Feminist Geography*, 11(1), 105–119. https://doi.org/10.1080/0966369042000188576.
Iglesias Prieto, N. (2004). Gazes and cinematic readings of gender: danzon and its relationship to its audience. *Discourse*, 26(1 & 2), 173–193.
Illouz, E. (1997). *Consuming the romantic utopia: love and the cultural contradictions of capitalism*. University of California Press.
Illouz, E. (2007). *Cold intimacies: the making of emotional capitalism*. Polity.
Javaid, A. (2019). *Masculinities, sexualities and love*. Routledge.
Jonze, S. (2013). Her. Warner Bros. Pictures.
Kaklamanidou, B. (2013). *Genre, gender and the effects of neoliberalism: the new millennium Hollywood rom com*. Routledge.
Kalviknes Bore, I.-L. (2011). Reviewing Romcom: (100) IMDb Users and (500) Days of Summer. *Participations*, 8(2), 144–164.
King, L. A. (2015). *Family men: fatherhood and masculinity in Britain, 1914–1960*. Oxford University Press.
Kitzinger, J. (1995). Qualitative research: introducing focus groups. *BMJ: British Medical Journal*, 311(7000), 299–308. https://doi.org/10.1136/bmj.311.7000.299.
Krueger, R. A. (1994). *Focus groups: a practical guide for applied research* (2nd edn). SAGE.
Krueger, R. A. (1998). *Moderating focus groups*. SAGE.
Kvale, S. (1996). *Interviews: an introduction to qualitative research interviewing*. SAGE.
Levinas, E. (1969). *Totality and infinity*. Duquesne University Press.
Livingstone, S. (1989). *Making sense of television: the psychology of audience interpretation*. Pergamon.
Luhmann, N. (1986). *Love as passion: the codification of intimacy*. Polity Press.
Marková, I. (Ed.). (2007). *Dialogue in focus groups: exploring socially shared knowledge*. Equinox.
Martin, M. W. (1993). Love's constancy. *Philosophy*, 68(263), 63–77. https://doi.org/10.2307/3751065.
McDermott, E. (2004). Telling lesbian stories: interviewing and the class dynamics of "talk." *Women's Studies International Forum*, 27(3), 177–187. https://doi.org/10.1016/j.wsif.2004.04.001.
McKee, A. (2009). What's love got to do with it? History and melodrama in the 1940s woman's film. *Film & History: An Interdisciplinary Journal of Film and Television Studies*, 39(2), 5–15.
Millward, L. (2012). Focus groups. In G. M. Breakwell, J. A. Smith & D. B. Wright (eds), *Research Methods in Psychology* (pp. 411–438). SAGE. https://doi.org/10.1016/S0272-4944(05)80228-80222.

Modleski, T. (2014). An affair to forget: melancholia in bromantic comedy. *Camera Obscura*, 29(2), 119–147.

Montell, F. (1999). Focus group interviews: a new feminist method. *NWSA*, 11(1), 44–71.

Morgan, D. L. (1996). Focus groups. *Annual Review of Sociology*, 22(1), 129–152. https://doi.org/10.1146/annurev.soc.22.1.129.

Morgan, D. L. (1997). *Focus groups as qualitative research* (2nd edn). SAGE.

Morgan, D. L. (1998). *Planning focus groups*. SAGE.

Morin, E. (2005). *The cinema, or, the imaginary man*. University of Minnesota Press.

Morris, C. E., Beaussart, M. L., Reiber, C., & Krajewski, L. S. (2016). Intrasexual mate competition and breakups. In M. L. Fisher (ed.), *The Oxford Handbook of Women and Competition* (Vol. 1). Oxford University Press. https://doi.org/10.1093/oxfordhb/9780199376377.013.19.

Nakassis, C. (2016). *Doing style: you and mass mediation in South India*. University of Chicago Press.

Neale, S., & Krutnik, F. (1990). *Popular film and television comedy*. Routledge.

Nowell-Smith, G. (1987). Minelly and melodrama. In C. Gledhill (ed.), *Home is where the heart is: studies in melodrama and women's film* (pp. 69–76). BFI Publishing.

Ortega y Gasset, J. (1957). *On love: aspects of a single theme*. Meridian Books.

Pini, B. (2002). Focus groups, feminist research and farm women: opportunities for empowerment in rural social research. *Journal of Rural Studies*, 18(3), 339–351. https://doi.org/10.1016/S0743-0167(02)00007-00004.

Potter, C. (2002). *I love you but … romance and comedy at the movies*. Methuen.

Radway, J. (1984). *Reading the romance: women, patriarchy and popular literature*. Verso.

Riessman, C. K. (1987). When gender is not enough: women interviewing women. *Gender & Society*, 1(2), 172–207. https://doi.org/10.1177/0891243287001002004.

Rosenfeld, M. J., & Thomas, R. J. (2012). Searching for a mate: the rise of the internet as a social intermediary. *American Sociological Review*, 77(4), 523–547. https://doi.org/10.1177/0003122412448050.

Roulston, K. (2008). Conversational interviewing. In L. M. Given (ed.), *The Sage Encyclopedia of Qualitative Research Methods* (pp. 127–129). SAGE.

Sennett, R. (1996). *The fall of public man*. Faber and Faber.

Sharot, S. (2010). Class rise as a reward for disinterested love: cross-class romance films, 1915–28. *Journal of Popular Culture*, 43(3), 583–599.

Shary, T. (2011). Buying me love: 1980s class-clash teen romances. *The Journal of Popular Culture*, 44(3), 563–582. https://doi.org/10.1111/j.1540-5931.2011.00849.x.

Shumway, D. R. (2003). *Modern love: romance, intimacy, and the marriage crisis*. New York University Press.

Silverman, D. (2013). *Doing qualitative research: a practical handbook*. SAGE.

Silverman, D. (2014). *Interpreting qualitative data* (5th edn). SAGE.

Skeggs, B. (1994). Situating the production of feminist ethnography. In M. Maynard & J. Purvis (eds), *Researching Women's Lives*. Taylor & Francis.

Skeggs, B. (1997). *Formations of class and gender: becoming respectable*. SAGE.

Smith Jr., G. D. (2009). Love as redemption: the American dream myth and the celebrity biopic. *Journal of Communication Inquiry*, 33(3), 222–238.

Standing, G. (2008). Economic insecurity and global casualisation: threat or promise? *Social Indicators Research*, 88(1), 15–30. https://doi.org/10.1007/s11205-007-9202-7.

Suárez, A. F. (2008). La sevicia en las masacres de la guerra Colombiana. *Análisis Político*, 63, 39–57.

Temple, B., & Edwards, R. (2002). Interpreters/translators and cross-language research: Reflexivity and border crossings. *International Journal of Qualitative Methods*, 1(2), Article 1. https://sites.ualberta.ca/~iiqm.

Uribe, M. V. (1990). Matar, rematar y contramatar: Las masacres de La Violencia en el Tolima, 1948–64. In Centro de Investigación y Educación (Vols 159–160). CINEP.

Uribe, M. V. (2004). *Anthropologie de l'inhumanité: essai sur la terreur en Colombie*. Calmann-Lévy.

Uribe, M. V., & Vásquez, T. (1995). *Enterrar y Callar: Las masacres en Colombia 1980–1993*. Comité Permanent por la Defensa de los Derechos Humanos, Fundación Terre de Hommes.

Vincendeau, G. (1989). Melodramatic realism: on some French women's films in the 1930s. *Screen*, 30(3), 51–65. https://doi.org/10.1093/screen/30.3.51.

Wahab, S. (2003). Creating knowledge collaboratively with female sex workers: insights from a qualitative, feminist, and participatory study. *Qualitative Inquiry*, 9(4), 625–642. https://doi.org/10.1177/1077800403252734.

Wartenberg, T. (1999). *Unlikely couples: movie romance as social criticism*. Westview Press.

Webb, M. (2009). (500) Days of summer. Fox Searchlight Pictures.

Wilkinson, S. (1998). Focus groups in feminist research: Power, interaction, and the co-construction of meaning. *Women's Studies International Forum*, 21(1), 111–125. https://doi.org/10.1016/S0277-5395(97)00080-0

Wilkinson, S. (1999). Focus groups: a feminist method. *Psychology of Women Quarterly*, 23, 221–244. https://doi.org/10.1111/j.1471-6402.1999.tb00355.x.

Williams, L. (1998). Melodrama revisited. In N. Browne (ed.), *Refiguring American film genres: history and theory* (pp. 43–88). University of California Press.

Zavella, P. (1993). Feminist insider dilemmas: constructing ethnic identity with "Chicana" informants. *Frontiers: A Journal of Women Studies*, 13(3), 53–76. https://doi.org/10.2307/3346743.

Zavella, P. (1997). Reflections on diversity among Chicanas. *Challenging fronteras: Structuring Latina and Latino Lives in the U.S.*, 12(2), 187–194. https://doi.org/10.2307/3346849.

1 Celluloid love
Romance, ideology and self-commodification

When it comes to cinema, few things are as fruitful for narratives as the trope of romantic love. The merging of the visual power of cinema with narratives of romantic love allows the latter to take on textures, forms and shapes it previously did not know beyond a reader's imagination. The visualisation and spread of these representations furthers their recognition across different classes and ages, prompting a distinct imagery and iconography to be associated with love; this includes sequences that we now 'knowingly' (Barker & Brooks, 1998) call romantic: the first kiss, the tender or erotic gaze from afar, the holding of hands, the sunset reunion. This is not to say that the images appearing in cinema are what construe certain actions and emotions as romantic in the first place, but rather that with the inception of film, there was an audiovisual way to 'standardise', 'consolidate' and 'reproduce' a common idea of romantic love.

Final Cut: Ladies and Gentlemen (2012) beautifully illustrates this point. Director and editor György Pálfi tells a story of a man who meets a woman, and falls in love with her on the first night they meet; he fights her former lover and marries her, only to be faced with the trials and tribulations of everyday life shortly afterwards. This is a story one has probably watched, read and heard countless times; Pálfi's accomplishment, however, lies in using clips from 450 different films to weave this narrative.

Roland Barthes (1990) had done something similar in his book *A Lover's Discourse: Fragments* recollecting fragments of books (fiction and non-fiction alike) and creating a typology of different situations, emotions, affects and ideas about romantic love. He calls these 'figures of love' that

> take shape insofar as we can recognize, in passing discourse, something that has been read, heard, felt. The figure is outlined (like a sign) and memorable (like an image or a tale). A figure is established if at least someone can say *'That's so true! I recognize that scene of language.'*
>
> (1990, p. 4)

From the 'first kiss', failure, jealousy, idealisation, atopos, this can't go on, love's languor to the moment of the 'nose' – when the lover recognises the first faults in the loved one's physique and character, Barthes' list of fragments is a rich list of elements of love that allows us to understand love not as a seamless unit, but rather as a pastiche of experiences, affects and practices that are in a constant struggle for coherence and harmony. That love lends itself to this sort of atomisation is exactly what makes it such a rich subject for cinema, malleable into a canon, a genre, a set of visual clues the audience can easily recognise. Furthermore, it is through the recognition of these figures that people organise their romantic identities in media representations and beyond, fragmentarily so, looking, longing and safeguarding coherence between the many figures.

This fragmentation can be found in all the approaches that have sought to study love to this day. This is not a mere coincidence, nor is it the caprice of stubborn researchers who attempt to wholly partition love into clean, non-overlapping elements. This, I argue, is because love is experienced, thought of, felt, idealised, remembered, seen and practised in fragments, in 'figures', more so than any other concept and/or idea one can think of (the 'one' here, as it is the concept of love, is circumscribed to Western societies and should not be construed as unproblematically applicable to other cultures and areas). This is not only because love can refer to love to a person, to a thing, to an animal, to an idea (religious and non-religious), but because love is more than the sum of its fragments, yet it can be fully expressed through them. This can be illustrated by the caricaturising of other concepts such as honesty and loyalty. It is possible to define honest as 'always telling the truth' and loyalty as 'staying by your side, no matter what', but if one tries, without alluding to the Judeo-Christian religious formulation of 'God is love', to do such a thing with love it is impossible. Instead, it inspires formulations such as 'love is finding he has left you half of the cake in the fridge despite it being triple chocolate', 'love is when he hugs you so hard after you've had a bad day', 'love is being able to speak without talking', 'love is when he makes you laugh even when you're mad at him' and 'love is that kiss you never forget'. These formulations, proposed by interviewees, are some of a plethora one can think, experience, remember and has seen. But to reduce love to one aphorism is impossible, even for the greatest of writers, thinkers and scholars.

Despite love's elusiveness to full categorisation, different disciplines have tried to come up with taxonomies, categories, sub-concepts, modes of operationalisation, theories and hermeneutics of love. Biological approaches like those of Harry Harlow and John Bowlby are two of many examples. Harlow (1958, 1974; Vicedo, 2010) worked with socialisation amongst primates and identified five different kinds of love: maternal, paternal, peer love, heterosexual love and the infant's love of the mother. This love, he argued, was based on both unlearned behaviours and sociocultural learned processes. This meant that an attachment process, beginning during infancy was crucial to develop into healthy mature individuals. Healthy here means successful sexual behaviour. In general, these approaches characterise themselves for considering love either a strategy or a trait for socialisation and group survival (Berscheid & Walster, 1974; Buss, 1988, 2006; Hatfield & Sprecher, 1986; Hazan & Shaver, 1987; Kenrick, 1987; Mellen, 1981; Rubin, 1970; Rubin, Peplau & Hill, 1981; Shaver, Hazan & Bradshaw, 1988; Fisher, 2004; Peele, 1975). In psychology, there's the work of Ellen Berscheid

(Berscheid, 1988, 1999, 2002; Berscheid & Regan, 2005; Berscheid & Walster, 1974), who categorised the different schemes of love into four different ones: attachment love, compassionate love, companionate love/liking and romantic love. Berscheid's theorising of love includes two further elements: the dyad of love/like and lust. Further, Susan and Clyde Hendrick (Hendrick, 1992; Hendrick & Hendrick, 1986, 1989, 2002) have, over the course of decades of work, developed a taxonomy and scale of love styles, inspired by John Alan Lee's (1973) love styles. These styles are divided in three primary and three secondary styles. The primary styles are: *eros, ludus* and *storge*. The secondary styles are: *pragma, mania* and *agape*. These are but a handful of examples in the ways scientific rigour has been applied to such complex and sometimes elusive phenomena.

However, I focus on psychoanalytic, philosophical and sociological approaches to love. The reason for this is that these disciplines recognise and value love as a cultural historical ideological construct that privileges certain forms of associations and sexual orientations over others.[1] That is to say, I am highlighting those approaches that have understood romantic love as a concept and as a practice.

I have omitted two major approaches to romantic love: literary and religious literature. The literary treatment and the religious literature (see Singer, 2009a, 2009b, 2009c for a three-volume abbreviated historical and philosophical discussion that contains multiple references to literature and Judeo-Christianity) is too vast to do justice to. Further, while it is undeniable that in a Western context talking about romantic love means connecting it to Christianity, religious literature contains an explanatory shift from the one opted for in this project. Religious literature is also more focused on divine love than is pertinent for this study. Such a focus is problematic as it makes human love only a subsidiary of the divine. Thus, any form of love is analysed insofar as it fits or does not fit the project of divine love. Such a lens displaces historical, economic, social and cultural contexts in which love is conceptualised and practised. Any links to the religious in this study will be made within secular philosophical and sociological frameworks, while the literary tradition is referenced only in so far as it is relevant to cinema.

Psychoanalytic theory and *eros*

A summary of the gargantuan number of concepts, theories, elements and critiques of psychoanalysis is outside the scope of this chapter. Here I will focus on how scholars have used, modified and critiqued concepts belonging to psychoanalysis to think about love. It should be noted that in psychoanalysis, love is characterised by two things: first, an intrinsic link with sexuality and the sex drive; and, second, it is almost entirely interested in the love between paternal figures and the infant. The love one experiences in these relationships is then seen as feeding and informing the kind of love one can develop towards everything else. In the subsections below, I will summarise and highlight a few concepts of psychoanalysis and socio-philosophical works and their relationship to romantic love.

Eros *and* Plato

One of the most important perspectives here that still informs a great deal of today's romantic discourse is Plato's account of love. It focuses on *eros* – usually understood to mean a sexual passion, a desire for an object – and the search of a greater good. Diotima/Plato (1953) understands both as the search and the end product to be the Form of Beauty. Beauty in Ancient Greece is *harmonious* and as such it is good because the parts that make it and their connections must be. Plato sees sexual attraction as a deficient step to truly love, to love Beauty, sanitising *eros* of its sexual component. Furthermore, he argues that love among people is not the greatest love to be had and thus is flawed, it is merely a path towards recognising beauty in a person's soul and then moving forward to recognise Beauty in itself. Plato puts forth the idea of a hierarchy of love, *scala amoris*, on top being Beauty, abstract Beauty. Plato insists that love must be reproductive, but for Plato this meant the reproduction, the conception of one's own theories and concepts, of knowledge; in short, love of Beauty should lead to philosophy.

There are two main critiques of this vision of love. First, it implies a quality-based love, denying the possibility of 'fully' loving a person (Vlastos, 1973). Second, there is an egocentric character, because it is focused on the lover's pursuit and not so much on the beloved, seen as an object of the lover's desires and goals (Nygren, 1969; Soble, 1989, 1990; Vlastos, 1973). This claim has been widely disputed on the basis that Plato never equated *eros* with desire as he believed desire was not dependent on the lack of something (Dixon, 2007; Haden, 1979; Kosman, 1976; Levy, 1979) like psychoanalytical theories of desire conceptualise it to be. Despite these philosophical criticisms, a more informal understanding of platonic love still permeates much of our understanding of romantic love as a love impossible, whatever the reasons might be, to fulfil and carry out in the realm of the everyday. Thus, platonic love and Plato's love are not the same thing nor do they refer to the same type of drive, but there are several elements they share and that are now common in other discourses of love. The hierarchical structure of this love, its conjecture as an upward path towards 'enlightenment' and the impossibility of its fulfilment in an earthly realm are all elements that have transpired and influence other discourses of love, including the discourse of intimacy which sets itself as a contemporary sublimation of these elements.

Sigmund Freud (1922), based on an arguably poor reading of Plato's work, conceptualised *eros* as an uncontrollable instinct to live. This, in Freud's work, was unavoidably linked to a sexual *drive* but he argued it also contained an energy to produce, to commune and create – a *drive* in psychoanalytic theory is an innate urge that seeks satisfaction in material objects or physical actions. In Plato, *eros* was an otherworldly energy void of sexuality that was unattainable as it wasn't embodied. Freud, however, thinks of *eros* as a sublimating power where the suppression of one's libido can be channelled to cultural pursuits. Furthermore, Freud goes on to oppose *eros* to Thanatos, the death drive (2010). *Eros* is the ultimate desire for wholeness, for the creation and preservation of life. *Eros*, driven by libidinal energy, is largely involved with sexuality but it is not explained fully by it.

Creativity, self-actualisation, self-fulfilment, cooperation and bonding are also expressions of *eros*. Thus, romantic love is one of the possible ways humans experience *eros*. The importance of *eros* as the life drive lies in its utopian dimension is clearly exemplified in Herbert Marcuse's (1966) work *Eros and Civilization*. Marcuse seeks to rethink Freud's dictum that humanity is organised around the repression of (sexual) instincts and their channelling into productive, organised endeavours. This repression causes guilt to be an organising principle of society and makes happiness unattainable. Following a Marxist-psychoanalytic line of thought, he posits the idea of a non-repressive society, where a pleasure principle (Eros) organises a new civilisation where creativity, automatised labour and libido instead of guilt are the drivers of progress. Aided by automatised material production, Marcuse believed a socialist society could accomplish this reconfiguration of societal organisation. The reality principle of repression finds its historically situated version in the performance principle,

> which is that of an acquisitive and antagonistic society in the process of constant expansion, presupposes a long development during which domination has been increasingly rationalized: control over social labor now reproduces society on a large scale and under improving conditions. For a long way, the interests of domination and the interests of the whole coincide: the profitable utilization of the productive apparatus fulfils the needs and faculties of individuals. For the vast majority of the population, the scope and mode of satisfaction are determined by their own labor; but their labor is work for an apparatus which they do not control, which operates as an independent power to which individuals must submit if they want to live. And it becomes the more alien the more specialized the division of labor becomes. Men do not live their own lives but perform pre-established functions. While they work, they do not fulfil their own needs and faculties but work in *alienation*.
> (1966, p. 45)

Thus, Marcuse recognises that work is a necessity of life, but he takes issue with what he terms surplus repression, or the organisation of labour not per the needs of the worker, but rather to the benefit of the capitalist. Thus, the reality and performance principles are capitalist drives that organise production and desires through oppression, domination and alienation. Against this, Marcuse champions a new intersubjective and libidinal subjectivity that seeks to break the separation between the senses and reason and that searches for harmony and gratification instead of domination and oppression (Kellner, 1999). This is what he terms a 'rationality of gratification', whereby *eros* reconfigures *logos* to help envision and build a better world.

Erich Fromm is another scholar who engaged in an ideological psychoanalytic-Marxist reading of love. In his book *The Art of Loving* (1974), Fromm rallies against the perception that love is something we *passively* fall into. Rather, he suggests that we think of it as a skill a man can teach himself. Quite notably, that up to this point, in the work of these three authors, *men are the ones who love, women are just the love object*. For Fromm, there are four core elements of love: knowledge, care, responsibility and respect. These elements are never clear-cut as they are bound to different sociocultural and historical understandings. Thus, a great deal about learning to love comes with the *real* understanding of these elements. A fifth element for Fromm which is crucial is self-love. Self-love means to know thyself, care for oneself, respecting oneself and being responsible for one's actions. Fromm identifies two problems that stops us from truly loving ourselves and others in capitalist societies. The first is that self-love turns into narcissism and egocentric attitudes towards loving another. This in turn means that we love some qualities of the beloved, not the whole of the beloved. In addition, Fromm also believed this fostered a harmful relationship to one's community as the lover was too focused on one single person to love all his community. The second, paradoxically as he accepts it, is that in our efforts to battle aloneness and alienation, we seek to fully merge with the beloved, which is problematic as we lose our individuality and, in the process, force the other to lose theirs. Fromm proposes the idea of a mature love, which he conceives as opposed to the narcissistic, goal-centred, functionalist, quality based immature love of Western societies. This type of love recognises the individuality of each being and does not attempt to either assimilate, merge or alienate, but to love (through a deep knowledge of) all of humanity. Fromm argues that mature love is best understood as a paradoxical thought of belonging to and not belonging (to a union of love) at the same time.

This is linked to the psychoanalytic distinction one can make between mature love and narcissistic love. According to Julia Kristeva (1987, p. 33), 'the lover is a narcissist with an *object*'. She further writes:

> The lover, in fact, reconciles narcissism and hysteria. As far as he is concerned, there is an idealizable other who returns his own ideal image (that is the narcissistic moment), but he is nevertheless an other. It is essential for the lover to maintain the existence of that ideal other and to be able to imagine himself familiar, merging with him, and even indistinguishable from him. In amorous hysteria the ideal Other is a reality, not a metaphor.
> (p. 33)

In psychoanalytic terms, this means that the ego has been able to deal with the trauma of the pre-Oedipal loss of the ideal by recognition of the *difference* of the *object*. This is mature love. 'Object' here is to be understood by another human being, initially the mother, and in Freud usually a woman (Kristeva is far more ambivalent). Narcissism, in Freud (1924), is divided in two: a primary/normal and a secondary narcissism. The primary/normal narcissism is the libidinal energy that is connected to the instinct of self-preservation that becomes one of the first mediations between the id and the ego. The secondary narcissism is when there is a withdrawal of libidinal energy towards objects and is fully directed at a self that is neither an ego ideal nor a subject. The harm contained in the secondary narcissism is that it withdraws the subject from the object-world. Narcissistic love is where the connection to the *real* object-world is rejected and the self becomes the model on which one chooses love-objects. As Sue Gottlieb (2011) argues, this means that narcissistic love is a quest for determination, control of the love-object to appease the anxiety of the self (see also Maurer, Milligan & Pacovská, 2014).

Narcissism, identification and difference

Marcuse and Fromm's work consolidated a line of ideological thought on love and capitalism that has been continued by other scholars and researchers. It follows a certain linear premise to love in a capitalist society:

- The human condition is one of isolation, solitude and damnation to aloneness.
- Humans live in a constant struggle for attachment, for appreciation, recognition and communion because of this.
- Because humans are, ultimately, selfish creatures they constantly fail in these pursuits. This failure and instinct of narcissism has been heightened by capitalism.
- This is so because capitalism has made of the self a quantifiable and divisible set of categories. This alienates humans from one another, making it impossible for them to truly recognise themselves as such and even less so others.
- Love is both a cure and a poison of this capitalist malady.
- It is a poison because 'loving capitalistically' is based around self-satisfaction, instead of intimating with the beloved, recognising and acknowledging them as human. That is, this love is more concerned with a narcissistic pursuit of self-pleasure and self-desire.
- Love can be a cure, a positive force, because it can help us, when 'properly' practised, to truly know other human beings and battle the alienation of capitalism. This positive force is very reminiscent of what Victor Turner termed as *communitas*.

Zygmunt Bauman and Alain Badiou are two scholars who fall in this line of thought. For Bauman (2003), love in a 'liquid world' is characterised by the consumerist co-optation of its ideals. That is, the bond, the relationship, becomes a commodity and the loved one is a bag of qualities we go out shopping for. When one gets bored of this 'bag', Bauman argues, we simply throw it away and go out shopping again, sometimes 'recycling' a few of the qualities. Of utmost importance for this 'liquid love' is to manage distances, to never fully commit to a relationship or a person, because in liquid modernity we are all uprooted and narcissistic. The main quality of a liquid lover then is one who can navigate the line of connection with others while preserving his/her own self-interests. As with much of his Eurocentric work, Bauman works in extremes. The liquid lover is a Western elite that oppresses, by emotionally and morally detaching from the underworld. Again, as is the case, consumerist romantic love is analytically extended to the impossibility of loving the Other. Bauman then asserts that there are no 'local solutions for globally produced problems' (p.115) and that to battle the never-ending individualisation and de-territorialisation of contemporary consumer globalisation, liquid individuals must seek globally aimed plans with local solutions. This uplifting glimmer of hope, however, cannot be retroactively sought after in couple romantic love.

This pessimistic outlook on love because of economic liberalism and 'rampant' narcissism has also been explored by authors like Christopher Lasch (1977), Ulrich Beck and Elisabeth Beck-Gernsheim (1995) and Richard Sennett (1998). These authors, lamented that love has become too narrowly focused; as Paul Adams (2005) suggests on Sennett's work:

> the fundamental problem was a lack of balance between private and public worlds caused by an overemphasis on love at the expense of cool and detached modes of engagement ... what we see is a collapse of attachment and involvement to a narrow sphere – from the cosmos to the hearth, from civil society to the narcissistic and possessive microcosm of family and friends.
> (p. 53)

Thus, one can recognise two types of love. One is telluric, broad and community based. This love was corrupted by capitalism and turned into a narcissistic, (semi-)detached, narrow love. The invasion of love into a public, civil sphere is understood as damaging and undermining more rational, manly forms of attachment and social engagement. The heterosexist and patriarchal connotations of this opposition have been critiqued and explored at length by feminist scholars, most notably Lauren Berlant (2008, 2000, 2012).

Alain Badiou (2009) follows a similar logic to Bauman's but he does believe in the possibility of a 'true' romantic love that is not subservient to consumer capitalist logic. *In Praise of Love* continues the nostalgia of a seemingly lost, utopic uncorrupted love by capitalism, while acknowledging three elements characteristic of it. First, is that love is impossible without a degree of risk. In 'true love', a person must make a leap of love, must adventure, must be prepared to risk and be nastily surprised, yet also accept being overwhelmed by affection. This is why, Badiou argues, to position love as a sort of economic exchange of favours (sexual and otherwise), qualities and traits is nothing but vulgar narcissistic hedonism made possible and fostered by a liberal capitalist logic that looks to minimise risks everywhere. In this notion of risk as inherent in true love, Badiou nods to both Plato and Christianity, but rather than looking at love as having a transcendental otherworldly quality – which is part of the root of the problem – he pleads with us to understand love as having an immanent quality:

> Christianity grasped perfectly that there is an element in the apparent contingency of love that can't be reduced to that contingency. But it immediately raised it to the level of transcendence, and that is the root of the problem. This universal element I too recognize in love as immanent. But Christianity has somehow managed to elevate it and refocus it onto a transcendent power. It's an ideal that was already partly present in Plato, through the idea of the Good. It is a brilliant first manipulation of the power of love and one we must now bring back to earth. I mean we must

demonstrate that love really does have universal power, but that it is simply the opportunity we are given to enjoy a positive, creative, affirmative experience of difference. The Other, no doubt, but without the 'Almighty-Other', without the 'Great Other' of transcendence.

(pp. 65–66)

In this view, the possibility of love lies in the recognition and push for an immanent experience of difference. Contrary to the religious sublimation of love towards a transcendent power (god), Badiou considers this search and experience of difference as a combative, grounded pursuit. This position is akin to ones taken by scholars like Emmanuel Levinas, Martin Buber and Jacques Derrida in regards to how *the experience of difference can be a tool against the alienation of contemporary capitalist societies*. He, however, is against a politics of love, as in love one does not deal with enemies – as one must in politics – only with the creative play between identity and difference. Thus, for Badiou, love remains anchored in the intrapersonal and intimate, and in linking it back to Plato, he argues that it is based on a 'truth procedure' of two. A truth procedure is the continuous, strenuous yet rewarding quest for truth of exploring, experiencing and developing the world from the perspective of difference and not identity. It is in this search of truth that love is universal, yet personal. This makes Badiou's project distinct from *agape* insofar as *agape* is the downward sublimation of *eros* through a sanctioned religious union and his is grounded in an earthly other. This is reminiscent of Freud's (1922) position on the intensity of the couple, where its intertwining is one of the most subversive energies one can envision.

Contrary to Badiou, Antonio Negri and Michael Hardt (Hardt, 2011, 2014; Hardt & Negri, 2000, 2004, 2011; see also Horvat, 2016) have recently pursued a politics of love. Their position is decidedly agapic and community based. The origin of this pursuit, Hardt says, lies in that feeling 'like love' one feels in the 'really good' protests. Initially, Hardt and Negri proposed that

Love – in the production of affective networks, schemes of cooperation, and social subjectivities – is an economic power. Conceived in this way love is not, as it is often characterized, spontaneous or passive. It does not simply happen to us, as if it were an event that mystically arrives from elsewhere. Instead it is an action, a biopolitical event, planned and realized in common.

(2011, p. 180)

Here, these authors are echoing the notion of love as active, not passive like authors such as Fromm proposed. Furthermore, they also highlight the need to go beyond an intimate and private conceptualisation of love. In other words, a loving subject is not *just* an intimate subject, must also be a civil one. Thus, a political notion of love would

First . . . have to extend across social scales and create bonds that are at once intimate and social, destroying conventional divisions between public and private. Second, it would have to operate in a field of multiplicity and function through not unification but the encounter and interaction of differences. Finally, a political love must transform us, that is, it must designate a becoming such that in love, in our encounter with others we constantly become different. Love is thus always a risk in which we abandon some of our attachments to this world in the hope of creating another, better one. I consider these qualities the primarily pillars of a research agenda for discovering today a political concept of love.

(Hardt, 2011, p . 678)

Hardt and Negri reject identity politics as a base for a politics of love as, even when they are in the service of a subordinate minority, these movements are too narrow in their scope and run the risk of being reactionary. Love, according to these two scholars, can be one of the powerful forces that could eventually replace private property, as it is in the strength and endurance of the social bond love can (ideally) provide that they encounter its transformative power, both individually and socially.

There are a few elements that tie all these authors to Freud and his work on the concept of *eros*. First, they all believe, as Freud proposed, that delayed gratification is a nobler pursuit than immediate (read: sexual) gratification. This is because it permits to think, experience and promote love at a level beyond the closed, intimate space of the family and friends. Second, love is ultimately and mostly a positive thing with a negative underside that should and can be fought against. It is also hardly surprising that this negative aspect is usually related to a sexual drive, intimate hedonism and personal narcissism. These elements are understood as the corruption of the noble, anti-capitalistic side of love; much like Freud advocated for the repression of the sexual drive to delay gratification and channel this energy towards cultural pursuits. This side of love is experienced and lived first as a couple, and through this experience we can, and should, extend it to bond with Others. Only by refusing to yield to the personal and individual Same is it possible to truly love.

Feminist and queer theories on love

Feminist and queer scholarship has had a long-standing interest in a critical engagement with romantic love, its forms, practices (both public and private), ideology and affects. A full engagement with the enormous body of work put out over the decades by feminist and queer scholars is simply impossible in here. I will, for the sake of clarity, divide the positions here as 'positive' and 'negative' in relation to love. This should not be understood as a fatalistic and deterministic outlook on romantic love, but rather as showing how different authors have argued that love, in its entirety or because of some ideological elements of it, is ultimately a positive or negative ideological force, with an emphasis on its material and psychic effects for women.

Given the renewed interest by philosophers and researchers on the political possibilities of love, feminist and queer scholars have engaged in dialogue and critique of certain elements contained in the work of these authors, particularly in the case of Hardt and Negri. In this section, I will delineate the most important elements of these critiques as they help to nuance and complicate the panorama of the politics of love. Eleanor Wilkinson (2016) has criticised their conceptualisation of love on two grounds: first, for creating a too fixed hierarchy of 'loves' and, second, for not considering the negative affects contained in the experience of love-as-communion. Berating identity politics and self-love as too narrow, reactionary and against the 'love of difference' misses the importance that these movements

> can be about both self-actualization, *and* a way of transcending the self, as a way to imagine 'relationality' 'outside the elisions of identity politics' … We must recognize the absolute crucial political role of both self-love and identity politics, specially for those who have spent their lives oppressed, excluded, silenced, and subject to violence. Self-love and identity politics are not narcissistic distractions, they are lifelines.
>
> (Nash, 2013, pp. 5–6)

Thus, there is a conflation of the types of love that lead to a rejection of difference, just like Sarah Ahmed (2004) has already criticised in her work on white-nationalist movements that speak of 'love your own race' to give a positive spin to a supremacist ideology with subaltern groups that speak of self-love as a reaffirmation of their worth in the face of oppression, violence and precarious conditions, like feminist Chicana movements.

Hardt's account of love, Wilkinson argues, is too homogenising in the experience of love as it pays little to no attention to how different bodies experience a communal event like a protest. In other words, just because Michael Hardt has felt something like love during a protest, this does not mean everyone else has felt in this way. People can feel angry, bored, scared, harassed, unsafe, thrilled and so on. Omitting the differential way we experience love leads Hardt to have a vision of love as joy that does not conceive of the less desirable aspects of an affective experience that can also have political potential like anger and frustration. For Wilkinson (2016), this means that 'rather than dividing love into good and bad forms, a truly political understanding of love would recognise the messiness, ambiguities and unruliness of affective life' (p. 10). This point of critique is further elaborated by Lauren Berlant (2011) in her response to Hardt's theory. Berlant calls for a consideration of ambivalence in any attempt to properly conceptualise love. Ambivalence in love means to understand its potentially non-reciprocated form, or asymmetrically so. It also contains the understanding that love, or intimacy in Berlant's work, can be irrational, and that the lines between egalitarian exchanges and subtle domination attempts over love objects can be easily lost at any point. Thus, for Berlant it is better to start at the point of attachment rather than of love as, in this way, love would be but one of the ways in which we relate to the world without reducing it to a desired-for world that love aims for.

Berlant (1997, 2001, 2008, 2012) has also written extensively on love and intimacy. Researching news, films, books and other cultural texts, Berlant has traced a shift in the separation between the public and private spheres, particularly in the US. This shift, she argues, is that intimate and 'private' matters have been increasingly brought to a public discussion on citizenship. This discussion of citizenship looks to regulate and sanction heteronormative, coupled sexual and romantic behaviour (here understood primarily through marriage) as the highest and solely acceptable form of romantic attachment. This has been accompanied then by a cultural output that has sought to legitimise a certain feminine subject:

> the woman who was adequate to its version of normal femininity was as powerful as a feminist would aspire to be, but she was *mainly* invested in the family and cognate emotional networks. She was socially important because she could mediate the worldly temptations of capitalist culture and the processes of family intimacy. Then, as payback for her absorption in the service economy of family life and social reproduction *and* for her own mental and physical health, she was encouraged to fulfil her sexuality, but only through monogamous heteromarital practice.
> (2008, pp. 178–179)

This mixture of liberties and constraints then sets the stage for the unequal ground on which romantic relationships are built. Furthermore, it is because of these tensions that the project of a normal ideology of love has been filled with self-help and therapeutic manuals to help once the project of love fails. This point has also been explored by Eva Illouz (2012) who considers that it is in the institutionalisation of romantic arrangements and the uneven expectations and promises they deliver to men and women that the emancipatory and egalitarian project of romantic love turns instead to pain and misery. Despite this, both Illouz and Berlant remain 'cautiously optimistic' about love. This is in part because, just like Janice Radway (1984) and Lynne Pearce and Jackie Stacey (1995), these authors share a belief that, given romantic love's narrative pervasiveness in our culture, explorations in the subversive potential of its narrative conventions can provide women with ways to fashion alternatives towards more egalitarian modes of romantic relationships while still recognising its utopian dimension.

One of the earliest critiques of romantic love can be traced back to Simone de Beauvoir's *The Second Sex* (1972). Beauvoir writes about love as a gendered experience that is in the periphery of a man's life but at the core of a woman's, or so it has been socially constructed. Thus, a woman is *a woman* as she confirms her lovingness, whereas a man is constituted as such through his success elsewhere. Thus, altruism, self-abnegation and devotion to an Other are pillars of a woman's *womanliness*. This, according to Beauvoir, is neither innate nor from time immemorial. It is a patriarchal historical and economic ideology that ultimately serves a phallic logic of servitude for women. This patriarchal ideology works through two overarching dualisms: 'Life versus Spirit' and 'immanence versus transcendence.' These aren't clear cut from one another but the first, life vs spirit, can be understood in terms of the orientation of one's own life purpose. A life oriented towards Life is repetitive, confined and not a proper human life. It is not so because it simply aims to replicate life. In contrast, a life oriented towards the Spirit is one that looks above biological imperatives and is instructed by creativity and a desire to build, invent, master, control something. The second dualism is immanence versus transcendence. This dualism refers to actions and the attitudes towards life contained therein. An immanent life is one of repetition, stagnation and conservation of the already known. A transcendent life, on the contrary, seeks originality and looks to shape *possible* futures to his/her own accord. This type of life is Beauvoir's most highly valued, very much a Platonic position.

These dualisms take on a social and embodied life through life instructions and situations that are differently scripted for men and women, such as child bearing, career seeking, marriage and so on. These lead Beauvoir to place these dualisms jointly with that of men vs women because the cultural, social and economic scripts tend to put women, throughout her lifetime, in the Life-immanent extreme. The role of love here is to make a woman believe that it is in her complete identification, merger and submission (through marriage and child bearing) to a man that her life is fulfilled. This role of romantic love is both facilitated and augmented by the economic, educational, and social constraints and precariousness of women. Thus, it is possible to speak of a romantic ideology that acts on three different aspects. The first is that womanhood is insufficient without the companionship offered by a man. Second, enabled by the first element, a woman's sexuality is both enabled and legitimised as part of her identity by such companionship. Finally, the value of such sexualised identity is valued largely depending on how men decide to value this at the time of romantic engagement. Simone de Beauvoir is unmistakably pessimistic about romantic love as a form of existential fulfilment because it deprives women of the possibility of self-determination.

This asymmetry of power in relationships and the primacy of couple love and marriage as the highest/noblest forms of love has been the source of much feminist critique (Bell & Binnie, 2000; Berlant, 2008, 2012b; Ferguson & Jonasdottir, 2014; Firestone, 1979; García Andrade, Gunnarsson & Jónasdóttir, 2018; Johnson, 2012; Jonasdottir, 1991; Wilkinson, 2013; Wilkinson & Bell, 2012). Beauvoir's work is not only still relevant by itself, but also in how it resonates, as Paul Johnson remarks, with the hierarchies of romantic love(s) when one adds the monogamous–polyamorous and heterosexual versus non-heterosexuals dyads. He argues that it is in the denial of considering polyamory, same-sex love, episodic sexuality and other non-conventional relationships the quality of love discourses that the supremacy of the supremacy of the heterosexual, marriage-sanctioned and reproductive love is based on. This asymmetry is connected to the analytical axis of this book in two ways. On the one hand, film representations of romantic love can help to reinforce reactionary, patriarchal ideologies of romantic love and gender identities. On the other hand, audiences articulate their reading of the romantic narrative and the gender-roles they portray based on their own position, which involves the possibility of transgressive, compliant or retrograde readings.

Thus, the work of much feminist scholarship about love can be divided as being concerned with two things. The first is challenging the economic, social and cultural inequalities and structure that furthers a patriarchal heterosexist ideology of love in favour of a wider conceptualisation of love. As an example, in film and film studies, this can be related to Laura Mulvey and Annette Kuhn's (Kuhn, 1994; Mulvey, 1989) proposal of a feminist film practice. This proposal was articulated on several levels: to challenge the male gaze that dominates narrative cinema by exploring possible female gazes and their narrative possibilities. Part of this was done by encouraging women to create cinematic experiences as well as demanding better gender equality in casts and crew. Renatta Grossi (2014) has written how heterosexual couple love, as sanctioned by marriage, is written in the very legal frameworks governing many nation-states, leaving out until recently other forms of love. Ana Jónasdóttir (1991; Jónasdóttir & Ferguson, 2014) has coined the term 'love power' to refer to the empowerment and possibility of flourishment that a subject receives when he is loved by another subject. This love power is a necessity for individuals to nourish and live socially, both giving and receiving it. She argues that the way that our love relationships are structured are ones in which men, through the exploitation of a woman's love power, come to have a 'surplus worthiness' that allows them to define themselves in and out of the relationship. Women, on the other hand, are left in the precarious position of being dependent on the constant giving away of their love power in order to get some recognition. Alongside Ann Ferguson, they argue that a feminist conceptualisation of love must challenge couple love and marriage as the objective of a woman's life while recognising the potential of other types of bonds.

Second, it has also meant an engagement with ideas of heterosexuality, monogamy and gender roles. The concern here is how to conceive, live and practise more egalitarian interpersonal relationships. This means addressing the expectations, roles and ideas of coupledom and romantic love as they are socioculturally scripted and lived out. This entails a politicisation of the intimate, the personal and private as loci of struggle and reconfiguration. Luci Irigaray (2012) argues that the key for this to happen lies in the recognition that our current way of amorous relationship is dominated by subject–object relationships and that a shift towards subject–subject relationships is necessary. She proposes to change from 'I love you' as the 'you' in this expression is an object of my desire to 'I love to you'. This entails, according to Irigaray, a recognition of the 'twoness' of a relationship. By recognising this, it is possible to love a subject while respecting their 'otherness' instead of reducing them to an appendix of oneself. What's left to enquire is whether such a technical change in language can overcome material, symbolic and other inequalities in relationships.

A similar position can be seen in bell hooks' *All about Love* (2000) in which hooks proposes that we ought *to understand love as a verb, rather than a noun*. She suggests that by understanding just how much work is needed for love to work and how it can be found in more than the expected places (nuclear family and partner), it is possible to go further from the narcissistic, sex- and desire-driven version of love towards one where service with and for others is valued by all parties. For hooks, this means that men must learn to receive and give love instead of basing their love on sexual performance. For women, she argues that self-love is necessary if women are to establish relationships that are not toxic and based on antiquated gender roles. This self-love includes a search for self-determination that includes both their relationship with others and a personal self-fulfilment. Thus, for hooks, as for many other feminist scholars (K. R. Allen & Walker, 1992; Bryson, 2014; Gordon et al., 1996; Lynch, 2014), there must be a consensual redefinition of the ethical and political dimension of caregiving within relationships as work with value valuable that cannot be reduced to just a woman's 'role' or 'duty'. This dimension of redefining care-giving, self-determination, monogamy, marriage and heteronormativity is a concern of all three research questions of this project, as this is a continuous project of romantic self that cuts across class, gender, representations and affects.

Historical and sociological approaches to love

Here I outline approaches to love that sidestep both psychoanalytic and Marxist conceptual frameworks. The first is Denis de Rougemont's *Love in the Western World* (1983), a historic-literary study of the roots and elements of romantic love that has been hugely influential, in particular with its dissection of the different elements of romantic love in literature and popular culture. The second are three sociological studies on love in contemporary societies that have generated much dialogue surrounding the ideas contained therein: Eva Illouz's study of the evolution of contemporary relationships, Niklas Luhmann and Anthony Giddens' study on the transformation of intimacy and romantic relationships.

Denis de Rougemont and the foundational myth of romantic love

In his book *Love in the Western World* (1983) Rougemont argues that the myth of Tristan and Isolde is the foundational myth of romantic love – also called courtly love – as it contains all the elements we identify with romance in it. This myth, in turn, is structurally and narratively a mixture of the meeting of several cultures and ideas of passion. There are three main sources which provide the character of courtly love. First off there's Platonism, which provides the idea of the divine nature of the loved one, the idea of the otherworldly feeling of love and the idea of love as transcending to a higher state. Second, from the druidic beliefs of the north we have the idea of woman as a divine being, as Eros; the idea of chivalric pride and the separation between light and shadow. Finally, from Manichaeism we owe the dualist conception of love and the idea that the material realm is perennially unhappy, so true happiness can only be found after death. While some of these traits are far more easily relatable to modern notions of love, one need think no further than films like *Ghost* (Zucker, 1990), *P.S. I Love You* (LaGravenese, 2007) and *If I Stay* (Cutler, 2014) to see how death, the afterlife and other elements listed above are still in play in narratives of romantic love. These examples also illustrate that their use nowadays is far more ludic and playful than the strict and structured explanation Rougemont offers in their medieval use.

Besides these sources, Rougemont identifies the triadic structure of love, as many other authors do as well, as its basic narrative element. This means that love contains two subjects who display affection towards each other and a third subject acting as the obstacle which stands in between the consummation of the first two's love. Likewise, he considers desire, even if coincidentally, much like in psychoanalysis, increasing as the distance from the subject and the desired object increasing and only possible as long as such distance exists. In other words, it is only possible to desire that which we do not possess. According to Rougemont, from this idea springs the difference between loving another subject and loving the idea of love. This, in turn, constitutes the great opposition he finds in romantic love: that between *agape* and *eros*. It's an opposition that further develops into the binaries of loveless marriage and passionate affair, before-marriage and after-marriage, love-as-passion and love-as-constancy, to name a few. This opposition has been extensively worked in film, in particular during the first half of the twentieth century (see Potter, 2002; Shumway, 2003).

Rougemont typifies this tension between *eros* and *agape* as a clash between the destructive, individualistic, fatalistic *eros*/romantic love and a communal, perseverant, virtuous *agape*/marriage. This is in line with his views on marriage, the increasing divorce rates of the first half of the twentieth century and the First World War, which led him to argue that stronger communal ties were needed to avoid the dissolution of society. Furthermore, his argument speaks of a fundamental shift in the nature of marriage: the introduction of personal choice and, in consequence, of love, which will be crucial in decades to come. While marriage as an institution dates even further back than the twelfth century, it is only until the seventeenth–eighteenth century that its nature starts to experiment significant changes. Previously an institution that sought to maintain and create kinship, wealth and affinities, marriages were arranged and sought after depending on their social and economic viability for both parties involved. With the popularisation of free choice in marriage – which is linked as well to new forms of wealth acquisition and distribution that were not related to one's family – romantic love starts to play an increasingly important role in bringing and maintaining couples together. The promise of love and fulfilment thus becomes internal and intrinsic to the idea of marriage.

Although impossible to unite all works of romance under one rubric, it is possible to collect a set of elements they all share, and indeed, that all romantic stories touch upon, even if it is only tangentially. First is the triadic structure of romantic love, which I have mentioned above, in which there is a subject that loves, a subject that is loved and a disruptive element comes into play. This pull-and-push between the three creates a necessary second element: distance. Love, sometimes in the guise of desire or lust, cannot work without a distance between the lovers, a distance usually brought on by the third element (e.g. a paternal figure, divorce, war, a journey). This distance, in turn, requires a resolution, usually by bridging it through marriage (at least in these works) or by death, the tragic ending par excellence. It is only a recent development that such distance remains either unabridged or left in a limbo, like in the film *Beginners* (Mills, 2011). A fourth factor is individualisation and the privatisation of desire. By privatisation of desire I mean not only the choosing of partner through romantic love rather than through social obligations but also how romantic love operates inwards, towards the individual, rather than towards broader social phenomena. The dissection of Rougemont's work here serves one crucial function: to illustrate the different narrative, ideological and affective elements of romantic love for both audiences and films and thus to guide much of the analysis on romantic love.

Intimacy in contemporary sociological approaches to love

Niklas Luhmann's work *Love as Passion: The Codification of Intimacy* (1986) elaborates in a distinct way the opposition between *eros/agape* that Rougemont also wrote about. Starting with the seventeenth and eighteenth centuries, Luhmann argues that because of the division between married life and romantic passion, in literature, romance novels, theatre and in behaviour manuals, a codification of love begun to be widespread. This codification of love is a set of rules, tropes, oppositions and stages that everyone goes through in their intimate relationships. The learning and living out of these codes was possible, according to Luhmann, because for the first time it was possible for women to reject the advances of their suitors. Not only this, but Luhmann suggests that 'interpersonal interpenetrations' between two lovers acquire a highly individualised and precarious nature. Interpersonal interpenetrations are the communicational exchanges people have where they showcase their qualities, preferences, flaws and other individual traits. Luhmann argues that communicating these can be incredibly difficult because of the unstable nature and downright incommunicability of some. It is through the codes of love that the gaps in this communication can be bridged. Finally, for Luhmann, it is important that this codification of love serves a higher social purpose, as remaining in a highly individualised, atomised communicational exchange threatens to erode the foundation of the social. This foundation is the family and, thus for Luhmann, the ideal ending is marriage.

Luhmann's view of love as mostly a communicational, disembodied practice is outdated and not without criticism (see Illouz, 1997). However, his argument that there was a shift during the seventeenth–eighteenth century in the codification of intimacy has been echoed by Anthony Giddens (1992) when he wrote:

> Romantic love, which began to make its presence felt from the late eighteenth century onwards, drew upon such ideals and incorporated elements of *amour passion,* while nevertheless becoming distinct from both. Romantic love introduced the idea of a narrative into an individual's life – a formula which radically extended the reflexivity of sublime love. The telling of a story is one of the meanings of 'romance', but this story became individualised, inserting self and other into a personal narrative which had no particular reference to wider social processes ... The complex of ideas associated with romantic love for the first time associated love with freedom, both being seen as normatively desirable states. Passionate love has always been

liberating, but only in the sense of generating a break with routine and duty. It was precisely this quality of *amour passion* which set it apart from existing institutions. Ideals of romantic love, by contrast, inserted themselves directly into the emergent ties between freedom and self-realisation.

(pp. 39–40)

Romantic love's individualised, normative and liberating condition sets it as the intimate paradigm that sought to reconcile *eros* and *agape*, the all-encompassing sexual desire of amour passion with the routine and duty of married life. At the same time, the idea of the narrative and its individualised nature begins a process of romantic rationalisation whereby the lover believes it is in her/his power to control the decisions that lead to her/his happiness and romantic fulfilment. Giddens argues that by uprooting the intimate from transgenerational practices, socioeconomic contracts and kinship alliances, this risked creating anxieties and ontological insecurities in an individual's romantic life. By ontological insecurity, Giddens refers to the gradual loss of grip by traditions and social institutions in an individual's life (he attributed this to modernisation as a process in general). This in turn, generates the anxiety of searching how to anchor one's position in society through processes of personal and interpersonal realisation. In regards to romantic relationships and intimacy, it meant that the constraints of the family, arranged marriages, class, race and space were greatly diminished, if not completely evaporated, in favour of making love one of the most noble forms of self-realisation. However, no longer did a romantic relationship warrant the economic, social and personal security it did in times past.

Giddens has coined the term 'pure relationship' which

> refers to a situation where a social relation is entered into for its own sake, for what can be derived by each person from a sustained association with another; and which is continued only in so far as it is thought by both parties to deliver enough satisfaction for each individual to stay within it.
>
> (1992, p. 58)

This pure relationship, Giddens argued, was the ideal culmination, in the late twentieth century, of the consolidation of the individualised nature of intimacy and romantic love. This was helped by its democratisation, understood here as the access of women to education, the job market, by processes of globalisation and the growth of expert systems. For Giddens, expert systems are forms of organisation and management of large bodies of information that help rule our lives in contemporary societies. In the case of the pure relationship, the main expert systems are those of therapy, self-therapy and constant self-interrogation. Thus, this means that the pure relationship is based around a project of self-disclosure, sexual and communicational intimacy and the promise of self-development. Films like *When Harry Met Sally* (Reiner, 1989), *Sleepless in Seattle* (Ephron, 1993), *You've Got Mail* (Ephron, 1998) provide examples of the idealised realisation of the supposedly 'pure' relationship. According to Giddens, the problem with the pure relationship is that the ties one builds with another can, at any point, be dissolved as they are not anchored in any social, cultural or economic institution. The anxiety contained in pure relationships leads to addictive behaviours, such as alcoholism, eating disorders, drug abuse and sex addiction. The latter is partly attributed to an increased period of sexual experimentation and avoidance of commitment. This mind-boggling analytical jump from the frailty of contemporary relationships to their addiction substitutes underlines Giddens' own detachment with empirical work (see Gross & Simmons, 2002; Sica, 1986). The idea of the pure relationship has been criticised for its lack of understanding of the gendered inequality of many contemporary relationships in regards to housework, gender roles, sexual satisfaction, monetary control, child care and caregiving arrangements, and men's emotional stunted development (Connell, 2000, 2006; Jamieson, 1999). I, too, critique the idea of the 'pure relationship' as too easily claiming victory in a heavily classed world.

Self-commoditised love

Eva Illouz's *Consuming the Romantic Utopia: Love and the Cultural Contradictions of Capitalism* (1997) traces the changes the concept of love has experienced at the turn of the twentieth century and its growing intermeshing with the sphere of consumption, focusing on the study of several media outlets and contemporary romantic practices. From the beginning of the twentieth century, Illouz argues there is a shift from Victorian 'private' ideals and utilitarian customs to a more 'public' and hedonistic consumer/leisure-oriented *practice* of love. She identifies two main changes: the boom of 'dating' and the abandonment of the 'visits' and a dual process she calls of 'romanticisation of commodities' and 'commodification of romance'. Based on this shift, she argues that both how we talk about love (and, connected to this, how we conceive it) and our romantic practices are informed by our class position. Furthermore, there is an existing tension about the cultural competences – borrowing the term from Bourdieu (1984) – and a self-perceived lack of them, the 'ironic distance' of the middle and upper classes clashing continuously with the apparent 'over-identification' of the working class.

She examines the boom in dating through the idea of the liminoid, arguing that romantic activities common on dates possess many of the elements of a *secular ritual* and indeed position themselves in a temporality that is different from that of everyday life, a *romantic love time*. This liminoid time, increasingly defined by consumption – ritualistic activities that privilege lavish spending and luxury – coexists with activities that only indirectly or explicitly reject the mediation of consumption and consumer culture. The latter kind of activities appeal to the element of selflessness, the rejection of material inclinations of the self that is so enticing to the bourgeois postmodern *ethos*. This, according to Illouz, points to a tension and a game of class positions and the different enjoyments and valuations each individual derives from a given romantic activity. The dialectic between the pleasure of love and the class games it invokes in contemporary societies becomes a source of much rationalisation and self-control from lovers. As a final point, Illouz argues that an individual's love discourse is influenced by her/his class position twofold: it articulates with a self-perception of one's 'cultural competences' or lack of them and a position in the spectrum of cultural identification or of 'ironic distance' taken in regards of the practices of love.

Romantic identity

As evident thus far, with romantic love there is a great emphasis nowadays on the self-fashioning of one's own romantic self. The narrativisation of one's own romantic ideals, attitudes, practices, affects and experiences is a constitutive element of what I call 'romantic identity'. Considered as a subset of a person's identity, other elements are gender, sexuality, race, class, age, education level and religiosity. In this section, I will succinctly outline a few of the elements of sociological conceptualisations of identity. I do not consider psychoanalytic and psychological long histories with the concept for the main reason that they are hyper-individualistic and largely non-ideological. Thus, the starting points of consideration of the notion of identity in this project are sociological in nature. First is the idea of the instability of identities. Identities are unstable because they are constantly negotiated, contingent and self-reflected on. Authors like Zygmunt Bauman (2004) and Scott Lash (1990) have used the term *bricoleur*, borrowing it from Claude Lévi-Strauss, to refer to identity construction. A *bricoleur* is one who builds something with whatever is at hand. This means that identity is a continuous process, it is always incomplete. This lends a fragmentary, fluctuating character to late modernity identities that Bauman, in a similar vein to authors like Anthony Giddens (1991), assumes to be different from those of early modernity, which were anchored on kinship, myths, rites, religion and strong social ties. The 'whatever is at hand' in identity are historical and context-dependent ideological discourses of gender, sexuality, class, race, power, love, kinship and nation. Second, Bauman argues that in late (liquid) modernity identities are grounded in socialisation and self-reflection. In other words, identities are performative (see Berger, 1974; Goffman, 2004). Third is the tension between identification and distancing that produces identities. Stuart Hall argued (1996) that 'identities are constructed through, not outside, difference' (p. 4). This means that through a process of distinction, of exclusion of *what is not*, of marking differences, identities are constructed. This, he recognises, unavoidably begets a parallel process of the construction of a sameness. These two processes are in constant destabilising tension, individually, socially and ideologically. This means that the affirmation of a certain identity always contains the rejection, usually thought of as inferior, of another(s). This affirmatory/rejection struggle of identities is inscribed in larger ideological struggles over hegemony and sub-alterity.

With these points in mind, a 'romantic identity' is the union point between sexual, gender, class, race identities and the different subject positions taken in different aspects of the competing romantic ideologies of the moment. According to John Lee (1998), there are six main love 'styles': *eros, ludus, storge, pragma, mania* and *agape*. Each of these 'styles' had an accompanying sex style, or preferred sexual practices. Lee (1998) called them ideologies as they represented not just ideas in the abstract, but also practices and prescriptions that were socialised and lived out communally. As such, he believed that it was nigh impossible to find 'pure' states of the different kinds of love. The qualities, traits, affects and practices contained in these ideologies are gendered, as exemplified in figures such as Don Juan, the male ludic lover par excellence, or the femme fatale, the female erotic lover; and also in the privileging and expectation of caregiving roles that is usually pushed onto women vis-à-vis the providing role for men. In other practice-based terms, which are also gendered, it encompasses attitudes regarding things like: who pays on the first date, the dilemma of sexual intercourse after X amount of dates, household duties, to resolve an argument straight away or after sleeping on it, to name a handful. Though the heterosexual, coupled, married love continues to be the pervading hegemonic ideology surrounding much of the ideology of romantic love, to understand romantic love as a monolithic ideology would be counterproductive. In different studies of romantic films in North America, authors like David Shumway (2003) and Cherry Potter (2002) highlight that the romantic love is suffused with ideas of many differing other discourses (intimacy, devotion, friendship, Platonism, etc.) that act as counterweights, exert contradictions and open spaces for different modes of interpersonal associations. As both authors suggest, cinema has been the privileged vehicle for the reproduction, contestation and historical reflection on the larger shifts in intimacy and romantic love in the West, particularly in the twentieth century, a point I share, with an onus on ideology.

Projective identification

In addition to the three ways in which romantic love has been dealt with in cinema (see introduction), Edgar Morin (2005) developed the concept of 'projective identifications' to deal with how cinematic images influence an individual's construction and negotiation of her/his identity. Of all the 'polymorphic projective identifications' that cinema produces, Morin signals love as the ultimate one, because

> We identify with the loved one, with his joys and misfortunes, experiencing feelings that are properly his. We project ourselves onto him, that is, we identify him with ourselves, cherishing him, what is more, with all the love that we carry within ourselves. His photos, his trinkets, his handkerchiefs, his house, are all infused with his presence. Inanimate objects are impregnated with his soul and force us to love them.
> (2005, pp. 89–90)

I find Morin's proposition illuminating because it allows us to get away from the analytic binary of romantic love in film either reinforcing or contesting particular ideologies, as well as not understanding identification as being gender-fixed. Instead, the focus is on the *ambivalence* of love in film as both potentially reinforcing and contesting certain ideologies at different moments. Morin's concept is appropriate because it recognises that love is experienced, on- and off-screen, fragmentarily. Thus, the idea of projective identifications is one that is transversal to my arguments and findings. At the same time, this ambivalence is related to one of the characteristics of love-as-commodity, its liminality (Illouz, 1997). The liminal is a moment for utopian thinking, of exposing ideologies and subverting hierarchies but it can also help to reinforce them, to strengthen ideologies and to reduce the effectiveness of counter-hegemonic acts.

It is also important to understand the possibility of non-emotional projective modes of engagement as well as how the social context of consumption might affect identification and other modes of engagement (cf. McDonald, 2018). Martin Barker (1989, 2005) has criticised the concept of identification because, as he contends, it possesses little explanatory power for audience research because it has been taken as a simple synonym for engagement. In the words of Diane Carr (2005), 'the pleasures of "identification" are overrated. Or, perhaps such pleasures are dependent on the contexts of play' (p. 475). Therefore, while identity and identification play an important role for audiences, they are not the sole reason or motive people engage with films.

It is with this critique in mind that I will touch briefly on the concepts of liminality and ideology to further elucidate its importance to an understanding of the positioning of romantic love in contemporary popular films and by their audiences.

Ideology

Karl Marx's comprehensive volume of work, some in collaboration with Friedrich Engels, is the cornerstone of modern understandings and developments of the concept of ideology. Early on, Marx conceives ideology as a veil that acts and is present in the superstructure, obfuscating the economic base and production relationships within the system to the proletariat. This presents as a form of false consciousness acting on the working class that prevents them from acting, thinking and seeing in accord with their 'real' class positions and that benefitted the ruling class (Marx & Engels, 1972). Refining this premise, and broadening its reach, for Marx (Marx, 1970; Marx & Engels, 1967) ideology was the set of ideas of the dominant class, tied to their social, political and economic interests, that were passed down through different sociocultural elements/institutions of the superstructure in specific historical contexts.

From this follows an elaboration of ideology as a product of the superstructure and as a description of human beings. Ideology presents a distorted and deformed description of the real conditions of production and the life of people. This is partly what is known as 'false consciousness' (Eagleton, 1991). This distortion and deformation is a direct consequence of the elite's interest to keep their stronghold of dominance over the proletariat. This entails that all ideas are a product of this dominant elite, both the ideas of the ruling class – which Marx famously said 'are in every epoch the ruling ideas' (Marx & Engels, 1972) – and those of the dominated class. This is so because the ruling class owns not only the means of production of material goods but also the means of production of ideas and spiritual or cultural goods.

Several of these points were contested by Louis Althusser (Althusser, 1969; Althusser & Balibar, 1971; Althusser & Matheron, 1997). Influenced by the work of Jaques Lacan, Althusser argues for two major changes to Marx's early conceptions of ideology and human consciousness. First, he moved to focus on the structure and not the individual for we cannot fully recognise an individual prior to its societal interaction (Althusser & Balibar, 1971). Second, Althusser (1972) maintains we can never reach 'the real' and thus 'false consciousness' as a concept is of little use; we are stuck at the level of 'reality'. In this view, a subject's values, beliefs, preferences, biases, taste and taboos, then, are inculcated by what Althusser (1972) calls *ideological practice* which, in turn, is constituted by what he termed ideological state apparatuses (ISAs) – governmental bureaucracy, the church, the school, family, media institutions and so on. This would suggest that it is through interactions, rituals, exchanges and everyday flows between the ISAs and practices that individuals not only learn how to be subjects but come into being as ideological subjects. Althusser named this process *interpellation*. Since it is highly impractical for every individual to carry scripts for all the ideological subjects s/he will 'interpret' in her/his daily life, Althusser (1972; Althusser & Balibar, 1971) claims that ideology is ahistorical. Although it seems to solve one set of problems by refocusing attention onto the structures which inform human consciousness, this approach to Marxism has been criticised by scholars such as Stuart Hall (1985) as too rigid: Hall argued that Althusser's model left no room for the subject to resist or contest their so-called interpellation into ideology or indeed, to contest ideology itself.

Despite this, interpellation and Althusser's other conceptualisations have been widely used and appropriated within film studies. Christian Metz (1974, 1981) and Jean Louis Baudry (1978, 1985) both use the concept of interpellation extensively to inform their theory of the cinematic apparatus. Known as the 'institutional' mode of spectatorship (Mayne, 1998), it posits that through an analysis of the film-as-text, it is possible to theorise and account for the subjects cinema construction. In other words, it is possible, according to these authors, to know how audiences *read* a particular film and are *interpellated* as subjects of a given ideological formation through a careful analysis of the text and its underlying production elements (see Baudry, 1985; Metz, 1981). This sense making is facilitated through the 'reality effect' the cinematic apparatus provides, easing the film viewers' resistance and co-opting them to comply ideologically. Despite the further critiques of this model (Bordwell & Thompson, 2010; Hall, 1985; Mayne, 1998; Mulvey, 1989; Shohat & Stam, 1996) stemming from both inside and outside of film studies, the idea that a film provides the viewer with certain *ideologically charged subject positions* and interpellates her/him through these positions is still widely accepted. Equally problematic is the corollary idea that for scholars working solely under this perspective, it is possible to discern the 'spectator' from theory alone and the ideological relationship between spectator and film.

A major problem with Althusser and those he inspired – and worked with – was the overemphasis on the power of the structure, leaving little room to reflect on the possibilities and shapes of agency. Directly or not, many have sought to address this flaw in Althusser's work. The act of wilfully opposing ideal subject positions, as they are put forward by dominant ideologies, is one with a long-standing history in all inhabited spaces. In the case of cinema, against this perspective of the infantilised, passive, imprisoned, co-opted spectator, it is possible to find an author like bell hooks (hooks, 1999), who uses her experiences as a member of an oppressed and discriminated social group to theorise what she terms an 'oppositional gaze'. This oppositional gaze is an act of looking, of choosing not to identify with the subjects presented by primarily white popular cinema; it is an act engaged first by black female spectators who, aware of their own race, class and gender position, resist, reject, mock and appropriate through this gaze the subjectivities (white/Hollywood) cinema presents. This unsettling of the universal categories of spectator and interpellation is not an isolated response but part of a larger set of scholarship by scholars who, although with a shared interest in Marxism and struggles by minoritised and oppressed groups, have considered ideology more in tune with the writings of Antonio Gramsci.

Gramsci and counter-hegemony

Antonio Gramsci (1971) identifies two forms of political control: domination or direct physical coercion (e.g., police and the military) and *cultural hegemony* which refers to both ideological control and consent. Gramsci argued that no regime or system can sustain itself on the basis of coercion and brute force and that in the long run it has to appeal to its foundation, its inhabitants. In order to do so, the dominating class utilises moral, religious, ethical beliefs and practices that help and support their project, something he coins 'hegemony'. Its presence and dispersion throughout society means, for Gramsci (Gramsci, 1971), that it is internalised, naturalised by the population and becomes 'common sense'. As pointed out previously, Gramsci coins the term *counter-hegemony* to account for when individuals and groups challenge ideology through actions, movements and thoughts (1971, 1995). Since for Gramsci all humans were intellectuals (some were trained as such, called traditional intellectuals) the first step to build a *counter-hegemony* was to lift the 'veil' of ideology, to be able to see the conditions of production of material objects and conditions. It is important to understand that struggles over hegemony entail the production of new hegemonic ideologies that look to displace prevailing ones. Gramsci saw this as a positive characteristic of hegemony, as it could provide the mass of the population with, in the case of Gramsci, ways to contest fascism through different means.

Gramsci is an influential thinker of a shift in certain theories of ideology towards a more 'humanistic' perspective, privileging culture as the locus of ideological reproduction and contestation (Eagleton, 1991; Gardiner, 1992; Thompson, 1990; Žižek, 1994). Raymond Williams (1977), Stuart Hall (1973), Ien Ang (1985), David Morley (1980, 1986) and John Fiske (1987) are some of the scholars who took on this Gramsci-influenced approach. Focusing on television rather than film, scholars within this tradition, later known as 'British cultural studies', researched the audiences' responses, activities and readings of different shows. In them, they sought to study and focus in the counter-hegemonic practices of different subjects and groups. For example, Ien Ang (1985) studied the letter responses of women to the soap opera *Dallas*. According to Ang, the understandings of these women were informed by two main elements: knowledge of the elements of a 'melodramatic imagination', borrowing the term from Peter Brooks (1995), and 'emotional realism'. The latter can be understood as a reading at a more connotative level, an internal level of what is felt to be real. This realism stands in contrast with an empirical realism, according to Ang, but they are situated and address different levels and, I would add, moments of readings.

This division between 'emotional' and 'empirical' realism is crucial to consider the relationship between what is shown on screen, what and how is it read, what is felt and what is experienced. This helps to articulate the contradictions, contestation and embodiment of hegemonic discourses. At the same time, I also consider that there is an uneven entry level of cultural competences when it comes to enjoying a romantic film. But while Brooks' concept is suitable, I will adhere to the works of authors like Annette Kuhn (1994), Sara Ahmed (2004) and Lauren Berlant (1997, 2000, 2008), who have all written and worked on film, romance, intimacy, gender, emotions and ideology. These authors agree that romance contributes to the construction of gendered subjects according to the dominant patriarchal ideology where the female is subordinated to a male partner, only complete when she is with him (see also Chaudhuri, 2006; De Lauretis, 1986; Ebert, 1988). This has contributed to construct gender and interpersonal relationships as a binary and in a fatalistic, natural way. These authors also argue that cinema and love also offer possibilities to disrupt and contest the dominant ideologies, but they consider, in the case of cinema, alternative textual options, not the audiences as the locus of this.

This leads me to the final consideration of the role of ideology. Both 'sides' of ideology provide a solid foundation on which to study texts and audiences. Gramsci and cultural studies move away from the textual-centric view of the Althusser-influenced film studies and in a way permit us to 'expect the unexpected' from the text–audience interaction, particularly from the latter. On the other hand, the idea of subject positions already contained within the film text allows for a preliminary consideration of a possible typology of viewers, modes of viewing, ways of readings and pleasures derived which is not only analytically insightful but was methodologically helpful.

Liminality and ideology

Arnold van Gennep (1960) first coined the term 'liminality' in 1960. His work served as a basis for Victor Turner's (1977) work, which popularised its use. Van Gennep considers liminality as the 'extraction', the displacement of something (or someone) during the ritual to detach him/her from cultural boundaries or to transform it into something anew. As a stage of a ritual, it has both an entry and exit point, constrained by time and space. Turner expands on this idea, this threshold between worlds, to develop the role of the liminal in symbolic acts, in rituals. As an anthropologist particularly interested in rites of passages, Turner considered one of its stages was the liminal stage, where the boundaries of the sacred and the profane, the taboo and the normal were subverted, inversed or wiped out for as long as the ritual took place. Turner, based on an evolutionary view of societies, differentiates between the 'liminal' (pre-industrialised societies) and 'liminoid', the stage of the industrialised rituals. Contrary to the strict and solemn traits of liminality and its rituals, where entrance is compulsory, liminoid rituals require the individual's *will* to enter. For example a person wishing to see a movie will voluntarily queue up (or go online) to buy her/his tickets and later, sit down and enjoy the film. Based on this, Turner (1982) argues that liminal phenomena tended to be 'eufunctional' – that is, beneficial – to the structure of a system while liminoid phenomena, 'on the other hand, are often parts of social critiques or even revolutionary manifestoes . . . exposing the injustices, the inefficiencies, and immoralities of the mainstream economic and political structures and organizations' (p. 86). Then, the liminoid ritual performance can constitute an action that disrupts and is subversive to hegemonic formations and ideological precepts, as Homi Bhabha argues (1994). If this is so, then romance on- and off-screen can't be easily discarded or glorified as servile or counter-hegemonic to a cultural elite. Rather, it is the *ambiguity* of romantic love, working for and against cultural mandates, as the satires of Douglas Sirk show (Gledhill, 1987), that provides a rich and vast space for liminality to enter and 'play'. Then, it is part of this project to look for those moments in the text, in the audience and in the couple where a 'politics of romantic love' and the role of the liminal/liminoid can be discerned, classified and studied.

In line with this, performativity theorists like Judith Butler (1990, 1993) and Elin Diamond (1996) suggest these liminoid moments can allow for an embodiment, a way of revealing the patriarchal ideology of gender roles and gender construction by denaturalising that which in the everyday is taken for granted. The opposite can also happen. That is, subjects who otherwise are highly alert to reactionary and retrograde ideologies and understandings of race, class, gender and so on can find themselves in a liminoid moment where this alertness gives way to compliance or at least to complacence. For example, a scorned lover who resorts to a misogynist/misandrist discourse to cope with heartbreak. Or a football fan who during the match resorts to pejorative adjectives for those of the opposing team but who'd normally preach humanistic-cosmopolitan values. There are fracture lines through which affect and liminality show up and act as a counter-balance at different levels of the exchange between the media product and the audience. But while there might be room for 'optimism', David Shumway (2003) argues that screwball comedies and their revival in the 1980s and 1990s work as a mystification of marriage. In a critique of Stanley Cavell (1981), who wrote on screwball comedies and their potential to spark a reflection on marriage, Shumway argues that marriage is portrayed antithetically to romance in these comedies and their successors. This leaves the latter as too 'unreal' to be true, strengthening, according to Shumway, marriage as the unequivocal, unavoidable, desirable 'real' ending (cf. Glitre, 2006). But, as I already pointed out, Shumway only focuses on the textual level, without giving any weight to the audience, who are seen only as dupes of the mystification of the film ideology. Thus, I consider that to avoid falling into either extreme of the romantic love–ideology characterisation, it is necessary to further delve into the text–audience dyad and how it can be said to work with and against romantic love.

Thus, liminality and the liminoid as concepts are related to romantic love and film on at least two levels: first, on a textual level and, second, accounting for the experience of cinema-going as a liminoid ritual. On the first level, Roland Barthes (1990), in his famous *Lovers Discourse*, says that relationships have no place, they are an *atopos*, impossible to locate anywhere. Barthes argues that love is experienced as something different, where one is not oneself but rather one's own image acting out one's love towards the beloved. José Ortega y Gasset (1957) also writes about the experience of love being different from any other because it is as if it were from a different dimension, from a distinct and unique world composed of two. In other words, this distinctiveness of love, of the relationship, of the lover and the beloved of a different time and space is highlighted by Eva Illouz (1997) who claims contemporary romantic practices invoke a liminal time lived and experienced differently from the non-romantic time of our lives, a moment she calls 'romantic time'. This 'romantic time' is characterised by a reluctance to be constrained by economic or social factors, a desire to go past them and a search for unique experiences. This, Illouz continues, relates to the ideology of commoditised romantic love, where leisure is considered to be a *sine qua non* condition of the consumer and free spending during leisure time is compliant with neoliberal capitalist consumer politics of personal expression. Textually then, romance operates by positioning this 'romantic time' at the forefront, juxtaposed to the monotonous everyday life in various ways. In so doing, the narrative opens the way for ideological reproduction and/or critique.

Second, Ella Shohat and Robert Stam (1996; Stam, 1989) point out spectatorship can be a liminal experience. Loosely borrowing from Mikhail Bakhtin's notion of the carnival (1984), they argue that cinema as a space brackets and voids sociocultural identities and allow for a period of 'dreams and self-fashioning' (p. 165). Likewise, Steve Derné (2000), in his ethnography of cinema-going in India, argues that men like to watch films as a 'liminal escape' from reality. In them, they like progressive, adventurous, feisty women; stories of marriages for love, of 'fighting for love', of going against the chaste system and overcoming the family opposition to a marriage of love. But as much as his respondents liked these characters and the plot twists 'at odds' with Indian traditions, they also stated their preference to marry somebody within their own caste, to settle down with girls who were more conservative and overall not as feisty as their filmic counterparts. In short, 'liminality', when related to cinema going, can constitute a moment sought after for its promise of freedom, of unconstrained daydreaming and inversion of the everyday. But this can be experienced as a magical moment, an escape to a fantasy, an impossible world that makes it able to cope with the 'real world'.

Alongside this, historical research on audiences and cinema-going through different periods, contexts and circumstances has shed light on the practices, the motives and the significance of the experience of cinema-going. Robert C. Allen (1990) identified four major aspects of historical research on film audiences: exhibition (the how and where films were screened), audiences (social composition), performance and activation/meaning-making.[2] Here I emphasise contributions about the historical social experience of female cinema-going and how these might help to understand cinema-going itself as a *romantic activity*. I do this because as Peter Krämer (1998) argues, 'until the mid-1960s, Hollywood had viewed women, particularly mature women in charge of regular film outings with their husbands and children, as the key audience with a range of films, including the industry's most important releases. (p. 615; see also Richards, 1994). Miriam Hansen (1991), focusing on North American silent cinema, writes that the possibility of cinema-going, infused with an egalitarian appeal, to an extent, granted visibility for women and immigrants (see also Haller, 2012). This she connects to a transformation in the public sphere, an incipient feminisation of it. At the same time, the cinema was becoming an alternative public sphere, one of relative inclusion for the middle class. Janet Staiger's (1992, 2000) work, based on a breadth of case studies from the silent era up to the films of Woody Allen[3] – taking what she terms as a historical materialist approach to cinema – is a response to a focus on the text–reader relationship. It highlights how historical contexts and their shifts or changes as well as the audience's intersectional identities affect the reception of texts. That is, how context, at micro and macro levels, influences the reading of a text at any and various points in time. Jackie Stacey's (1994) seminal work *Star Gazing: Hollywood Cinema and Female Spectatorship* uses fan letters from *women* and a questionnaire to sketch the relationship that female audiences had with the movie stars of 1940s and 1950s Britain. In a critique of psychoanalytic, ahistorical spectatorship studies, Stacey argues for the historical and local positioning of the audience to understand the *gendered* relationship audiences develop with cinema-going, movies and movie stars.

She delineates three main discourses arising from the letters written to her: identification,[4] consumption and escapism. The latter is linked to the cinema as a physical, sensuous space to escape the material precarity of home at times of war. During the period discussed, identification was based on the differences between audiences and the movie stars, while after the war, with the post-war consumption boom, this shifted to emphasise their similarities, aided by a plethora of available commodities with which to accomplish this. Annette Kuhn builds on Stacey's work with a project of cinema reception and consumption in Britain during the 1930s. She uses the term 'ethnohistory' to signal her determination in using oral accounts (gathered through extended interviews and questionnaires) as well as archival material to draw out the myriad accounts – their motives, pleasures, logics and codes – of the practice of cinema-going. One of these accounts is that of courting and romance during cinema-going. Kuhn points out that the experience of the romantic film, narratively, while important for some in its enabling of identifications, idealisations and projections of the audience onto and from the text, is just a fraction of the 'all-encompassing somatic, sensuous and affective involvement in the cinema experience' (p. 147). Kuhn (2002) writes:

> Cinemas are remembered as places where courting could be conducted in relative comfort and privacy ... associated exclusively with one kind of cinema: the sumptuous new picture palace [super-cinema] ... These cinemas are the heterotopias[5] of courtship ... Cinemas as physical spaces – as *places* – embody all these qualities of **liminality** and heterogeneity: they are very much part of the built environment, and yet they conjoin the mundanity and materiality of bricks and mortars with the worlds of fantasy and imagination.
>
> (pp. 140–141, bold mine)

Kuhn also points out that, at the time, an invitation to go to the cinema was an express signal of (heteronormative) romantic interest. This wasn't to any cinema, but to a super-cinema, with additional treating to food and sweets, and, ideally, to the back row, where double seats were available. For some, this was the (highly codified) entry-point to courting.[6] Thus, the experience of cinema-going was an important 'romantic time' (Illouz, 1997), conditioned by economic conditions, that contrasted with the everyday. Importantly, it also signalled an entry into (young) adulthood. Part of this meant a connection between courting, cinema and sex, often evoked by the pictorial depictions. The work of these authors contributes to the understanding of romance, cinema and liminality as playing out on various (affective, cognitive social and ideological) levels, some of which have continued to this day, others not so much.

Conclusion

The concept of love used here understands the importance of historical shifts in our understanding, experience and conceptualisation of it. Again, I emphasise that I only speak of love insofar as contemporary, urban, Western societies are concerned, as some of the points I have elaborated have different experiential histories and are lived out differently in other areas of the world. The works of Anthony Giddens (1993), Eva Illouz (1997, 2012) and some of the Marxist positions of Badiou, Fromm and Hardt bring up several points necessary for context. First, the consideration of love as a social and ideological construct. Second, the individualisation of interpersonal relationships from the social and kinship contract-transaction they used to be. Third, the narrativisation of one's romantic self, based on a constant dual process of self-disclosure and self-interrogation. Fourth, the contingency of contemporary relationships and the anxiety this generates. Based on these points, the concept of romantic identity as I outlined it is crucial. It helps to highlight the aspects of romantic love that are fragmentary, ambivalent and always in a process of construction. Fifth, the commoditisation of romance in late capitalism. This commoditisation, experienced acutely in the practices of romantic love, makes the concept of the 'liminoid' of interest to pursue. Giddens and Illouz's positions are largely apolitical and detached, and thus inadequate to understanding fully the politics of the intimate. However, the Marxist positions are also too narrow in their understanding of love, creating oppositions between 'good' and 'bad' love that privilege a communal, public/civic-based love while deriding the intimate as a site of political struggle.

I find in the feminist critique of these seemingly critical (yet all written by men) positions that there is a richer position to understand romantic love as an academic and political concept. In this regard, the starting point of the conceptualisation of romantic love here is the understanding that patriarchal, hetero-marital couple, romantic love is the hegemonic ideology of love – thus understanding ideology and hegemony from the point of Antonio Gramsci's work. This ideology contains a gendered and class division of roles that has been constructed to privilege men's position subordinating and sub-valuing women, their emotions, care-giving, roles and demands. At the same time, the concept recognises the utopian, positive dimension that the pursuit of such romantic love holds for many women (and men). A feminist conceptualisation of love understands the ambivalence, potentially divergent, fragmentary and intersectional experience of this hegemonic romantic love and the counter-hegemonies that feminist and queer theories have pushed forward, theoretically and practically. At the same time, a feminist concept of love seeks to *widen* its acceptable forms, personal and social undertakings beyond hetero-marital, coupled love to promote the acceptability pluralistic sexual, romantic and intimacy ethics. I move on to the next chapter to articulate how these concepts will be articulated in representations of romantic films and their audiences.

Notes

1 A slew of theories and perspectives such as social penetration theory, expectancy violation theory and the systems perspective have also theorised love. However, their focus on the communicational aspects of love leaves them ill-equipped to deal with the practices contained beneath this concept. For anyone wishing to pursue this further, Dainton & Zelley (2015) give a relatively strong summary of some of these theories and perspectives.
2 The whole issue of *Memory Studies*, 2017, vol. 10, no. 1, is devoted to memory and the historical experience of cinema-going. The link between cinema and memory is twofold. On the one hand there is the memory of the place and experience of cinema-going, as social as it is individual. Then there's the construction of the larger place (neighbourhood, community, society, nation) and the larger experience through the recollection of representations in cinema. These two links are not separate from one another of course, as cinema has had an increasingly important role in the construction, shaping and reproduction of the historical collective memory of many nations in the twentieth and twenty-first centuries. One only has to think of the plethora of action films produced by Hollywood at the end of the Cold War and their mythic heroes and villains (see Biltereyst, Lotze & Meers, 2012; Biltereyst, Maltby, & Meers, 2011; Kuhn, Biltereyst & Meers, 2017; Maltby, Biltereyst & Meers, 2011 for a compilation and overview of studies and contributions in this area).
3 For an example of the opposite, a dedicated case study of one film, *Gone with the Wind* (Fleming, 1939), see Helen Taylor's (1989) *Scarlett's Women: "Gone with the Wind" and its Female Fans*.

4 Contrary to the use in psychoanalysis, where the emphasis lies in unconscious processes, Stacey's elaboration of identification focuses on conscious memories, although it recognises the importance that fantasy plays in these.
5 See Foucault (1986) for a definition of the concept and Kuhn (2004) for her elaboration of it.
6 See McIver (2009) for a case study of one cinema in Liverpool during the same time period. Significantly, in McIver's findings, the finding of a partner also meant the end of cinema-going.

References

Adams, P. C. (2005). *The boundless self: communication in physical and virtual spaces*. Syracuse University Press.
Ahmed, S. (2004). *The cultural politics of emotion*. Edinburgh University Press.
Allen, K. R., & Walker, A. J. (1992). attentive love: a feminist perspective on the caregiving of adult daughters. *Family Relations*, 41(3), 284–289. https://doi.org/10.2307/585192.
Allen, R. C. (1990). From exhibition to reception: reflections on the audience in film history. *Screen*, 31(4), 347–356. https://doi.org/10.1093/screen/31.4.347.
Althusser, L. (1969). *For Marx*. Pantheon Books.
Althusser, L. (1972). *Lenin and philosophy, and other essays*. Monthly Review Press.
Althusser, L., & Balibar, E. (1971). *Reading Capital*. Pantheon Books.
Althusser, L., & Matheron, F. (1997). *The spectre of Hegel: early writings*. Verso.
Ang, I. (1985). *Watching Dallas: soap opera and the melodramatic imagination*. Methuen.
Badiou, A. (2009). *In praise of love*. Serpent's Tail.
Bakhtin, M. M. (1984). *Rabelais and his world*. Indiana University Press.
Barker, M. J. (1989). *Comics: ideology, power and the critics*. Manchester University Press.
Barker, M. J. (2005). *The Lord of the Rings* and 'identification': a critical encounter. *European Journal of Communication*, 20(3), 353–378. https://doi.org/10.1177/0267323105055262.
Barker, M., & Brooks, K. (1998). *Knowing audiences: Judge Dredd, its friends, fans and foes*. University of Luton Press.
Barthes, R. (1990). *A lover's discourse: fragments*. Penguin.
Baudry, J.-L. (1978). *L'Effet cinéma*. Albatros.
Baudry, J.-L. (1985). Ideological effects of the basic cinematographic apparatus. In B. Nichols (ed.), *Movies and methods*, vol. 2 (pp. 531–542). University of California Press.
Bauman, Z. (2003). *Liquid love: on the frailty of human bonds*. Polity Press.
Bauman, Z. (2004). *Identity*. Polity Press.
Beauvoir, S. de (1972). *The second sex*. Penguin.
Beck, U., & Beck-Gernsheim, E. (1995). *The normal chaos of love*. Polity Press; Blackwell.
Bell, D., & Binnie, J. (2000). *The sexual citizen: queer politics and beyond*. Polity Press.
Berger, P. L. (1974). Modern identity: crisis and continuity. In W. Dillon (ed.), *The cultural drama: modern identities and social ferment* (pp. 158–182). Smithsonian Institution Press.
Berlant, L. G. (1997). The queen of America goes to Washington city: essays on sex and citizenship. In *The queen of America goes to Washington city: essays on sex and citizenship* (pp. 1–221). University of Chicago Press. https://doi.org/10.2307/2927393.
Berlant, L. G. (2000). *Intimacy*. University of Chicago Press.
Berlant, L. G. (2001). Love: a queer feeling. In T. Dean & C. Lane (eds), *Homosexuality and Psychoanalysis* (pp. 431–452). Chicago University Press.

Berlant, L. G. (2008). *The female complaint: the unfinished business of sentimentality in American culture*. Duke University Press.
Berlant, L. G. (2011). A properly political concept of love: three approaches in ten pages. *Cultural Anthropology*, 26(4), 683–691.
Berlant, L. G. (2012). *Desire/love*. punctum books.
Berscheid, E., & Walster, E. (1974). A little bit about love. In T. L. Huston (ed.), *Foundations of Interpersonal attraction* (pp. 355–381). Academic Press.
Berscheid, E. (1988). Some comments on love's anatomy: or, whatever happened to old-fashioned lust? In R. Sternberg & M. L. Barnes (eds.), *The psychology of love* (pp. 359–374). Yale University Press.
Berscheid, E. (1999). The greening of relationship science. *The American Psychologist*, 54 (4), 260–266. https://doi.org/10.1037/0003-066X.54.4.260.
Berscheid, E. (2002). Searching for the meaning of "love." In R. Sternberg & K. Weis (eds), *The new psychology of love* (pp. 171–183). Yale University Press.
Berscheid, E., & Regan, P. C. (2005). *The psychology of interpersonal relationships*. Pearson Prentice Hall.
Bhabha, H. K. (1994). *The location of culture*. Routledge.
Biltereyst, D., Lotze, K., & Meers, P. (2012). Triangulation in historical audience research: Reflections and experiences from a multimethodological research project on cinema audiences in Flanders. *Participations*, 9(2), 690–715.
Biltereyst, D., Maltby, R., & Meers, P. (eds.). (2011). *Cinema, audiences and modernity: new perspectives on European cinema history*. Routledge.
Bordwell, D., & Thompson, K. (2010). *Film art: an introduction* (9th edn). McGraw-Hill Higher Education.
Bourdieu, P. (1984). *Distinction: a social critique of the judgement of taste*. Routledge & Kegan Paul.
Brooks, P. (1995). *The melodramatic imagination: Balzac, Henry James, melodrama, and the mode of excess*. Yale University Press.
Bryson, V. (2014). Time to love. In A. Jónasdóttir & A. Fergusson (eds), *Love: a question for feminism in the 21st century* (pp. 113–126). Routledge.
Buss, D. M. (1988). Love acts: the evolutionary biology of love. In R. Sternberg & M. L. Barnes (eds), *The psychology of love* (pp. 100–117). Yale University Press.
Buss, D. M. (2006). The evolution of love. In *The new psychology of love* (pp. 65–86). https://doi.org/10.1037/019904.
Butler, J. (1990). *Gender trouble: feminism and the subversion of identity*. Routledge.
Butler, J. (1993). *Bodies that matter: on the discursive limits of "sex."* Routledge.
Carr, D. (2005). Contexts, gaming pleasures, and gendered preferences. *Simulation & Gaming*, 36(4), 464–482.
Cavell, S. (1981). *Pursuits of happiness: the Hollywood comedy of remarriage*. Harvard University Press.
Chaudhuri, S. (2006). *Feminist film theorists: Laura Mulvey, Kaja Silverman, Teresa de Lauretis, Barbara Creed*. Routledge.
Connell, R. W. (2000). *The men and the boys*. Polity Press.
Connell, R. W. (2006). *Masculinities*. Polity Press.
Cutler, R. J. (2014). If I stay. Warner Bros. Pictures.
Dainton, M., & Zelley, E. D. (2015). *Applying communication theory for professional life: a practical introduction* (3rd edn). SAGE. https://us.sagepub.com/en-us/nam/applying-communication-theory-for-professional-life/book238885
de Lauretis, T. (1986). *Feminist studies, critical studies*. Palgrave Macmillan.

Derné, S. (2000). *Movies, masculinity, and modernity: an ethnography of men's filmgoing in India*. Greenwood Press.
Diamond, E. (1996). *Performance and cultural politics*. Routledge.
Dixon, N. (2007). Romantic love, appraisal, and commitment. *The Philosophical Forum*, 38(4), 373–386. https://doi.org/10.1111/j.1467-9191.2007.00275.x.
Eagleton, T. (1991). *Ideology: an introduction*. Verso.
Ebert, T. L. (1988). The romance of patriarchy: ideology, subjectivity, and postmodern feminist cultural theory. *Cultural Critique*, 10, 19–57.
Ephron, N. (1993). Sleepless in Seattle. TriStar Pictures.
Ephron, N. (1998). You've got mail. Warner Bros. Pictures.
Ferguson, A., & Jonasdottir, A. (2014). *Love: a question for feminism in the twenty-first century*. Routledge.
Firestone, S. (1979). *The dialectic of sex: the case for feminist revolution*. Women's Press.
Fisher, H. *Why we love: the nature and chemistry of romantic love*. Henry Holt.
Fiske, J. (1987). *Television culture*. Routledge.
Fleming, V. (1939). Gone with the Wind. Loew's Inc.
Foucault, M. (1986). Of other spaces. *Diacritics*, 16(1), 22–27.
Freud, S. (1922). *Beyond the pleasure principle*. International Psycho-Analytical. http://www.bartleby.com/br/276.html.
Freud, S. (1924). *Zur Einführung des Narzissmus*. Internationaler Psychoanalytischer Verlag.
Freud, S. (2010). *Civilization and its discontents*. Martino Publishing.
Fromm, E. (1974). *The art of loving*. Harper & Row.
García Andrade, A., Gunnarsson, L., & Anna G.Jónasdóttir. (2018). *Feminism and the power of love: interdisciplinary interventions*. Routledge.
Gardiner, M. (1992). *The dialogics of critique: M.M. Bakhtin and the theory of ideology*. Routledge.
Gennep, A. van. (1960). *The rites of passage*. University of Chicago Press.
Giddens, A. (1991). *Modernity and self-identity: self and society in the late modern age*. Polity Press in association with Basil Blackwell.
Giddens, A. (1992). *The transformation of intimacy: sexuality, love and eroticism in modern societies*. Polity Press.
Gledhill, C. (1987). *Home is where the heart is: studies in melodrama and the woman's film*. BFI Publishing.
Glitre, K. (2006). *Hollywood romantic comedy: states of union, 1934–1965*. Manchester University Press.
Goffman, E. (2004). *La presentación de la persona en la vida cotidiana* (5th edn). Amorrortu.
Gordon, S., Benner, P., & Noddings, N. (1996). *Caregiving: readings in knowledge, practice, ethics, and politics*. University of Pennsylvania Press.
Gottlieb, S. (2011). The capacity for love. In D. Mann (ed.), *Love and hate: psychoanalytic perspectives* (pp. 68–87). Routledge.
Gramsci, A. (1971). *Selections from the prison notebooks of Antonio Gramsci* (ed. Q. Hoare & G. Nowell-Smith). Lawrence & Wishart.
Gramsci, A. (1995). *Antonio Gramsci: further selections from the prison notebooks* (ed. D. Boothman). Lawrence & Wishart.
Gross, N., & Simmons, S. (2002). Intimacy as a double-edged phenomenon? An empirical test of Giddens. *Social Forces*, 81(2), 531–555.
Grossi, R. (2014). *Looking for love in the legal discourse of marriage*. ANU Press.
Gyorgy, P. (2012). Final cut: ladies and gentlemen. HvD Productions.

Haden, J. (1979). On Socrates, with reference to Gregory Vlastos. *The Review of Metaphysics*, 33(2), 371–389.
Hall, S. (1973). *Encoding and decoding in the television discourse*. Centre for Contemporary Cultural Studies.
Hall, S. (1985). Signification, representation, ideology: Althusser and the post-structuralist debates. *Critical Studies in Mass Communication*, 2(2), 91–114.
Hall, S. (1996). Who needs "identity"? In S. Hall & P. Du Gay (eds), *Questions of Cultural Identity* (pp. 1–17). SAGE.
Haller, A. (2012). Diagnosis: Flimmeritis: female cinemagoing in Imperial Germany, 1911–18. In D. Biltereyst, R. Maltby, & P. Meers (eds), *Cinema, audiences and modernity: new perspectives on European cinema history* (pp. 130–141). Routledge.
Hansen, M. (1991). *Babel and Babylon: spectatorship in American silent film*. Harvard University Press.
Hardt, M. (2011). For love or money. *Cultural Anthropology*, 26(4), 676–682.
Hardt, M. (2014). The power to be affected. *International Journal of Politics, Culture and Society*, 28, 215–222. https://doi.org/10.1007/s10767-014-9191-x.
Hardt, M., & Negri, A. (2000). *Empire*. Harvard University Press.
Hardt, M., & Negri, A. (2004). *Multitude: war and democracy in the Age of Empire*. Penguin.
Hardt, M., & Negri, A. (2011). *Commonwealth*. Belknap Press of Harvard University Press.
Harlow, H. F. (1958). The nature of love. *American Psychologist*, 13(12), 673–685. https://doi.org/10.1037/h0047884.
Harlow, H. F. (1974). *Learning to love*. Jason Aronson.
Hatfield, E., & Sprecher, S. (1986). Measuring passionate love in intimate relationships. *Journal of Adolescence*, 9(4), 383–410. https://doi.org/10.1016/S0140-1971(86)80043-80044.
Hazan, C., & Shaver, P. (1987). Romantic love conceptualized as an attachment process. *Journal of Personality and Social Psychology*, 52, 511–524.
Hendrick, C., & Hendrick, S. (1986). A theory and method of love. *Journal of Personality and Social Psychology*, 50(2), 392–402. https://doi.org/10.1037/0022-3514.50.2.392.
Hendrick, C., & Hendrick, S. S. (1989). Research on love: does it measure up? *Journal of Personality and Social Psychology*, 56(5), 784–794. https://doi.org/10.1037/0022-3514.56.5.784.
Hendrick, C., & Hendrick, S. (2002). Styles of romantic love. In R. Sternberg & K. Weis (eds), *The new psychology of love* (pp. 149–170). Yale University Press.
Hendrick, S., & Hendrick, C. (1992). *Romantic love*. SAGE.
hooks, b. (1999). The oppositional gaze: black female spectators. In J. Belton (ed.), *Movies and mass culture* (pp. 247–265). The Athlone Press.
hooks, b. (2000). *All about love: new visions*. Perennial.
Horvat, S. (2016). *The radicality of love*. Polity Press.
Illouz, E. (1997). *Consuming the romantic utopia: love and the cultural contradictions of capitalism*. University of California Press.
Illouz, E. (2012). *Why love hurts: a sociological explanation*. Polity Press.
Irigaray, L. (2012). *The way of love*. Continuum.
Jamieson, L. (1999). Intimacy transformed? A critical look at the 'pure relationship.' *Sociology*, 33(3), 477–494.
Johnson, P. (2012). *Love, heterosexuality, and society*. Routledge.
Jonasdottir, A. (1991). *Love power and political interests: towards a theory of patriarchy in contemporary western societies*. University of Örebro.

Jónasdóttir, A. and Ferguson, A. (eds). (2014). *Love: a question for feminism in the twenty-first century*. Routledge.

Kenrick, D. T. (1987). Gender, genes, and the social environment: a biosocial interactionist perspective. In P Shaver & D. T. Kenrick (eds), *Sex and gender* (pp. 14–43). SAGE.

Kosman, L. A. (1976). Platonic love. In W. Werkmeister (ed.), *Facets of Plato's philosophy* (pp. 53–69). Van Gorcum.

Krämer, P. (1998). Women first: "Titanic" (1997), action-adventure films and Hollywood's female audience. *Historical Journal of Film, Radio & Television*, 18(4), 599–619.

Kristeva, J. (1987). *Tales of love*. Columbia University Press.

Kuhn, A. (1994). *Women's pictures: feminism and cinema* (2nd edn). Verso.

Kuhn, A. (2002). *An everyday magic: cinema and cultural memory*. Tauris.

Kuhn, A. (2004). Heterotopia, heterochronia: place and time in cinema memory. *Screen*, 45(2), 106–114. https://doi.org/10.1093/screen/45.2.106.

Kuhn, A., Biltereyst, D., & Meers, P. (2017). Memories of cinemagoing and film experience: an introduction. *Memory Studies*, 10(1), 3–16. https://doi.org/10.1177/1750698016670783.

LaGravenese, R. (2007). Ps I love you. Momentum Pictures.

Lasch, C. (1977). *Haven in a heartless world: the family besieged*. Basic Books.

Lash, S. (1990). *Sociology of postmodernism*. Routledge.

Lee, J. A. (1973). *Colours of love: an exploration of the ways of loving*. New Press.

Lee, J. A. (1998). Ideologies of lovestyle and sexstyle. In V. C. De Munck (ed.), *Romantic love and sexual behavior: perspectives from the social sciences* (pp. 33–54). Praeger.

Levy, D. (1979). The definition of love in Plato's Symposium. *Journal of the History of Ideas*, 40(2), 285–291.

Luhmann, N. (1986). *Love as passion: the codification of intimacy*. Polity Press.

Lynch, K. (2014). Why love, care, and solidarity are political matters: affective equality and Fraser's model of social justice. In A. Jónasdóttir & A. Fergusson (eds), *Love: a question for feminism in the 21st century* (pp. 173–189). Routledge.

Maltby, R., Biltereyst, D., & Meers, P. (eds.). (2011). *Explorations in new cinema history: approaches and case studies*. Wiley-Blackwell.

Marcuse, H. (1966). *Eros and civilization; a philosophical inquiry into Freud*. Beacon Press.

Marx, K. (1970). *A contribution to the critique of political economy*. International Publishers.

Marx, K., & Engels, F. (1967). *Capital; a critique of political economy*. International Publishers.

Marx, K., & Engels, F. (1972). *The German ideology* (trans. C. J. Arthur). International Publishers.

Maurer, C., Milligan, T., & Pacovská, K. (2014). *Love and its objects: what can we care for?* Palgrave Macmillan.

Mayne, J. (1998). *Cinema and spectatorship*. Routledge.

McDonald, H. (2018). *Digital love: romance and sexuality in video games*. CRC Press.

McIver, G. (2009). Liverpool's Rialto: remembering the romance. *Participations*, 6(2), 199–218.

Mellen, S. L. W. (1981). *The evolution of love*. Freeman.

Metz, C. (1974). *Film language; a semiotics of the cinema*. Oxford University Press.

Metz, C. (1981). *The imaginary signifier: psychoanalysis and the cinema*. Indiana University Press.

Mills, M. (2011). Beginners. Focus Features.

Morin, E. (2005). *The cinema, or, the imaginary man*. University of Minnesota Press.

Morley, D. (1980). *The nationwide audience: structure and decoding*. British Film Institute.

Morley, D. (1986). *Family television: cultural power and domestic leisure*. Comedia.

Mulvey, L. (1989). *Visual and other pleasures*. Macmillan.
Nash, J. (2013). Practicing love: black feminism, love-politics, and post-intersectionality. *Meridians: Feminism, Race, Transnationalism*, 11(2), 1–24.
Nygren, A. (1969). *Agape and Eros*. Harper & Row.
Ortega y Gasset, J. (1957). *On love: aspects of a single theme*. Meridian Books.
Pearce, L., & Stacey, J. (1995). *Romance revisited*. New York University Press.
Peele, S. 1975. *Love and addiction*. Taplinger Publishing Co.
Plato. (1953). *The dialogues of Plato* (ed. B. Jowett) (4th edn). Clarendon Press.
Potter, C. (2002). *I love you but... Romance, comedy and the movies*. Methuen.
Radway, J. (1984). *Reading the romance: women, patriarchy and popular literature*. Verso.
Reiner, R. (1989). *When Harry Met Sally...* Columbia Pictures.
Richards, J. (1994). Cinemagoing in worktown: regional film audiences in 1930s Britain. *Historical Journal of Film, Radio and Television*, 14(2), 147–166. https://doi.org/10.1080/01439689400260131.
Rougemont, D. de (1983). *Love in the Western world*. Princeton University Press.
Rubin, Z. (1970). Measurement of romantic love. *Journal of Personality and Social Psychology*, 16(2), 265–273. https://doi.org/10.1037/h0029841.
Rubin, Z., Peplau, L. A., & Hill, C. T. (1981). Loving and leaving: sex differences in romantic attachments. *Sex Roles*, 7(8), 821–834.
Sennett, R. (1998). *The corrosion of character: the personal consequences of work in the new capitalism*. Norton.
Shaver, P., Hazan, C., & Bradshaw, D. (1988). Love as attachment: the integration of three behavioral systems. In R. J. B. Sternberg & M. L. Barnes (eds), *The psychology of love* (pp. 68–99). Yale University Press.
Shohat, E., & Stam, R. (1996). *Unthinking Eurocentrism: multiculturalism and the media*. Routledge.
Shumway, D. R. (2003). *Modern love: romance, intimacy, and the marriage crisis*. New York University Press.
Sica, A. (1986). Locating the seventeenth book of Giddens. *Contemporary Sociology*, 15, 344–346.
Singer, I. (2009a). *The nature of love 2: courtly and romantic*. MIT Press.
Singer, I. (2009b). *The nature of love 3: the modern world*. MIT Press.
Singer, I. (2009c). *The nature of love I: Plato to Luther*. MIT Press.
Soble, A. (1989). *Eros, agape, and philia: readings in the philosophy of love*. Paragon House.
Soble, A. (1990). *The structure of love*. Yale University Press.
Stacey, J. (1994). *Star gazing: Hollywood cinema and female spectatorship*. Routledge.
Staiger, J. (1992). *Interpreting films: studies in the historical reception of American cinema*. Princeton University Press.
Staiger, J. (2000). *Perverse spectators: the practices of film reception*. New York University Press.
Stam, R. (1989). *Subversive pleasures: Bakhtin, cultural criticism, and film*. Johns Hopkins University Press.
Taylor, H. (1989). *Scarlett's women: "Gone with the wind" and its female fans*. Virago.
Thompson, J. B. (1990). *Ideology and modern culture: critical social theory in the era of mass communication*. Stanford University Press.
Turner, V. W. (1977). *The ritual process: structure and anti-structure*. Cornell University Press.
Turner, V. W. (1982). *From ritual to theatre: the human seriousness of play*. Performing Arts Journal Publications.
Vicedo, M. (2010). The evolution of Harry Harlow: from the nature to the nurture of love. *History of Psychiatry*, 21(2), 190–205. https://doi.org/10.1177/0957154X10370909.

Vlastos, G. (1973). *Platonic Studies*. Princeton University Press.
Wilkinson, E. (2013). Learning to love again: 'broken families', citizenship and the state promotion of coupledom. *Geoforum*, 49, 206–213. https://doi.org/10.1016/j.geoforum.2013.02.012.
Wilkinson, E. (2016). On love as an (im)properly political concept. *Environment and Planning D: Society and Space*, 35(1), 1–15.
Wilkinson, E., & Bell, E. (2012). Ties that bind: on not seeing (or looking) beyond "the family." *Families, Relationships and Societies*, 1(3), 423–429.
Williams, R. (1977). *Marxism and literature*. Oxford University Press.
Žižek, S. (1994). *Mapping ideology*. Verso.
Zucker, J. (1990). Ghost. Paramount Pictures.

2 Audience research, audiences of romance

The film audience, as Tomas Austin (2002) points out, is an under-researched area in an otherwise saturated field.[1] The reasons for this are debatable. However, amongst the ones consistently cited, first and foremost is the difficulty of physically locating and defining these 'audiences' as media become more diffuse and de-territorialised. Others, like Jostein Gripsrud (2002), counter that quantitatively, given film's paradigmatic status as mass-medium early in the twentieth century, scholarly interest and research on film audiences and related themes outnumber any other type of research and writing on the film medium. Further, Gripsrud highlights that this empirical interest in audiences was somewhat lost in the sixties and seventies, being replaced with an interest in film as art and as text. Since, then two primary strands of research have dealt with film in one way or another and neither has considered it a priority to study audiences. The first is the approach usually termed 'Screen theory', where the text is not only privileged in analysis, but it is considered enough to suggest modes of spectatorship allowed by a given text. That is, as Judith Mayne (1998) suggests, researchers in line with this considered that a subject's reading of a text could be extracted from the ideological or psychoanalytic analysis of a film's narrative with its encoded intended meanings.

Banaji (2006) argues that the spectator in such an analysis is a result of textual processes posed by the film, a monolithic vessel of monological synthesis. Instead of research into actual audiences, audiences are assumed to be at one with the spectral viewer, a generally ideologically compliant ideal. This approach was extremely popular across Europe in the seventies, and though it has met enormous criticism since then, it still provides several valuable ideas which I will explore in later chapters. Laura Mulvey's (1975) provocative essay on cinematic pleasure and the male gaze is considered a seminal example of this tradition. In it, Mulvey argues that the female cinematic spectator enjoys filmic texts, accepts the patriarchal ideology presented therein, identifies with a passive female image, and only through an adoption of a male gaze gains a form of masochistic pleasure. Mary Ann Doane (1982) builds on and counters Mulvey's argument with the suggestion that the female spectator, because of the psychic steps required to enjoy mainstream films – which she terms as cross-dressing or masquerading – leaves female spectatorship open to the possibility of subverting the ideological naturalisation of gender.

DOI: 10.4324/9781003164289-3

Doane does concede, however, that when it comes to women's films, the pleasure is masochistic given that the identifying process is masculine. Both Mulvey's and Doane's account of the (female) spectator have faced many criticisms, primarily for their complete omission of actual film audiences and the complex and contradictory viewing positions taken up (Banaji, 2002; De Lauretis, 1994; Doane, 1982; Silverman, 1996). This position, as Mayne suggests, stems from

> The assumption of 1970s' film theory was that the particular characteristics of the classical cinema encourage oedipal desire through the looking structures that make the woman object of the look and man its subject, as well as through conventions of plot and characterization ... oedipal desire suggests that the subject of the classical cinema is male.
>
> (1998, p. 23)

In *Loving with a Vengeance: Mass-Produced Fantasies for Women* (1984), Tania Modleski analyses soap operas, romances and gothic novels in an effort to understand exactly what makes these mediated narratives so appealing to women. Through a psychoanalytic and clinical psychology framework, Modleski characterises romance readers as hysterics and soap-opera viewers as housewives, suggesting that these cultural products act as an addiction-fuelling narcotic that leave their subjects hopeless patriarchal junkies. Female spectatorship, according to Modleski, is divided into two types: an ideal mother and a villainess. In the text, the villainess is the character set up to be hated by women, thus reinforcing their position as mothers. Seiter et al. (1989) criticised Modleski for pushing what they view as her middle-class armchair analysis of these texts without bothering to pursue actual readers and viewers. While this critique is fair, it is also interesting to consider how Modleski's own condition influenced the decision to pursue a textual analysis and her subsequent work. In their ethnographic study, Seiter et al. found very differing views from their working-class participants. They argued that

> The 'successful' production of the (abstract and 'ideal') feminine subject is restricted and altered by the contradictions of women's own experiences. Class, among other factors, plays a major role in how our respondents make sense of the text. The experience of working-class women clearly conflicts in substantial ways with the soap opera's representation of a woman's problems, problems some women identified as upper or middle-class. This makes the limitless sympathy that Modleski's textual position demands impossible for them. The class discrepancy between textual representation and their personal experience constituted the primary criticism of the programs.
>
> (1989, p. 241)

The dichotomy of Modleski's model is undone, in part, by the class position of the audience. Moreover, Seiter et al. add that their participants were not interested in the sympathy of the mother and did not despise the villainess. Rather, they admired her transgressions. This is because Modleski's division does not account for the possibility of spectatorship being a fragmentary activity (Banaji, 2006) where different aspects of a subject's intersectional experience of womanhood are engaged in different ways, at different times. Modleski's work sits between Screen theory and the then booming academic interest in academic studies of romance, straddling the two without seriously challenging the monolithic view of spectatorship outlined above.

Around the same time as Modleski's work, literary critics Ann Barr Snitow (1979) and Kay Mussell (1984) published their studies on romantic fiction. Both authors regard the genre, pejoratively, as a fantasy (Snitow specifically refers to it as pornography for women) that prevents women from truly living in the real world by infantilising them and detaching them from their actual material conditions This is related to classic Marxist accounts of false consciousness. Influenced by these accounts, albeit with a slightly more sociological approach, it is possible to find the work of Annette Kuhn (1994) and Elizabeth Cowie (1997), who take gender and film working primarily from an ideological basis, yet open to contestation. Cowie challenged the idea of a singular text–reader position, suggesting instead that the relationship between spectator and text is constituted by a set of continuous looks that constantly (re)positioned the text–subject. The intermittency of these looks and subjectivities provides only partial identifications for women. Kuhn argued that sociological approaches to cinema were based around judgements and valuations made by critics, which took these valuations at face value, with a gross neglect of the cinematographic elements. In her structural analysis, Kuhn highlights five elements to understand how meaning is produced *for* the subject of the filmic text: textual gratification, cinematic address, suture, cinematic apparatus and the look. Significantly, in these categories and their articulation, neither text-as-meaningful nor the subject exist a priori from one another. However, the subject, because of the interpellation of the ideologies in the text, is shaped by the text. This crucial analytical link is what permits these works to talk about spectators, of subjectivities. These are discursive by-products of ideological, textual and subtexts within a particular style of film, in this case classical cinema, never actual flesh-and-blood viewers of films.

The construction of an interpellatable and interpellated subject through a filmic text is only possible because it operates on the assumption that such texts are narrative attempts to create an illusion of reality. In scenic terms, and following Jacques Aumont (1992), the illusion of reality is only possible because every film, besides developing in time and producing a sensation of volume, possesses a fiction effect. The illusion presents itself in terms of the image perception and credibility, provoking an impression of reality in the spectator through scenic rules and specific codes – close-ups, depth of field, film editing and so on. For example, in a film like *(500) Days of Summer* (2009), there are close-ups of the female lead, focusing on several of her facial and body features with a voiceover of the male lead praising them while they are together, and berating them when brokenhearted. The combination of this element seeks to emulate the mental images we all have of the traits we praise of the beloved. The illusion or effect of reality attributed to narrative cinema has been treated in terms of verisimilitude.

Tzvetan Todorov (1970, 1977) lists several meanings of the term verisimilitude. To Aristotle, verisimilitude was the grouping of what is possible to the common view, in opposition to the set of what is possible to the wise people. Post-enlightenment tradition recovered that idea enhancing it with a second type of verisimilitude, not so different from the first and not entirely absent from the Greek philosopher's thought: it's the verisimilitude that adjusts to the laws of an established genre. In these two cases, verisimilitude is defined by discourses and presents itself as a *corpus effect*: the rules of a genre emanate from the previous works of the genre. Finally, nowadays another use is predominant:

> one talks of the verisimilitude of a work to the extent in which it tries to make us believe it conforms with the real and no to its own set of norms; put in another way, verisimilitude is the mask with which the text laws are disguised, and that we must assume as a direct relationship with reality.
> (Todorov, 1970, p. 11, my translation)

Cinematographic verisimilitude, according to Christian Metz (1991, 2002), can be understood on two levels. There was a time when cinema had its well-defined genres – western, crime drama, melodrama – and they would not mix. Each genre had its own verisimilitude, so any other possibilities were impossible. However, these genres aged and they started to confound with each other. With the evolution of the industry, nowadays genres mix up is something usual –for example, *District 9* (Blomkamp, 2009) combines false documentary with science fiction, and *They Came Together* (Wain, 2014) combines romantic comedy with parody. This genre mix up can be understood through Rick Altman's (1999) semantic/syntactic/pragmatic approach to genre. Arguing against synchronic, ahistorical and semiotic approaches to genre, Altman initially proposed understanding genres as a combination of 'inclusion' and 'exclusion'. The semantics were the list of recognisable elements of a genre (locations, characters, situations, shots, etc.), while the syntactics was related to the established and possible relationships between these elements. Altman later included the pragmatics, to accounts for both institutions (studios, film producers) and audiences (critics, scholars, laymen), highlighting the importance of *users* and *uses* in contributing to shape genres.[2] Thus, in this view, the combination of genres can be understood (depending on the mix up) as part of cycles responding to historical changes and pushes from producers seeking to cater to broader audiences. Thus, genre repackaging has become a standard practice in the post-classical film production. Yet, the verisimilitude is maintained through the maintenance of certain key semantic and syntactic elements (e.g. the romantic couple, the final hero–villain encounter).

In a more general perspective, cinema has functioned as one vast genre, with its list of specific authorised contents and its catalogue of filmable subjects and tones. This last one is the censorship of verisimilitude: it doesn't deal with the subjects, but with how to approach them; it is concerned with the very own content of the movies. It targets the forms, the way in which the movie talks about what it talks, what it says and the explicit face of its content. For this reason, the constraint of verisimilitude is aimed at every film, independent of its subject.

That's how, supposedly, cinema defines what Foucault (1977) called 'the limits of the speakable'. The verisimilar feature attempts to persuade that the conventions used to restrict the possibilities are not discursive or writing rules, they are not conventions at all. The effect of this, as envisioned and done by the film director, verifiable in the content of the film, is actually the effect of the nature of things and answers to the intrinsic characteristics of the represented subject. The verisimilar feature thinks of itself – and pretends that we comply – as directly translatable in terms of reality. There verisimilitude finds its full use: it's about making the whole thing look real.

Thus, narrative cinema, in its fabrication of an illusion of reality, is an ideological work that seeks the status of natural, normal and acceptable to the detriment of others (such as contestation, multiple discourses, potentially competing versions of reality). The key word here is illusion, as it both constitutes the 'ideal' positioning of the subject as *the* meaning to be taken from a text and opens the possibility of subversion, however minor in narrative (fictional) cinema. This idea of verisimilitude and the division between reality and illusion it invites, plus the recognition of media texts as ideological texts, has also been researched by scholars in the British cultural studies tradition, usually referred to as 'modality'. The difference, as is well known, is that the latter worked empirically to understand the relationship between audience and texts.

In the next section, I move on to a brief outline of some of the works of the school of British cultural studies, which will be seen to have been an evident inspiration for the study discussed in this book.

The incorporation/resistance paradigm and the ethnographic turn

This paradigm of which the British cultural studies tradition is a big part came about partly as a response to the effects theory tradition and also as a response to literary criticism of the 1970s. It also obeyed certain historical circumstances, like the post-war consumer boom and globalisation (Katz, 1980). Following Perti Alasuutari's (1999) division of three waves in audience reception studies, throughout the 'discipline's' history there has been a measured but mechanistic approach to audiences (exemplified by Hall's initial writings), an over-celebration of the audience's agency and a call back to the examination of the political, ideological and economic constraints on such agency (see Morley, 2006). Much work in this area owes a debt to Stuart Hall's (1973) seminal work on 'encoding/decoding'. Hall breaks down the model into 'moments': the moment of encoding, the moment of the text and the moment of decoding. Hall was particularly interested in how social class played a role in differentiating the decoding of a message. His interest was twofold. First, how the uneven distribution of knowledge and cultural competences necessary to decode a message affect the assumed competences and knowledge at the moment of encoding. Second, how the class-position affects the reading of the text and the articulation of identity.

The encoding/decoding model shifts from a technical understanding of the media text to an ideological-semiotic one. This shift understands the text working on two levels: denotation and connotation. A technical understanding of the media, say of a romantic film like *Gone with the Wind*, posits that the message of the film is that of a woman and her romantic affairs and misfortunes with two men, with the American Civil War as the background. Hall's model would add that there is a connotative level where race, class and gender hegemonic ideologies, like the glorification of slavery and the idealisation of the upper class, are also at play.

Perhaps one of the most important studies to follow Hall's encoding–decoding theory and further develop it is David Morley's *Nationwide* (1980) study. One of the developments Morley found was on how members of particular subcultures tended to interpret things in similar ways. This, he argued, made it possible to frame individual readings within shared cultural practices and hermeneutics. Thus, sharing the same class background was not enough to warrant the same type of interpretation. Morley argued it was extremely important to pay attention to the different institutions and contexts in which subjects of a similar milieu were positioned to understand why they provide different interpretations.

Originally a theoretical 'work-in-progress', another refinement of the model through an empirical study of the Sony Walkman, gave way to what is known today as the 'circuit of culture' (Du Gay et al., 1997). The authors argued that meaning-making was articulated in several interconnected sites that fed onto one another at different points. This allowed the approach to bypass textual, ideological and materialist assumptions of signification. They identified five main points to be studied in the circuit of culture: production, consumption, regulation, identity and representation. In order to study culture, then, 'one should at least explore how it is represented, what social identities are associated with it, how it is produced and consumed, and what mechanisms regulate its distribution and use' (p. 3). It is through this constant dialogue that notions of power, fixation of meaning and possibilities of resistance come to the fore.

The circuit of culture and the encoding/decoding model were a theoretical side of a burgeoning interest on audiences as a pivotal element of media research. Alongside Hall and du Gay, researchers like John B. Thompson (1995), John Fiske (1987, 2010), Paul Willis (1990) and James Lull (1988) also contributed to a dialogue about audiences, their roles, their readings, their relationship with the media they consume. This dialogue has shaped a radically different picture of what researchers conceptualise audiences to be. Alasuutari (1999) suggests that after the first wave of reception studies, there was a turn towards *ethnographies of the audience*. He highlights three reasons that contributed to this gradual shift. First, due to the influence of burgeoning feminist theory, there was an increased interest in identity politics, in particular with regard to gender – Abercrombie & Longhurst (1998) have termed this the shift from the incorporation/resistance paradigm to the spectacle/performance paradigm. Second, with a growing interest in the social use and lives of television and finally, researchers became more interested in doing work from the 'audience's end of the chain' (p. 7). Thus, it should come as no surprise that from the mid-eighties and early nineties, some of the most recognisable works dealt with media texts that had a clearly marked gendered appeal, soap operas in particular

Moving on then, I will draw attention to the important literature on melodrama, woman's film and romantic comedies, focusing on their narrative and ideologically discursive characteristics. The discussion here will highlight changes and continuities in order to understand the liminal possibilities of watching cinema as mapped out by the texts, starting with the textual approaches and ending with the seminal and newer works of romantic audiences research.

From the women's films and melodrama to the bromance

In film, the genres that have been theorised and understood to appeal the most to women, and/or which scholars suggest cater to and are aimed at them, are: melodrama, woman's film (also known as weepies), screwball comedy and romantic comedy (see Evans & Deleyto, 1998; Gledhill, 1987a). For simplicity's sake, I will outline the characteristics of each genre in this order, emphasising the romantic comedy and its shifts, departures and continuities with other genres. Because it is outside the scope of this chapter, novels, theatre plays, romances and other cultural texts that feature women and were written by and apparently for them will not feature (see Frantz & Murphy Selinger, 2012; Mussell, 1984; Owen, 1997; Radway, 1984 for different research on women's texts and popular romance fiction). I do recognise, however, the significant impact that these texts had on the construction of the canon and characteristics of the film genres I will speak of.

Despite numerous studies of each, there is no clear-cut conceptual distinction between melodrama and the woman's film. Melodrama, in its simplest definition, is a dramatic mood or technique, in which the heightening of emotions through the narrative, characters and mise-en-scène (where applicable) is sought as a means to evoke strong affective reactions from the audience. Having disturbed the status quo of suburban family life or small-town existence via a sense of menace and excess, this device usually concludes a film or sequence on a morally reassuring note. Melodrama, then, can be understood as a form of storytelling adaptable to many artistic needs and forms. In cinema, melodrama is used extensively across many genres and narratives. Its origins can be traced to the eighteenth century, to the then illegal forms of theatre, the ban on the spoken word, sentimental drama and French post-revolutionary romantic dramas (see Elsaesser, 1987; Gledhill, 1987a). However, as Peter Brooks (1996) and Christine Gledhill (1987b) have pointed out, in its modern incarnation, melodrama is too fragmented to truly fit the category of a genre. That is not to say that there are not some continuities across the different dramatic mediums that utilise melodrama. As Brooks highlights, melodrama follows an 'expressionist aesthetic' (which varies in intensity depending on the medium), music and non-verbal language play an important role in its signifying practices and the importance of some psychoanalytic themes, such as the rule of the father.

Saliently, Brooks also adds that melodrama focuses on personal relationships and their conflicts, micro-struggles of power usually put forward as moral contradictions to be solved. This involves a 'simplification' (projection) of moral, social and psychological signs into characters; usually victims, heroes, couples and/or virtuous. This projection of moral absolutes, as Ien Ang (1985) highlights, is substituted in soap operas with contradictions and ambivalences of characters that allow these texts to delay melodrama's reassuring ending. Thomas Elsaesser (1987), in his seminal essay on melodrama, establishes these points and develops them in relation to cinema, highlighting that

> [m]elodrama is iconographically fixed by the claustrophobic atmosphere of the bourgeois home and/or the small town setting, its emotional pattern is that of panic and latent hysteria, reinforced stylistically by a complex handling of space in interiors . . . to the point where the world seems totally predetermined and pervaded by 'meaning' and interpretable signs
>
> (p. 62)

Melodrama can thus be understood as encompassing four major themes: sexuality, relationships, class and space. These themes have received widespread attention from researchers who linked them to issues around realism, ideology, hegemony and feminism (see Doane, Mellencamp & Williams, 1984; Gledhill, 1987a; Kaplan, 2000; Radner & Stringer, 2011; van Zoonen, 1994). The treatment of these is of interest here in regards to two forms melodrama has taken in cinema: the family melodrama and the woman's film. The former, broadly speaking, deals with family relationships and the creation of such bonds, usually through marriage. When it comes to the woman's film, Gledhill says that 'there appears to be no absolute line of demarcation between melodrama and the woman's film but rather, a contest between them over the construction and meaning of the domestic, of personal life, and the place of men and women in this' (1987b: 36). That is, embedded across supposed differences between melodrama and woman's film is a larger question regarding representation, ideological positions and address. The woman's film is better understood through its address to a (female) audience. Maria Laplace (1987) suggests that women's films can be

> distinguished by its female protagonist, female point of view and its narrative which most often revolved around the traditional realism of women's experience: the familial, the domestic, the romantic – those arenas where love, emotion and relationships take precedence over action and events. One of the most important aspects of the genre is the prominent place it accords to relationships between women. A central issue, then, in any investigation of the woman's film is the problematic of female subjectivity, agency and desire in Hollywood cinema.
>
> (p. 139)

The 'problem' of female subjectivity remains a pivotal point of romantic films nowadays, especially in relation to how it enables and/or disables male subjectivity in line with patriarchal norms for specific cultures. In classic Hollywood cinema (and with notable exceptions such as *Now, Voyager* (Rapper, 1942)), this was usually through the eventual subordination of the former to the latter. The films analysed here present a slightly different picture. Laplace highlights the repression (and subsequent education) of female sexuality, the confinement of the female lead to domestic, closed-off spaces and the victim status of the female lead as key features of the woman's film. Laplace also identifies three discourses that came from a woman's circuit of culture to inform the genre: consumerism, the female's star persona and women's fiction. The latter, produced by and for women albeit with little distinction between or attention to issues of intersectionality regarding race and class, served as a way to create interstices in the otherwise patriarchal hegemonic discourse of Hollywood.

After the heyday of the woman's film and melodramas of classic Hollywood, the popularity of romantic comedies increased substantially. Although romantic dramas still occupy a privileged position, they have increasingly become epochal or fantastic films, set in another time and exploring different conditions of love and relationships to those audiences might themselves experience. Examples of this can be seen in *Titanic* (Cameron, 1997), *Anna and the King* (Tennant, 1999), *The English Patient* (Minghella, 1996), *Pride and Prejudice* (Wright, 2005), *Atonement* (Wright, 2007), *Ghost* (Zucker, 1990), *Forever Young* (Milner, 1992), *City of Angels* (Silberling, 1998) and *Shakespeare in Love* (Madden, 1998). Such isolation from the everyday permits the rescue of reactionary ideas of heterosexual love and *amour passion* which entail a return to melodramatic forms of narrative articulation. By distancing narratives from present sociocultural and economic contexts, nostalgia and a presumption of 'authenticity' permit the idealisation of a romantic love narrative set in another time. The narrative, while not directly, then opposes its version of a 'truer' love against a contemporary one, which is represented as cynical, jaded or of lesser value. Thus, many romantic films can be understood as providing a thorough exploration of atavistic and escapist forms of romantic love. On the other hand, from the 'sex comedies' of the 1950s and early 1960s, the 'nervous romances' of the 1970s, the 'new romances' of the 1980s to the 'self-conscious romances' and 'friendship romances' of the 1990s and the 'post-modern romances' of the 2000s (Dowd & Pallotta, 2000; Evans & Deleyto, 1998; McDonald, 2007; Neale & Krutnik, 1990), a constant of the genre has been its resilience through its ability to adapt to historical changes while maintaining a rigid codified structure (Neale & Krutnik, 1990). The genre is particularly responsive to what some term as 'crises of marriage' and shifting attitudes towards sex, romantic love and relationships (Deleyto, 2003; Lent, 1995; Shumway, 2003).

Furthermore, as Shumway (2003) argues, romantic comedies have adopted and explored competing and contradictory discourses of love, juxtaposing romantic love with intimacy and companionate love. This means that while many of the elements, themes and traits of melodrama and the woman's film have remained a staple of romantic comedies, romantic comedy has sought to actively play, contravene and explore canon deviation in one or several of these aspects. Thus, it can be argued that the history of romantic comedy is one of both progressive and reactionary discourses pulling against each other and being meshed into individual narratives that concede in some ideological aspects while also looking to explore ambiguities, contradictions and changes in others. Shakuntala Banaji (2007) has identified this tension also in her discussion of Indian cross-border (with Pakistan) romances. There she argues for

> the need for an understanding of Hindi film spectatorship as being heterogeneous, psychologically contradictory, always emotionally engaged – whether through individual or altruistic fantasies and critiques. Such spectatorship is also always built around the potential of texts to be read as fragmentary and internally divergent, articulating radical positions at odds with their own (frequently socially retrograde) dominant discourses but also inviting complex – and threatening – pleasures through fleeting or more extended participation in compelling 'reactionary' ideological positions and equally compelling 'anti-authoritarian' personal ones.
>
> (pp. 174–175)

A clear example of the fragmented and divergent potential of texts can be seen in the film *Friends with Benefits* (Gluck, 2011), which takes as its starting point the figure of heterosexual friends with benefits, a new form of relationship where friends with no apparent or agreed need for a deeper emotional connection acknowledge their physical desire and have occasional sexual intercourse. The film starts by exploring how this somewhat new configuration of a relationship might work for the different parties involved and moves through the tensions when their understandings of friendship, love and need clash. It ends, however, by having the two lead characters declare their wish to enter a conventional heterosexual romantic relationship.

This 'pull-and-push' has been taking place also in the trends scholars have identified throughout decades of the romantic genre:[3] from the near-global conservative backlash against women's independence in the fifties, the burgeoning youthful hedonism of the sixties, the re-evaluation of masculinity (embodied in a new beta male figure) and the incursion of feminism into popular culture (see Potter, 2002), to the 'neo-traditionalist' or even post-feminist comedies of the eighties and nineties that sought to revitalise hegemonic gender roles and the institution of heterosexual marriage (McDonald, 2007). During the nineties and the 2000s, two things have characterised the romantic comedy genre: friendship and a renewed interest in gender roles, in particular the role of men. The first element has already been pointed out by Celestino Deleyto (2003) who suggested:

> It is as if the new climate of social and sexual equality between men and women had rendered heterosexual desire less vital, as if the perfectly codified conventions that have been valid for so long had lost much of their meaning and become nothing more than picturesque museum pieces – to be admired but not believed. Disenchanted by this state of affairs the genre has started to explore other types of relationships between people and to consider their incorporation into their plots … Friendships between men, between women,

or between men and women have started to proliferate in the space of romantic comedy.

(pp. 181–182)

This exploration of the tensions between friendship qua friendship and friendship as a prelude to romantic love in romantic comedy is not new, however. In Bollywood this tension is highlighted in the romantic triangle of *Kuch Kuch Hota Hain* (*Something's Happening*, Johar, 1998) discussed at length by Banaji (2006), while *Annie Hall* (Allen, 1977) foregrounds this topic and films like *When Harry Met Sally* (Reiner, 1989), *My Best Friend's Wedding* (Hogan, 1997) and *Four Weddings and a Funeral* [4] (Newell, 1994) explore it in depth. They all are, not coincidentally, some of the most enduring romantic films of the past decades because, as David Shumway (2003) argues, they blend the discourse of romantic love with a modern sensibility towards the discourse of intimacy that is lacking in other films, while including differing nods to possible shortcomings of marriage as institution. The novelty lies in the emergence of same-sex friendship eclipsing or replacing the typical heterosexual romantic ending. Although there have been recent examples of female friendship comedies, from *Bridesmaids* (Feig, 2011) and *The Heat* (Feig, 2013) to the recent remake of *Ghostbusters* (Feig, 2016),[5] this tendency has been dominated by male friendships, fittingly named (bro)mances.

The 'bromance' subgenre of romantic comedies can be characterised by an acute recognition of the genre's conventions and an exploration of masculinity, homophilia, homophobia, misogyny and romantic love (Alberti, 2013a, 2013b; DeAngelis, 2014; Greven, 2011; Peberdy, 2011; Rehling, 2009). Long a staple of Indian cinema in various languages, but pioneered in Hollywood by Judd Apatow, bromances are part of a larger trend that includes 'beta male' comedies, like *Forgetting Sarah Marshall* (Stoller, 2008) and *The 40-Year-Old Virgin* (Apatow, 2005), where a latent crisis of white, straight, (mostly) American masculinity finds expression through the figure of the 'abject' (if one is to follow psychoanalytic analysis, see Kristeva, 1987; Modleski, 2014), the idea of the bifurcated male hero (see Alberti, 2013a) and the 'redeemed male loser' (Greven, 2011). Greven and Alberti suggest that the novelty of bromances and beta male comedies lies in the 'homo-confused' bond that male characters endure, which presents a challenge – or even a threat – to the culmination of heterosexual relationships in marriage, without challenging the hegemonic desirability of marriage as a goal. Furthermore, in these comedies that seek to appeal to both men and women, homoerotic moments and homophilic tension often replaces sequences of heterosexual attraction. Despite this, the resolution of these conflicts and obstacles is what paves the way for heterosexual relationships to take place. Thus, the exploration of already adult male coming-of-age, pathos and new forms of male relationships are embedded in a framework of the melodramatised, feminised man-child who must overcome his sexual anxieties and reconfigure his own *maleness* in order, yet again, to woo a woman. Lastly, women in these type of films are hardly present, and in a sense misogynised and masculinised. Successful, assertive, pragmatic, they represent a trigger for the male characters' anxieties and a constant reminder of the self-loathing and deprecation this new masculinity must endure before a finale which reasserts patriarchal order.

In parallel to these two subgenres are 'anxious romances', as Alberti (2013b) terms them. These can be broadly understood as the independent or semi-independent productions of North American cinema, particularly 'mumblecore'. Mumblecore is a style of film that privileges dialogue, is low budget, uses improvisation and largely deals with the lives of white, college-educated, urban, mostly heterosexual people in their 20s and 30s. The term 'anxious' refers to both the continuation from the nervous romances and their questioning of marriage, romantic love and relationships and the personal, professional and economic instability that surrounds their own personal lives. The so-called 'crisis of marriage' that fuelled the nervous romances, the third source of anxiety, has become a commonality of the twenty-first century. This means that these films cannot be considered 'comedies of remarriage' as marriage itself is either marginalised or not present at all.

In the remainder of this chapter I explore the other part of the dyad: audiences. I will emphasise how audience research has dealt specifically with romantic audiences.

Romantic audiences

One of the most recognisable aspects of audiences' relationship with romantic media texts is the double articulation of liminality they bring. On one hand, there is the physical retreat from everyday concerns. On the other, there is the psychic retreat that these films might provide. This has usually been termed 'escapism', or is usually linked to notions of verisimilitude and fantasy, but as work on audiences shows, this 'escape' is not as straightforward as conceived in earlier spectatorship studies. Richard Dyer (2002) links this to the utopian sensibilities and possibilities that the consumption of media can warrant for audiences as they are juxtaposed with the scarcity and precarity (moral, material, emotional) of contemporary everyday life, a point also elaborated by Jackie Stacey.

Working with this juxtaposition between everyday life and the realm of the possible, three of the most important works of audience research to come from the ethnographic turn in reception studies and the increasing influence of British cultural studies are Janice Radway's *Reading the Romance: Women, Patriarchy and Popular Literature* (1984), Sonia Livingstone's *Making Sense of Television* (1989) and Ien Ang's *Watching Dallas: Soap Opera and Melodramatic Imagination* (1985). Two reasons lead me to pursue these works instead of others. First, their differing theoretical and methodological approaches to audiences. Second, their considerations of romance as a *feminine* genre and the relationships and attitudes women develop towards it. In other words, while aforementioned accounts like Modleski's, Mulvey's and (early) Kuhn's chose an authoritative voice to speak for women, these works are characterised by their awareness of listening and 'letting' women speak. Radway's departure from a dominant textual approach – like Ann Barr Snitow's that proposed romance novels to be pornography for women that subdued them to a patriarchal ideology; Snitow never spoke to actual romance readers – by remarking on the need to approach romance novels not just from the comfort of the critic and the text but to complement, compare and analyse readers' responses as well was a pioneering decision at the beginning of the 1980s. She interviewed 42 women from a small town in the Midwest of the United States and coupled it with a brief questionnaire and textual analysis. The crucial importance of this move is generally recognised as twofold. First, she showed empirically how interpretative communities differ in the prioritisation, identification and selection of narrative elements in their readings. Thus, while feminist literary critics using textual analysis derided the female protagonists for ending up subservient to the hero, female readers admired features that suggested heroines were strong, independent women. Second, her work brought to the fore the discussion of *pleasures* from the text as a plausible form of ideological resistance, not as a form of false consciousness as discussed by the Frankfurt School (Adorno, 1976; Adorno & Horkheimer, 2002; Adorno & Rabinbach, 1975; Kracauer, 1947, 1995).[6] It must be noted, however, that the understanding of pleasures in Radway's work was very much inscribed in the incorporation/resistance paradigm; that is, as positions regarding power distribution asymmetries. On pleasure, she argues that

> Dot and her customers see the act of reading as combative and compensatory. It is combative in the sense that it enables them to refuse the other directed social role prescribed for them by their position within the institution of marriage. In picking up a book ... they refuse temporarily their family's otherwise constant demand that they attend to the wants of others even as they act deliberately to do something for their own private pleasure. Their activity is compensatory, then, in that it permits them to focus on themselves and to carve out a solitary space within an arena where their self-interest is usually identified with the interests of others and where they are defined as a public resource to be mined at will by the family. For them, romance reading addresses needs created in them but not met by patriarchal institutions and engendering practices.
>
> (p. 211)

That is, Radway conceived that the pleasure readers derived from the heroines as escapist and compensatory of the material situation many found themselves in. She argued this had to do with the possibility of resisting, ephemerally so, by abandoning their everyday life and identify with heroines, situations and emotions that provided them with the nurture that their family life did not. Furthermore, this was not a mere individual pleasure; rather it was shared with others from a similar milieu and situations. Coupled with this was a clear distinction between 'ideal' and 'failed' romances, where the difference lay in that the misdemeanours, mistakes and hurtful attitudes of the man were either explained by a background to make sense of them (and thus, redeemable) or not. Yet, despite the oppositional and utopic potential of readings of the narrow circumscription of their role as wives, mothers and housewives, romance narratives are still normative and patriarchal and did not ultimately challenge the social values, relations and structures of patriarchal marriage.

Sonia Livingstone's (1989, 1991) work on the soap opera *Coronation Street* is an attempt to go beyond the dominant textual and dominant audience perspectives that ruled the field throughout the eighties. Livingstone chose a narrative from the show, prepared a questionnaire and administered it to 42 regular viewers. Participants were asked to *retell* a plot of the show: A woman returned to town to live with her father and his new wife. The daughter began a romance with an older man who had had an affair with the father's current wife some time ago. The father opposed the marriage of the two based on this. It is clear this choice of narrative is reminiscent of romantic love's foundational myth, Tristan and Isolde. Livingstone argued there were two main possible positions in this case: a) true love would triumph over the paternal opposition (embodied in the father's aversion and prejudices) or youthful naivety and relentlessness topples paternal wisdom. This argument is reminiscent of Hall's encoding/decoding model and the three possible readings it suggested (dominant, negotiated and oppositional). The first position she termed as 'romantics', the latter as 'cynics'. As a necessary step to show how complex the text–reader relationship is, she further adds two other positions: the 'negotiated romantics' and the 'negotiated cynics'. These two positions mainly sided with true love or paternal wisdom respectively, but also conceded that there might be an element of truth in the father's warnings (negotiated romantics) and/ or that the father's opposition was too stern (negotiated cynics). Interestingly so, across all these positions there was a spectrum of opinions about the couple's love, ranging from complete belief to utter mistrust. Livingstone argued that meaning and sense emerged from the interaction between text and reader where neither exerted complete control or had absolute freedom over the other.

The third of the seminal works of the 1980s audience reception studies came from Ien Ang (1985) and her study of letters from the audience of the TV show *Dallas*, a North American night-time soap opera at the peak of its popularity globally at the time. In it, Ang read and analysed over 40 letters from viewers of the show and what it meant to them, how they articulated and understood the narrative with its plot twists and devices. Ang showed that rather than being duped by the contradictions and excesses of the text, the viewers are aware of its fantastic nature. One of the work's most ground-breaking contributions to the field was on the aspect of pleasure. During the 1980s, the cultural ambience was very much dominated, at least with respects to cultural elites, by the post-Marxist disdain of the popular and American forms of culture. Hall's encoding/decoding model and subsequent work thus had no consideration for the possibility of enjoyment of a text; only the dialectical struggle had relevance. Ang's work reacts to this, suggesting that the pejorative outlook on *Dallas* had to do with the consideration of its viewers as duped masses and, by and large, feminised.

The development of a politics of pleasure from a feminist perspective was, then, one of the main objectives of the book. This gave context to the overarching response Ang received: viewers derived immense, diverse pleasures and identifications from the show yet constantly found themselves apologising for doing so.

Even 30 years later, my participants repeatedly expressed this sentiment, especially during the discussions of those films perceived to be middle/low-brow (*Don Jon, Once* and *(500) Days of Summer*). This apologetic pleasure comes from the difference between *Dallas* and its soap opera competitor *Dynasty*. While the former was a melodrama that demanded serious attachment, and exploited the pathos of the genre, *Dynasty* diverged in a self-reflexive, ironic camp detached style. In other words, 'by the 1990s "straight" melodrama has become unfashionable, while irony has become trendy and cool' (Ang, 2007, p. 22). This was further represented in the two types of pleasure Ang identified in her work: one that privileged the emotional realism of melodramatic imagination while the other was found in the distancing effect of ironic pleasure. The first kind of viewer enjoyed being swept away by the tragic structure of feeling, the overwhelming of emotions coming from countless plot twists, narrative devices and elements. Emotional engagement and attachment with characters or an element is crucial to this to this pleasure.

The second mode, ironic detachment, activated and operated a distance between the text and the viewer, a mode 'informed by a more intellectually distancing, superior subject position which could afford having pleasure in the show while simultaneously expressing a confident knowingness about its supposedly "low" quality' (Ang, 2007, p. 22). Irony as distance, Pierre Bourdieu (1984, 2010) also shows in his work about the social construction of taste, evokes a class difference marked by a clear symbolic violence between those unable to 'enlighten' themselves and recognise the lowly position a certain object inhabits in a given field and those who use different methods to create distance between them as subjects and that which they have a taste for. This distance, or lack thereof, is only possible if the subject possesses a cultural capital based around the field and the positions those objects inhabit. When it comes to night-time soap operas, then, it becomes a crucial distinction between seeing them as melodramas and thus as possible rapturous and captivating narratives and seeing them as soap operas, 'low-brow' entertainment. This does not mean some viewers have it and others do not. If you will, with the emotional pleasure, suspension of disbelief may also include a suspension of this knowledge. Discerning the type of aesthetics, technical, narrative and production elements being used permit this distance and bridge a schism between fiction and reality through irony, a more masculine pleasure. Those who do not develop a farcical relationship to the text allow themselves to travel back and forth from the text to their everyday. These two modes of enjoyment are, if not necessarily complete opposites, at least clearly partitioned as requiring and embodying two distinctive pleasures derived from a romantic text. Ang's study highlights the importance of the recognition of emotions in the process of interpretation, articulation and enjoyment.

These researchers were working in a new field and following a then widespread interest in the debate of media effects, ideology, power and subjective agency – later, identity, context and uses. While their contributions have been noted, there are a few aspects that further research, including my own, has sought to address. First, audiences constitute a key component in their works. However, be this as it may, they are overwhelmingly audiences of television, not of cinema. Second, their theorisation and understanding of romantic love was underdeveloped and they barely, if at all, mention cinema and its rich tradition of romances. Finally, the reception and articulation of romantic love depends on four factors: a melodramatic imagination/cultural repertoire of romance/ideal romance, the text, the intersectionality of audiences and the context of consumption. As illuminating and helpful as their typologies can be, they also commit to a facile division between the 'real' and the 'fantastic', between 'romantic imagination' and 'romantic practice'. Perhaps this division can be accepted more easily with the peculiarities of romances for television, but I find this is not the case for the realist tradition of cinema (of which all my selected films can be said to belong). It is possible to trace some new attempts to track and research film audiences or audiencing (still a somewhat marginalised topic) I would like to discuss, highlighting either their theoretical and/or methodological innovations and continuities focusing on romantic audiences of film.

New orientations in audience research

Between those studies' time and today, theories, debates, methods and concepts have changed significantly. The 'new audience research' tradition has been somewhat superseded by a focus on debates on participation and the 'audience or publics', convergence, mediation, participation, media practices and big data, fed in partly by changes to our relationship with media consumption (see Couldry, 2010; Jenkins, 2006; Livingstone, 2013; Mathieu et al., 2016; Silverstone, 2006). It must be noted, however, there is a certain conceptual and methodological continuum; surveys, interviews, focus groups and ethnographies continue to dominate, while questions of literacy, text–reader, and structure–agency are still prevalent in today's research agenda (see Livingstone & Das, 2013; Zaborowski & Dhaenens, 2016). In regard to the audiences or audiencing processes I am interested in, I have highlighted above three works on romance and its audiences, though these works were not alone in their interest of soap operas and text–audience relationships (see Brown, 1994; Hobson, 1982; Katz & Liebes, 1990). They encapsulate a refinement in methods and theoretical nuance and sophistication (at the time) we have grown used to in the field.

While it is possible to identify that in the last decade online media has become the mainstay interest of media scholars, there was an 'interim' period before its boom. During this period, the spectator/performance paradigm and debates around the 'active audience' dominated a great deal of academic attention up until a decade or so (Abercrombie & Longhurst, 1998; Alasuutari, 1999; Livingstone, 2000). The link between these two lie in the questions of power and context. While these distinctions are not to be taken as a clear-cut separation of interests, methods and concepts from previous paradigms or works, there was a distinct shift from questions of power and ideology to enquiries about identity and everyday life. The notion of the active audience was based around three ideas:

> First audiences must interpret what they see even to construct the message as meaningful and orderly, however routine this interpretation may be.

Second, audiences diverge in their interpretations, generating different understandings from the same text. Third, the experience of viewing stands at the interface between the media (and their interpretations) and the rest of viewers' lives, with all the concerns experiences and knowledge which this involves.

(Livingstone, 2000, p. 177)

Illustrative as this excerpt is of several points that the dominant audience perspective levelled against the dominant textual approach, it also highlights what the third paradigm sought to address in contrast to previous ones. Audiences began to be looked as a locatable, graspable, researchable 'thing', a misleading account that too easily missed the interaction between history–text–audience–context by treating the second and third as concrete wholes (Ang, 1990). Instead, John Fiske (1992) proposed the verb 'audiencing' to refer to the active and continuous process of cultural meaning making and exchange of these meanings instead of a sequestered private static event. The idea of the audience as performance, of the audience or audiencing as practice, has followed this idea, trying to add to the research foci of reception the elements of iteration and wider contexts of media consumption (see Nightingale, 2011). Though both considerations have proved crucial for researchers in the area, my focus lies with the latter as films do not necessarily evoke the repetitive interaction that television or new media do. More to the point, I deal with how the interpretative work of the audience speaks not just of individuals, but of larger social groups and attitudes towards, in this case, romantic love and interpersonal relationships.

New (studies of) romance

I will now highlight three different studies of audiences of romantic films that have incorporated the critiques above to produce more nuanced accounts of 'audiencing'. First, drawing from audience studies, film history and political economy, with an emphasis on marketing strategies, Thomas Austin's (2002) work on three Hollywood productions places importance on a multi-dimensional approach to films as socio-economic and cultural textual products. He uses as case studies, dubbing them 'event' films, three films: *Basic Instinct* (Verhoeven, 1992), *Bram Stoker's Dracula* (Coppola, 1992) and *Natural Born Killers* (Stone, 1994), dubbing them as 'event' films. An 'event' film is not only a wildly economically successful film but also one that generates public controversy, such as depictions of sexuality and violence in *Natural Born Killers*. With this consideration, Austin argues that 'understanding how cultural forms work within contemporary society also requires an investigation of institutional context and commercial strategies and practices, as media consumption clearly does not happen in isolation from these operations' (p. 14). For Austin, this entails understanding the films as a 'dispersible text'. That is, a text produced with certain commercial, economic and intertextual strategies and operations in mind. Further, these operations and strategies, which are targeted at specific groups of the population, attempt to influence and privilege certain readings of the film, though they do not fully fix them. Moreover, the marketing and distributional strategies employed serve to cement films as commodities. With a clear picture of how a given film is positioned, marketed (i.e. interviews with cast, media reports, press sensationalism), 'hyped' up and distributed, Austin's approach is completed via audience research on how contextually positioned subjects receive, interpret and articulate their pleasures of the film, its 'hype' (its contentious quality) and its commoditisation. Austin's work is ambitious in its scope and nuanced in its articulation of the different 'life' stages a film goes through economically, socioculturally and individually. From his work, I take into my own book the rationale of how to choose and study film, emphasising the continued life of films.

Norma Iglesias-Prieto's (2004) work on the reception of the film *Danzón* (Novaro, 1991) focuses on articulations and inflections of gender at three levels: first, on the feminine gaze of the director, María Novaro; second, on the construction of masculine–feminine subjectivities through cinema; and finally, on their reception by gendered subjects with specific sexual orientations. *Danzón* is about a woman who moves from Mexico City to Veracruz in search of a lost lover. Using discussion groups segregated by age, sexual orientation, gender and place of origin, Iglesias Prieto's research shows how a director's attempts at challenging dominant patriarchal cinematic codes are received, interpreted and given differing levels of significance depending on her four chosen variables. For example, for her female participants, the female lead of the film was celebrated because of her complexity. This was attributed in part because this is a female character with agency, contrary to dominant portrayals of the feminine in (Mexican) cinema. They also praised the film for its nuanced, feminine telling story of Mexico. On the other hand, the young, male, Mexican, heterosexual participants derided this type of storytelling, based around micro-stories with an emphasis on the sensual, as boring or lacking in 'transcendence'. In comparison, all variables constant bar place of origin, her Spaniard participants saw the film as a dual journey of the female lead towards her own liberation. Her analysis and research highlight how there are many inflective moments that affect the reception of the discursive aspects of a film, her focus on gender. The work of Iglesias-Prieto serves as an eloquent counter-argument to Barker's critique of identification. By segregating the groups and choosing the film she chose, her analysis highlights one of the most illuminating aspects of audiences' identification: the constant tension between self-affirmation and 'others', between specificity and generalisation.

Shakuntala Banaji's (2006, 2007, 2014) work on Bollywood audiences of primarily romantic Hindi films in Bombay and London has been central to driving forward a more complex and nuanced understanding of the processes of encounter, reformulation and meaning-making in which audiences are collectively and individually engaged. Her research is based on participant observation at over 80 film showings, brief public interviews and 36 extended in-depth interviews about politics, everyday life and film-linked meaning-making or behaviour. Working at two urban sites, her 2006 book explores different audiences' interpretations and pleasures, articulating connections between places of origin, gender, age, religious beliefs, sexuality, masculinities and femininities, ethnicity, violence, terrorism and nation. With a plethora of subjectivities explored, her work highlights that the interpretative act of an audience member reading and responding to a text is not a singular process but is a multi-dimensional matrix full of inflections, connections and counter-intuitive projections and disavowals. That is, interpretation is usually fragmentary, and, at points, contradictory. Banaji's analysis (2007, 2014) calls attention to the manner in which the intersectionality of audiences comes to the fore in pleasures and ideological critiques, and in the attribution of significance, and/or rejection of certain sequences and elements of a film and its ideological discourses. Banaji's work highlights the importance of *context*. Banaji argues

> *That the immediate context of the social act of viewing Hindi films in a group,* along with members of an audience, in a quasi-public space such as a cinema hall or a crowded living room, *can have a profound impact on the nature of spectatorship, inflecting and even colouring entirely the experience of film viewing and the interpretation of particular sequences in films.*
>
> (2006: 176; author's emphasis)

Context, in Banaji's work, can be understood as a relationship between the physical (cinema hall, living room) and social (alone, with relatives, with friends) condition of film viewing, and the *intersectionality* of a subject's identity, where intersectionality is understood as always politicised, and never a stand-in for some form of diversity. In addition to this, she suggests that it is important to pay attention to the larger historical and sociopolitical contexts in which a film is produced and released and how these affect the both momentary interpretation and audiences' memories of films. Given the intermeshing of the narrative, sensuous, sartorial, and musical elements 'it appears that *emotional and material realism are often mutually interdependent ... a suspension of disbelief has to be earned and is not automatically granted* to a ... film text' (2006: 168). This entails a further refinement of the politics of pleasure, of emotional engagement and ironic, rational detachment by admitting the possibility of their coexistence at the same time.

Further, Banaji argues that when understanding *why* audiences remember and articulate their pleasures and interpretations of sequences in different ways at different times, it is important to consider the experiences and background and social context of the interpreter as well as the different claims of truth of the text. Importantly, she argues that a detached mode of engagement with an element of a film becomes nigh on impossible for those audiences – and those scholars – who have experienced something similar in their lives. Her analysis showcases the importance of going beyond the text–audience dyad and understanding the psychosocial and political contextual nuances at every level that affect the interaction between films and audiences. Banaji's and Iglesias-Prieto's work, then, significantly influences several aspects of the research discussed in my book. First, the importance of understanding that the context of reception is influenced in myriad ways by the intersectionality of a subject. This entails understanding that interpretation can be contradictory, fragmentary and ambiguous. Thus, it is paramount, when highlighting variations and overlaps in perspectives, to also analyse how different subjects articulate particular elements of their subjectivity to understand these variations and overlaps. Further, that the construction of these interpretations differs from a group setting to an individual one, and that memory is a political and ideological act. Both of these theoretical positions have implications for methodology, and posit the sort of contextual engagement with audiences through talk, observation and discussion that is discussed here. Finally, I seek to further elucidate the multi-directional relationship that emotional realism, the verisimilar, ideology and pleasure have both in representations of romantic love, as well as in their interpretations.

Today's audiences

In the past decade, audience research hasn't relented, with a concern of performativity and new modes of media consumption and engagement drawing researchers to now look online for film audiences, taking online comments, reviews and forums as proxies to study attitudes, pleasures, interpretations and other elements audience research is known for (Bore & Hickman, 2013; Davis & Michelle, 2011; Kalviknes-Bore, 2011, 2012; Ridanpää, 2014; K. Weir & Dunne, 2014). Connected to the online, in today's media environment, researchers are also cognisant that people consume films in myriad ways. Constantine Nakassis (2016), in his study of Tamil cinema and youth in India, emphasises the importance of style and interdiscursivity in understanding film consumption. That is,

> Filmic *style* is inherently interdiscursive, always pointing to another *stylish* act. And it is reflexively so. Style, as I've argued, is always presenced in quotes. That which is cited is always marked in one way or another as not quite one's own, as a reanimation of some other act originating from another, more statusful subject or object. The performativity of film to do style is contingent on this citationality, the ability of the citation to figurate *this* performance here and now as an instance of *style* by virtue of its grounding in *another* cited performance, which, in being so cited, is figured as its originary moment.
>
> (p. 217)

What Nakassis highlights is that the film and the audience do not end when the film ends. Rather, by articulating their pleasures, and identities through specific elements of a filmic text, audiences reform and perform the text not just mimicking it, but by bricolaging it to fit their personal agenda. This citationality he speaks of is paramount to understand the allure films can have over our projects of self. In addition to this, it considers that a film's enduring cultural life is largely dependent on its performativity by audiences (see also Aran-Ramspott, Medina-Bravo & Rodrigo-Alsina, 2015; Hollinshead, 2011).

Connected to this recognition of modalities of consumption is also a renewed, if not novel, interest in the spaces of this consumption (Smets et al., 2013).[7] Others have looked at how contemporary geopolitics are represented and are involved in the negotiation of national, trans-national and local (urban/rural) identities (Anaz, 2014; Aveyard, 2012; Cochrane, 2011). Finally, ethnographic or participant observation exercises with particular groups also continue to be of interest, whether that be indigenous communities or film festival attendants (Bertolli Filho, 2015; Bradby, 2013; Iglesias-Prieto, 2012; Marx, 2014; Smets, 2012; Wilson & Stewart, 2008; Ateşman, 2015; Dickson, 2015; Martinez et al., 2015).

Conclusion

I have outlined some of the main theoretical and empirical approaches to reception studies. It is possible to divide these as textual and audience-driven studies. I mainly draw from the cultural studies tradition and, to a lesser extent, spectatorship studies. Like many other audience researchers interested in cinema, the inalienable relationship between psychoanalysis and cinema must be recognised (see Elsaesser, 2009; Mayne, 1998; Smelik, 2001). Early Screen theory, and to a lesser extent the film apparatus theory, offers an initially compelling way to understand the ideological messages embedded in narrative cinema, its claims to 'reality', pleasures and identities by the spectator. Through an ocularcentric appropriation of psychoanalysis, early Screen theory poses that the film text has a set of pre-inscribed meanings. These meanings, in narrative cinema,[8] because it aims to emulate reality, are dominant, patriarchal ideological tools that seek the status of 'normal'. Further, early Screen theory posits that given the affective and aesthetic qualities of cinema, it structures two main types of pleasures: scopophilia and narcissistic identification. In addition to this, the spectator of narrative cinema is considered as a passive entity that was submissive to the film ideological apparatus, partly enabled through the lure of the cinematic pleasures. Finally, Screen theorists emphasise the importance of gender in all these elements. I admit that there have been many developments of this early position sketched out here. Further, there has also been a turn towards phenomenology and the work of Gilles Deleuze in the past few years (see Plantinga, 2009; Rushton, 2009).

The criticisms of Screen theory, many of them coming from the British cultural studies tradition, help to enrich the picture of reception. First was the structural overemphasis on the text. This meant three things: a methodological neglect of the audience; an over-celebration of the authorial power of the writer to 'unveil' the psycho-ideological workings of the text; and a reductionist, monolithic account of spectator pleasures and identifications. While acknowledging media as ideological and with 'preferred readings', the work of audience researchers has shown the importance of 'speaking' to actual audiences. By doing so, we've come to understand the many ways people read texts, and articulate their pleasures and identities. Research from this tradition has shown that the meanings and claims of truth of any media text are read differently depending on the socioeconomic and historical context of the reception and the intersectionality of the subject reading. At the same time, by understanding the reading of a text as fragmentary, ambivalent at times and contradictory, it becomes possible to understand why certain ideological elements of a text are read in particular ways. This is not to say that there are an infinite number of possible readings, but rather that how subjects position themselves vis-à-vis the ideological positions of a text opens the way to indifference, ideological affirmation, resistance, incredulity, identification and other modes of engagement. Moreover, it is with the understanding that pleasures may be precarious and that identities are not fixed, yet neither of these are unbound, that it becomes important to understand how different modes of engagement speak of their relationship with the ideological work of the text and the reception of this work by the audience. In other words, it is important to consider that any given film contains ideologies that cut across gender, sex, race and class in a particular socioeconomic and historical context. At the same time, the intersectionality of a subject affects how at different moments of a reading different modes of engagement come to the fore.

Notes

1 A recent exception is the book *Making Sense of Cinema: Empirical Studies into Film Spectators and Spectatorship* edited by Carrie Lynn D. Reinhard and Christopher J. Olson (2016). It must be noted, however, that while the book showcases the different methodologies and disciplines interested in the interaction between film and audiences, none of the chapters contained therein deal with romantic audiences or films.
2 Altman uses the example of the woman's film and the scholarship in the seventies and eighties surrounding these films (some reviewed in this chapter) to highlight, according to him, the power of critics in shaping genre conventions and limits post facto (see Garrett, 2007 for a critique of Altman's position).
3 This is something not unique to the West, as the cases of Tehran, Bombay and Shanghai illustrate.
4 According to Diane Negra (2006), films like *Four Weddings and a Funeral, Notting Hill* (Michell, 1999) and *French Kiss* (Kasdan, 1995) were, alongside friendship, part of a trend to treat tourism and the luxury of mobility of white, (upper) middle-class women as a catalyst for self and/or romantic fulfilment, enabled by the encounter of the 'authentic', the 'real' (land and lover) elsewhere.
5 It is worthy of mention that the TV series *Friends* and *Sex and the City* are examples of this that preceded these films.
6 Adorno and Horkheimer (2002) wrote on pleasure: 'Pleasure hardens into boredom because, if it is to remain pleasure, it must not demand any effort and therefore moves rigorously in the worn grooves of association. No independent thinking must be expected from the audience: the product prescribes every reaction: not by its natural structure (which collapses under reflection), but by signals. Any logical connection calling for mental effort is painstakingly avoided' (p. 137).
7 For more literature on this project, see: Smets et al. (2016); Vandevelde et al. (2015); Smets (2012).
8 For those writing from a Screen or film apparatus perspective, there was a clear difference between narrative and art cinema. The former seeks to etch out contradictions in favour of a resolution of the conflict, in support of dominant ideologies. The latter, because it can blur ideological positions and have greater affective impact, has the potential to challenge the dominant gaze.

References

Abercrombie, N., & Longhurst, B. (1998). *Audiences: a sociological theory of performance and imagination*. Sage.
Adorno, T. W. (1976). *Television and the Patterns of Mass Culture*. Oxford University Press.

Adorno, T. W., & Horkheimer, M. (2002). *Dialectic of enlightenment: Philosophical Fragments* (trans. E. Jephcott). Stanford University Press.

Adorno, T. W., & Rabinbach, A. (1975). Culture industry reconsidered. *New German Critique*, 6(Autumn), 12–19.

Alasuutari, P. (ed.). (1999). *Rethinking the media audience: the new agenda*. SAGE.

Alberti, J. (2013a). "I love you, man": bromances, the construction of masculinity, and the continuing evolution of the romantic comedy. *Quarterly Review of Film and Video*, 30, 159–172.

Alberti, J. (2013b). *Masculinity in the contemporary romantic comedy: gender as genre*. Routledge.

Allen, W. (1977). Annie Hall. United Artists.

Altman, R. (1999). *Film/genre*. BFI Publishing.

Anaz, N. (2014). Geopolitics of film: surveying audience reception of a Turkish film, Valley of the Wolves: Palestine. *Participations*, 11(1), 5–30.

Ang, I. (1985). *Watching Dallas: soap opera and the melodramatic imagination*. Methuen.

Ang, I. (1990). *Desperately seeking the audience*. Routledge.

Ang, I. (2007). Television fictions around the world: melodrama and irony in global perspective. *Critical Studies in Television*, 2(2), 18–30.

Apatow, J. (2005). The 40-year old virgin. Universal Pictures.

Aran-Ramspott, S., Medina-Bravo, P., & Rodrigo-Alsina, M. (2015). Exploring the Spanish youth audience's interpretation of loving relationships. *Media, Culture & Society*, 37(6), 813–833. https://doi.org/10.1177/0163443715577243.

Ateşman, Ö. Ö. (2015). The politicisation and 'Occupy'sation of the Istanbul Film Festival audience. *Participations*, 12(1), 679–702.

Aumont, J. (1992). *Aesthetics of film*. University of Texas Press.

Austin, T. (2002). *Hollywood, hype and audiences: selling and watching popular film in the 1990s*. Manchester University Press.

Aveyard, K. (2012). Observation, mediation and intervention: an account of methodological fusion in the study of rural cinema audiences in Australia. *Participations*, 9(2), 648–663.

Banaji, S. (2002). Private lives and public spaces: the precarious pleasures of gender discourse in Raja Hindustani. *Women: A Cultural Review*, 13(2), 179–194. https://doi.org/10.1080/09574040210148988.

Banaji, S. (2006). *Reading "Bollywood" the young audience and Hindi films*. Palgrave Macmillan.

Banaji, S. (2007). Fascist imaginaries and clandestine critiques: young Hindi film viewers respond to violence, xenophobia and love in cross- border romances Book section. In M. Bharat & N. Kumar (eds), *Filming the line of control: the Indo–Pak relationship through the cinematic lens* (pp. 157–178). Routledge.

Bertolli Filho, C. (2015). Cine Real: ethnography of a movie theater for workers. *Revista Famecos*, 22(3), 110–128. https://doi.org/10.15448/1980-3729.2015.3.19301.

Blomkamp, N. (2009). District 9. TriStar Pictures.

Bore, I.-L. K., & Hickman, J. (2013). Continuing The West Wing in 140 characters or less: improvised simulation on Twitter. *Journal of Fandom Studies*, 1(2), 219–238. https://doi.org/10.1386/jfs.1.2.219_1.

Bourdieu, P. (1984). *Distinction: a social critique of the judgement of taste*. Routledge & Kegan Paul.

Bourdieu, P. (2010). *El sentido social del gusto: elementos para una sociología de la cultura*. Siglo veintiuno editores.

Bradby, B. (2013). Our affair with Mila Kunis: A group ethnography of cinema-going and the 'male gaze.' *Participations: Journal of Audience and Reception Studies*, 10(1), 3–35.

Brooks, P. (1996). *The Melodramatic Imagination: Balzac, Henry James, Melodrama and the Mode of Excess*. Yale University Press.

Brown, M. E. (1994). *Soap Opera and Women's Talk*. SAGE.

Cameron, J. (1997). Titanic. 20th Century Fox.

Cochrane, J. (2011). 6 years of alcohol: an allegory of a nation? *Participations*, 8(2), 308–326.

Coppola, F. F. (1992). Bram Stoker's Dracula. Columbia Pictures.

Couldry, N. (2010). Theorising media as practice. In B. Bräuchler & J. Postill (eds), *Theorising Media and Practice* (pp. 35–54). Berghahn.

Cowie, E. (1997). *Representing the woman: cinema and psychoanalysis*. University of Minnesota Press.

Davis, C., & Michelle, C. (2011). Q methodology in audience research: bridging the qualitative/quantitative "divide." *Participations: Journal of Audience and Reception Studies*, 8(2), 559–593.

De Lauretis, T. (1994). *The practice of love: lesbian sexuality and perverse desire*. Indiana University Press.

DeAngelis, M. (ed.). (2014). *Reading the bromance homosocial relationships in film and television*. Wayne University Press.

Deleyto, C. (2003). Between friends: love and friendship in contemporary romantic comedy. *Screen*, 44(2), 167–182.

Dickson, L.-A. (2015). 'Ah! Other bodies!': embodied spaces, pleasures and practices at Glasgow Film Festival. *Participations*, 12(1), 706–724.

Doane, M. A. (1982). Film and the masquerade: theorising the female spectator. *Screen*, 23(3–4),74–88. https://doi.org/10.1093/screen/23.3-4.74.

Doane, M. A., Mellencamp, P., & Williams, L. (eds). (1984). *Re-vision: essays in feminist film criticism*. American Film Institute.

Dowd, J. J., & Pallotta, N. R. (2000). The end of romance: the demystification of love in the postmodern age. *Sociological Perspectives*, 43(4), 549–580. https://doi.org/10.2307/1389548.

Du Gay, P., Hall, S., Janes, L., Mackay, H., & Negus, K. (1997). *Doing cultural studies: the story of the Sony Walkman*. SAGE.

Dyer, R. (2002). Entertainment and utopia. In *Only Entertainment* (2nd edn) (pp. 19–35). Psychology Press.

Elsaesser, T. (1987). Tales of sound and fury: observations on the family melodrama. In C. Gledhill (ed.), *Home is where the heart is: studies in melodrama and the woman's film* (pp. 43–69). BFI Publishing.

Elsaesser, T. (2009). Freud as media theorist: mystic writing-pads and the matter of memory. *Screen*, 50(1), 100–113. https://doi.org/10.1093/screen/hjn078.

Evans, P., & Deleyto, C. (eds) (1998). *Terms of endearment: Hollywood romantic comedy of the 1980s and 1990s*. Edinburgh University Press.

Feig, P. (2011). Bridesmaids. Apatow Productions.

Feig, P. (2013). The Heat. 20th Century Fox.

Feig, P. (2016). Ghostbusters. Sony Pictures Releasing.

Fiske, J. (1987). *Television culture*. Routledge.

Fiske, J. (1992). Audiencing: a cultural studies approach to watching television. *Poetics*, 21(4), 345–359. https://doi.org/10.1016/0304-422X(92)90013-S

Fiske, J. (2010). *Understanding popular culture*. Routledge.

Foucault, M. (1977). *Discipline and punish: the birth of the prison* (1st American edn). Pantheon Books.
Frantz, S. S. G., & Murphy Selinger, E. (2012). *New approaches to popular romance fiction: critical essays*. McFarland.
Garrett, R. (2007). *Postmodern chick flicks: the return of the woman's film*. Palgrave Macmillan.
Gledhill, C. (1987a). Home is where the heart is: studies in melodrama and the woman's film. BFI Publishing.
Gledhill, C. (1987b). The melodramatic field: an investigation. In C. Gledhill (ed.), *Home is where the heart is: studies in melodrama and the woman's film* (pp. 1–25). BFI Publishing.
Gluck, W. (2011). *Friends with benefits*. Screen Gems.
Greven, D. (2011). *Manhood in Hollywood from Bush to Bush*. University of Texas Press.
Gripsrud, J. (2002). Film audiences. In J. Hill & P. Church Gibson (eds), *The Oxford guide to film studies* (pp. 202–211). Oxford University Press.
Hall, S. (1973). *Encoding and Decoding in the Television Discourse*. Centre for Contemporary Cultural Studies.
Hobson, D. (1982). *Crossroads: the drama of a soap opera*. Methuen.
Hogan, P. J. (1997). My Best Friend's Wedding. TriStar Pictures.
Hollinshead, A. (2011). "And I felt quite posh!" Art-house cinema and the absent audience – the exclusions of choice. *Participations*, 8(2), 392–415.
Iglesias Prieto, N. (2004). Gazes and cinematic readings of gender: danzon and its relationship to its audience. *Discourse*, 26(1 & 2), 173–193.
Iglesias-Prieto, N. (2012). The U.S.–Mexico border and children's social imaginary: an analysis of *Wacha el Border* and *Beyond the Border*. *American Studies Journal*, 57. http://www.asjournal.org/57-2012/the-us-mexico-border-and-childrens-social-imaginary/
Illouz, E. (2012). *Why love hurts: a sociological explanation*. Polity.
Jenkins, H. (2006). *Fans, bloggers, and gamers: exploring participatory culture*. New York University Press.
Johar, K. (1998). Kuch Kuch Hota Hai. Dharma Productions.
Kalviknes Bore, I.-L. (2011). Reviewing romcom: (100) IMDb users and *(500) Days of Summer*. *Participations*, 8(2), 144–164.
Kalviknes Bore, I.-L. (2012). Focus group research and TV comedy audiences. *Participations*, 9(2).
Kaplan, E. A. (2000). *Feminism & film*. Oxford University Press.
Kasdan, L. (1995). French Kiss. 20th Century Fox.
Katz, E. (1980). On conceptualising media effects. *Studies in Communication*, 1, 119–141.
Katz, E., & Liebes, T. (1990). Interacting with 'Dallas': cross cultural readings of American TV. *Canadian Journal of Communication*, 15(1), 45–66.
Kracauer, S. (1947). *From Caligari to Hitler: a psychological history of the German film*. Princeton University Press.
Kracauer, S. (1995). *The mass ornament: Weimar essays* (ed. T. Y. Levin). Harvard University Press.
Kristeva, J. (1987). Tales of love. Columbia University Press.
Kuhn, A. (1994). *Women's pictures: feminism and cinema* (2nd edn). Verso.
Laplace, M. (1987). Producing and consuming the woman's film: discursive struggle in *Now, Voyager*. In *Home is where the heart is: studies in melodrama and the woman's film* (pp. 138–166). BFI Publishing.
Lent, T. O. (1995). Romantic love and friendship: the redefinition of gender relations in screwball comedy. In K. Karnick & H. Jenkins (eds), *Classical Hollywood Comedy* (pp. 314–331). Routledge.

Livingstone, S. (1989). *Making sense of television: the psychology of audience interpretation.* Pergamon.

Livingstone, S. (1991). Audience reception: the role of the viewer in retelling romantic drama. LSE Research Online.

Livingstone, S. M. (2000). Television and the active audience. In D. Fleming (ed.), *Formations: 21st century media studies* (pp. 175–195). Manchester University Press.

Livingstone, S. M. (2013). The participation paradigm in audience research. *Communication Review*, 16(1–2),21–30.

Livingstone, S. M., & Das, R. (2013). The end of audiences? theoretical echoes of reception amid the uncertainties of use. In J. Hartley, J. Burgess & A. Bruns (eds), *A Companion to New Media Dynamics* (pp. 104–121). Wiley-Blackwell.

Lull, J. (1988). *World families watch television.* SAGE.

Madden, J. (1998). Shakespeare in Love. Universal Pictures.

Martinez, J., Frances, M., Agirre, K., & Manias-Muñoz, M. (2015). Zinegin Basque film festival: a non-existent audience revealed. *Participations*, 12(1), 725–738.

Marx, L. (2014). Making cinephiles: an ethnographic study of audience socialization. *Participations: Journal of Audience and Reception Studies*, 11(1), 88–98.

Mathieu, D., Brites, M. J., Chimirri, N. A., Saariketo, M., Tammi, R., Torres, M., Silva, D., & Pacheco, L. (2016). *Methodological challenges in the transition towards online audience research.* 13(1), 289–320.

Mayne, J. (1998). *Cinema and spectatorship.* Routledge.

McDonald, T. J. (2007). *Romantic comedy: boy meets girl meets genre.* Columbia University Press.

Metz, C. (1991). *Film language: a semiotics of the cinema.* University of Chicago Press.

Metz, C. (2002). *Ensayos sobre significación en el cine (1964–1968).* Paidós.

Michell, R. (1999). Notting Hill. Universal Pictures.

Milner, S. (1992). Forever young. Warner Bros. Pictures.

Minghella, A. (1996). The English Patient. Miramax Films.

Modleski, T. (1984). *Loving with a vengeance: mass-produced fantasies for women.* Methuen.

Modleski, T. (2014). An affair to forget: melancholia in bromantic comedy. *Camera Obscura*, 29(2), 119–147.

Morley, D. (1980). *The Nationwide audience: structure and decoding.* British Film Institute.

Morley, D. (2006). Unanswered questions in audience research. *The Communication Review*, 9(2), 101–121.

Mulvey, L. (1975). Visual pleasure and narrative cinema. *Screen*, 16(3), 6–18. https://doi.org/10.1093/screen/16.3.6.

Mussell, K. (1984). *Fantasy and reconciliation: contemporary formulas of women's romance fiction.* Greenwood Press.

Nakassis, C. (2016). *Doing style: you and mass mediation in South India.* University of Chicago Press.

Neale, S., & Krutnik, F. (1990). *Popular film and television comedy.* Routledge. https://jykdok.linneanet.fi/vwebv/holdingsInfo?bibId=1098795;http://site.ebrary.com/lib/jyvaskyla/Doc?id=5003136.

Negra, D. (2006). Romance and/as tourism: heritage whiteness and the (inter)national imaginary in the new woman's film. In E. Ezra & T. Rowden (eds), *Transnational cinema: the film reader* (pp. 82–97). Routledge.

Newell, M. (1994). Four Weddings and a Funeral. Rank Film Distributions.

Nightingale, V. (2011). *The handbook of media audiences* (ed. V. Nightingale). Wiley-Blackwell.

Novaro, M. (1991). Danzón. Jorge Sánchez.
Owen, M. (1997). Re-inventing romance: reading popular romantic fiction. *Women's Studies International Forum*, 20(4), 537–546. https://doi.org/10.1016/S0277-5395(97)00042-00043.
Peberdy, D. (2011). *Masculinity and film performance*. Palgrave Macmillan. https://doi.org/10.1057/9780230308701.
Plantinga, C. (2009). *Moving viewers: American film and the spectator's experience*. University of California Press.
Potter, C. (2002). *I love you but … romance, comedy and the movies*. Methuen.
Radner, H., & Stringer, R. (2011). *Feminism at the movies: understanding gender in contemporary popular cinema*. Routledge.
Radway, J. (1984). *Reading the romance: women, patriarchy and popular literature*. Verso.
Rapper, I. (1942). Now, Voyager. Warner Bros. Pictures.
Rehling, N. (2009). Extra-ordinary men: white heterosexual masculinity in contemporary popular cinema. Lexington Books.
Reiner, R. (1989). When Harry Met Sally… Columbia Pictures.
Reinhard, C. D., & Olson, C. J. (2016). *Making sense of cinema: empirical studies into film spectators and spectatorship*. Bloomsbury.
Ridanpää, J. (2014). 'Humour is serious' as a geopolitical speech act: IMDb film reviews of Sacha Baron Cohen's *The Dictator*. *Geopolitics*, 19(1), 140–160.
Rushton, R. (2009). Deleuzian spectatorship. *Screen*, 50(1), 45–53. https://doi.org/10.1093/screen/hjn086.
Seiter, E., Borchers, H., Kreutzner, G., & Warth, E. M. (1989). *Remote control: television, audiences, and cultural power*. Routledge.
Shumway, D. R. (2003). *Modern love: romance, intimacy, and the marriage crisis*. New York University Press.
Silberling, B. (1998). City of angels. Warner Bros. Pictures.
Silverman, K. (1996). *The threshold of the visible world*. Routledge.
Silverstone, R. (2006). *Media and morality: on the rise of the mediapolis*. Polity Press.
Smelik, A. (2001). *And the mirror cracked: feminist cinema and film theory*. Palgrave.
Smets, K. (2012). Connecting Islam and film culture: the reception of *The Message* (*Ar Risalah*) among the Moroccan diaspora. *Participations: Journal of Audience and Reception Studies*, 9(1), 68–94.
Smets, K., Van Bauwel, S., Meers, P., & Vande Winkel, R. (2016). Film-viewing in Turkish and Moroccan diasporic families: a gender and place perspective. *Gender Place & Culture*, 23(4), 556–571.
Smets, K., Vandevelde, I., Meers, P., Vande Winkel, R., & Van Bauwel, S. (2013). Diasporic film cultures from a multi-level perspective: Moroccan and Indian cinematic flows in and towards Antwerp. *Critical Studies in Media Communication*, 30(4), 257–274.
Snitow, A. B. (1979). Mass market romance: pornography for women is different. *Radical History Review*, 20, 141–161. https://doi.org/10.1215/01636545-1979-20-141.
Stoller, N. (2008). Forgetting Sarah Marshall. Apatow Productions.
Stone, O. (1994). Natural Born Killers. Warner Bros. Pictures.
Tennant, A. (1999). Anna and the King. 20th Century Fox.
Thompson, J. B. (1995). *The media and modernity: a social theory of the media*. Polity Press.
Todorov, T. (1970). Introducción. In E. Verón (ed.), *Lo verosímil* (pp. 11–16). Tiempo Contemporáneo.
Todorov, T. (1977). *The poetics of prose*. Blackwell.
van Zoonen, L. (1994). *Feminist media studies*. SAGE.

Vandevelde, I., Meers, P., Van Bauwel, S., & Vande Winkel, R. (2015). Sharing the silver screen: the social experience of cinemagoing in the Indian diaspora. *BioScope*, 6(1), 88–106.

Verhoeven, P. (1992). Basic Instinct. TriStar Pictures.

Wain, D. (2014). They Came Together. Lionsgate.

Weir, K., & Dunne, S. (2014). The connoisseurship of the condemned: *A Serbian Film, The Human Centipede 2* and the appreciation of the abhorrent. *Participations*, 11(2), 78–99.

Willis, P. E. (1990). *Common culture: symbolic work at play in the everyday cultures of the young*. Open University Press.

Wilson, P., & Stewart, M. (2008). *Global indigenous media: cultures, poetics and politics*. Duke University Press.

Wright, J. (2005). Pride and Prejudice. Focus Features.

Wright, J. (2007). Atonement. Focus Features.

Zaborowski, R., & Dhaenens, F. (2016). Old topics, old approaches? "Reception" in television studies and music studies. *Participations*, 13(1), 446–461.

Zucker, J. (1990). Ghost. Paramount Pictures.

3 Love and technology
Control, affordances and prejudice

Introduction

Romantic love is such a versatile and popular (sub)plot in cinema partly because of the many ways in which it can introduce a second plot or structural element into the narrative. Family, class, euthanasia, immigration, technology, war, nation and nationalism, history, sexuality and mental health are but a few themes linked to romances over and over again. Before cinema, there was the novel in the eighteenth and nineteenth centuries when the two leading movements of the time were realism and romanticism. Three great examples of these links can be found in Leo Tolstoy's *Anna Karenina*, Johann Wolfgang von Goethe's *The Sorrows of Young Werther* and Gustave Flaubert's *A Sentimental Education*. Before and after the novel, though, it is possible to trace amatory fiction in Britain and romantic novels. These works of fiction were mass marketed and followed archetypical characters and deviated very little from their canon. The main storyline followed a couple facing some sort of obstacle who eventually surpass it and end up living happily ever after. Furthermore, they were written mostly by women for women (Jane Austen, Ann Radcliffe and Eliza Haywood, to name a few). Many of the authors of novels of the nineteenth century had relative degrees of contempt for these works. Flaubert's *Madame Bovary* is one of the most famous examples of this disdain. In recent years, films like *Amour* (Haneke, 2012), *The Immigrant* (Gray, 2013), *Like Crazy* (Doremus, 2011), *LOL* (Swanberg, 2006), *Broken Circle Breakdown* (Van Groeningen, 2012), *Weekend* (Haigh, 2011), *Omar* (Abu-Assad, 2013) and *Catfish* (Joost & Schulman, 2010) have touched on these subjects and gained critical and, on some occasions,[1] public acclaim (see Clare, 2013; García Guillem, 2015; Rosinski, 2015). This is not to say that they are ground-breaking in addressing these issues. It does suggest, however, that films which dare to mix love with more 'controversial' issues are gaining some traction in the narratives of cinematic love, ephemeral and frail as it may be.

Further, the genre of romantic love on screen, in its dramatic structure, grants enough liberties and plenty of recognisable elements to writers so that it achieves malleability far beyond that of any other theme. This, as mentioned previously, is possible not only because we share a sociocultural script and practices that allows us to recognise love on screen, cinema has its set of conventions that produce and reproduce certain representations of these scripts and practices. In addition, a crucial factor

DOI: 10.4324/9781003164289-4

in the longevity and continued cinematic interest in romantic love lies in the representations of the wider socioeconomic and cultural changes romantic love, intimacy and relationships undergo. Love is not an insulated, asocial or isolated emotional, individual phenomenon. Rather, it reverberates into other emotions and phenomena, and constantly feeds on them (see Evans, 2003; Kipnis, 2003; Wilkinson & Bell, 2012). Thus, successful romantic films often mix a subplot dealing with a contemporary issue whilst also touching on shifts and continuities of romance. Taking this into account, I chose *Her* (Jonze, 2013) and *Don Jon* (Gordon-Levitt, 2013) as the last films I screened in order to bring to the fore the discussions participants of other group interviews had shown great interest in. The former not only dealt with technology, but also portrayed a relatively novel type of masculinity, a beta masculinity. The latter was written as a sort of parody and meta-commentary on romantic comedies, following on from the trend of self-conscious romantic films, as well as dealing with perceived shifts in intimacy brought about by the mediatisation of sex (pornography) and romantic love (romantic comedies). But while the topics of technology and mediatisation did appear, and will be discussed where appropriate, *expectations* and *romantic affordances* were the two themes most frequently highlighted in films and by participants across all group interviews. These two topics, I argue, represent two pressing historical issues within interpersonal romantic relationships with two important shifts in the configuration of intimacy and relationships. Thus, I aim to elucidate how these two themes are linked with certain continued film narratives in the romance genre, and how considerations and discussions of these themes and their accordant representations on screen are conduits for audiences to speak their minds on issues they consider crucial to the ways romantic love is changing in their lives. Therefore, understanding how changes in expectations and romantic affordances are being represented on screen and how they are being read by audiences is crucial in building a clearer picture of the role played by cultural representation of romantic love in contemporary Western societies and in contemporary romantic relationships.

Before moving on to the analysis, I would like to briefly touch upon the fact that for this project in which I interviewed and worked with dozens of women I took into account ethical considerations to make the process as transparent and fruitful for all involved.

The interaction between interviewer and interviewee is neither neutral nor symmetrical (Atkinson & Silverman, 1997; Fontana & Frey, 2008; Kvale, 1996; Scheurich, 1995). This interaction, at the same time, is burdened by the question of trusting (empathy) or suspecting the reality claims of what the interviewee says (Silverman, 2014; Willig, 2014). Third, it is the interviewer who selects, cuts and interprets the interview in the final text. Thus, drawing on feminist literature (DeVault & Gross, 2012; Doucet & Mauthner, 2012; Finch, 1984; Hesse-Biber, 2012; Reynolds, 2002; Skeggs, 1997, 2001; Thapar-Björkert & Henry, 2004), it is possible to envision this as a non-exploitative project as long as three things are considered. The first is adopting a constructionist perspective that understands and accepts women's ways of knowing. The second is an acknowledgement of my gendered position and an active effort to collaborate, empower and reciprocate the time and effort of my participants.

The third is that power relationships in the interview setting are not fixed and are negotiated throughout the process. The first consideration for this was whether to interview participants individually or in groups. Following the experience of Radhika Parameswaran's (2001) ethnographic work on elite Indian women reading Western romance novels, where she struggled to get her participants to do individual interviews and thus decided to first interview them in groups, I considered following suit, despite the marked contextual differences.

Further, as Esther Madriz (Madriz, 1998) writes:

> Focus groups allow access to research participants who may find one-on-one, face-to-face interaction 'scary' or 'intimidating'. By creating multiple lines of communication, the group interview offers participants ... a safe environment where they can share ideas, beliefs, and attitudes in the company of people from the same socioeconomic, ethnic, and gender backgrounds
>
> (p. 835)

Madriz's work is with working-class Latina women for whom the group setting became a moment of catharsis, empowerment and bonding. While the contextual differences are important, I would like to highlight the idea of a 'safe space' (reminiscent of the therapeutic one) for women and men to talk about these subjects with others and myself. Finally, by investing a lot of energy and emotion, I managed to create a good rapport with most of my participants. This does not mean I consider that I was talked to *as if I were a woman*. Rather, by the end of the discussion, I was, at least, a man who *listened* actively to women (and to other men). Clearly not all the time by all participants, but it is my contention that the quality of the data presented in these pages attests to this. With this is in mind, it is also important to point out that this knowledge should be considered as a social co-production of notions and ideas of romantic love and cinema based on the flow and exchange of ideas that took place

Commodified love, commodified subject

The concept of commodification of romance has been used by several authors, notably Colin Campbell (1987),[2] Eva Illouz (1997) and Zygmunt Bauman (2003). As I mentioned previously, Illouz traces the shift, in Western societies, from Victorian ideals and customs to a more 'public' and consumer/leisure-oriented practice of love. From chaperoning and visits to the boom of dating, she argues this has entailed a dual process of 'romanticisation of commodities' and 'commodification of romance'. Thus, romantic love, marriage and relationships go from a utilitarian, status-seeking (or maintenance) social contract to an individual pursuit. Illouz argues as well that love becomes a place for a *visual utopia*, contrary to its oral and print presence in the past two centuries respectively. Bauman (2003) argued that (online) dating was like scrolling through a mail-order catalogue where one need never buy. Further, as Dröge and Voirol (2011) suggest, online dating sites

> By the way they present the profiles of potential partners in exactly the same manner as items on eBay, Amazon or other shopping sites, with their complex search forms that allow to define the own preferences in mate selection with a precision unknown before, with the tools they offer to evaluate one's own market value and to enhance this value if possible –with all these elements borrowed from modern forms of consumerism and the economic sphere, they suggest a subject position which is very close to what we have outlined above as the main characteristics of a calculating subject in the realm of the market. It is the position of an economic agent who compares offers on a level of equivalence and tries to maximize his own interests. At the same time, it is the position of a self-marketing 'supplier' in a very competitive 'economy of attention'.
>
> (p. 346)

They further argue that this economic rationalisation is in constant tension with the discourse of romantic love and its search, causing ambivalences and contradictions the users must navigate. The exhilaration, the promise of finding love is met with rational, market-based strategies that look to maximise efficiency of search and diminish frustrations and disappointments. In an early exploratory study of online dating, researchers agreed with Bauman's statement, suggesting that 'like the shelves of a supermarket, the Internet offers endless variety, unlimited choice and great convenience' and that 'marketplace values are evident both in the way users market themselves, and in terms of how they look through profiles and photos to identify an "evoked set" of potential partners' (Maclaran et al., 2005, 41–44). However, they also rejected his pessimism, as I do too, contending online dating also allowed for deep bonds to nourish. Further, while this study is specific to online dating, the market and rational decision logic Bauman highlights *aren't*. Commodification of romance, then, is a deeply ingrained process of contemporary romance whereby subjects and their traits enter a transactional market place. The entanglement of late capitalism, romantic love and commoditisation has not desecrated some nostalgia-ridden idea of love, it has brought new affordances, pain, frustrations and for some, joy, love and stable relationships. Technology's main role has been to exacerbate it all.

Further, as Illouz (2012) argues, the discourse of love now is not only interconnected with that of psychotherapy but also with that of suffering. This is not the romantic suffering of established fiction texts (e.g. *Romeo and Juliet*), but a self-conscious suffering constantly levered against the benefits. She attributes this shift largely to the influence of psychoanalysis and its emphasis on understanding the self as an 'ongoing process of self-understanding and careful self-monitoring of the psyche' (p. 163). She continues:

> The model of mental health which massively penetrated intimate relationships demanded that love be aligned to definitions of well-being and happiness, which ultimately rejected suffering, and commanded one to maximize one's utilities ... To love well means to love according to one's self-interest. The emotional experience of love increasingly contains and

displays utilitarian project of the self, in which one has to secure maximum pleasure and well-being. Suffering is progressively foreign to his new cultural idiom of love.

(pp. 164–165)

Illouz's point is that through this shift, love becomes a reflexive, rationalised act, one particularly oriented towards an egotistical happiness. Or, in the very least, as she puts it, to 'maximize one's utilities' (p. 182). Thus, the commodification of romance is intertwined with the avoidance of suffering and the maximisation of pleasure.

While it is important to acknowledge certain features of contemporary dating and how they may exacerbate toxic ideologies, the perspective of economic rationalisation risks becoming reductionist insofar as it fails to acknowledge that looking for shared values, attributes and pass times is one of the first things we do when we meet a potential new partner. Not just now. Anton Chekhov's (2010) short story 'The Kiss' is a good example. A brigade of Russian soldiers on campaign are hosted by a nobleman. One of the soldiers, Ryabovitch, gets lost in the mansion, entering a dark room. In this room, a woman kisses him, only to recoil knowing it was not the man she was expecting. Ryabovitch, on the other hand, euphoric, starts to aggrandise this moment as if it were a declaration of never-ending love. When they leave the mansion, Ryabovitch struggles to 'put together' the woman: her smell, her arms around him, her shoulders, her lips and so on. Because he never saw her, he tries to do this bricolaging through the physical features of the other women he saw in the mansion. Soon afterwards, after understanding it was a fleeting moment, he berates himself for expecting news and a magical reappearance of she who kissed him. Chekhov's story points to the importance a seemingly trivial moment can have in our lives, but I want to single out that even if there was not a 'loved one', Ryabovitch's attempt at a reconstruction, through the prominent physical features of other women is resonant with the idea that highlighting certain aspects of the other is a long-standing feature of romantic love. Further, doing so is also linked to the activation of desire finding these traits has and, in turn, to the expectations this creates. Needless to say, this is not limited to physical traits.

How, then, do the commodification of romance, the individualised pursuit of romantic love, expectations and affinities relate to one another? Don Jon's story and reception provide an interesting perspective on this. At the outset of the film, Jon, played by director Joseph Gordon-Levitt, is a man of a strict routine: watch porn, gym, church, dinner with the family, going to a bar, picking up a woman, have sex with her, watch porn. In a voiceover commentary after a montage implicating several sexual encounters (naked women dropping on the same bed one after the other) cutting to a blurred computer screen showing porn, Jon expresses his discontent with real life sexual intercourse compared to pornography. He remarks on the positions and attitudes he finds in porn missing in all his sexual partners. The sequence of events and places that takes us through Jon's life highlights the link between his lack of intimacy and his unrealistic sexual expectations. His mirrored self is Barbara, played by Scarlett Johansson, who Jon meets and picks up at a bar. Barbara, unlike other women, does not have sex with Jon on the night they meet, or even the first week. The reason behind this is that Barbara believes she can't do this for the relationship with her Prince Charming to work – a belief informed by her fascination with romantic films. Thus, Barbara's intimacy is informed by an ideal man from romantic films. Eventually, they have intercourse. Jon is disappointed by it while Barbara shrugs it off as not as important. The relationship between the two fail as Jon is unable to stop watching pornography, something Barbara can't tolerate. In their final meeting, Jon apologises for having done so while also remarking she asked too much of him, her expectations unachievable. Barbara leaves unhinged, asking Jon never to contact her again. While this resolution is problematic as it leaves the female character as the hopeless ideological dupe of romantic films, narratively it helps to drive the male protagonist towards his acquiescence of 'true' intimacy with Esther. Further, it helped participants to express a wide range of perspectives on the topic of expectations. Thomas and Rupert, a professional couple in their late 20s, had this exchange:

RUPERT: Thomas was filling out one of those silly quizzes like 'who's your celebrity husband?' and we ended up talking about who we each thought would end up with.
THOMAS: Yeah, it's bizarre because you can have so many crazy ideas of what you want, but when we listed them the other day, we were both 'those people just can't exist'.
BENJAMIN: In what sense, if I may?
THOMAS: Well, maybe for straight people is different, but for us the porn bit wasn't as strong as romantic films. But you know, like with Barbara, you wish for somebody with nice hair, a lovely accent, great in bed, but an amazing listener, ambitious but also down to earth, you want them to like the same things …
RUPERT: And you go on and on, sort of daydreaming about all the things, not just physical, that you really hope to find in someone and I think that's the worst bit, or at least what we discussed … like deep inside you really don't want to 'settle' for anything less than something way out of your league but things never work that way. I think that's what I didn't like so much about the movie, like everyone knows that a bit of daydreaming is good and all, but at the end of the day, you have to appreciate how lucky you are to have somebody love you.

Martina, a 32 year-old private tutor, chimed in with her experience:

MARTINA: I think films and online dating have definitely created this attitude of perfection and unreal expectations when you meet someone. I remember I met this guy at a party and we clicked. We went out a few more times, but I could never shake this feeling of 'missing out' on my actual true love because I didn't continue looking it up online, or because I was missing out on other parties, you know, like in films where the person you should be was always there but you weren't looking … me and plenty of my friends sometimes talk that we will end up alone, but that's preferable over settling down over someone who doesn't meet your expectations.

BENJAMIN: And you strongly feel this way?
MARTINA: Not all the time, sometimes I do feel we are just too picky, people cling to anything they don't like so they won't commit but at the same time through online dating and living in a place like London I do feel you can meet so many people that it's impossible not to feel you are missing out …

These two excerpts express the general consensus of my participants who find themselves as if trapped in a double bind of some sort. On the one hand, there is a recognition of the fantastical nature of many personal expectations. This trait, in turn, is linked to media narratives of romantic love. As argued in previous chapters, many romantic films provide a smoothed-out, conflict-free version of love that can be easily recognised and desired, as with Martina's mention of the unnoticed love trope. However, to solely accuse films is to grossly misunderstand how desire works, while also assuming that audiences, like Barbara in the film, can't tell the difference between fiction and reality. Yet, there was a general acknowledgement that cultural phenomena such as romantic films and pornography help inflect many of our attitudes and frustrations with off-screen romantic love and sexual intimacy.

On the other hand, the context of contemporary romantic practices in a city like London, with a large population of single people, provides a setting where the idea of the commoditisation of expectations becomes a troubling, yet fundamental aspect of the romantic search. These attitudes undoubtedly pervade the logic and practice of contemporary romantic love, insofar as there persists the belief that one's ideal match can be found in a 'never-ending' aisle of potential lovers, and thus an 'infinite' pool of traits, affinities and beliefs that can be moulded into one's perfect match. Online dating has helped to foster this attitude. Illustrative are the cases of Amy Webb (2014) and Christopher McKinlay[3] (2014). At some point in their lives, they were looking for love. Given their expertise with mathematics, algorithms and data, both developed models in order to increase the likelihood of a positive romantic match. They did. This mathematical approach to the romantic search, possible through their knowledge and online dating, is indicative of the logic of expectation management of which the film and my participants speak. The difference lies, first, that not everyone possesses the same knowledge as McKinlay and Webb to 'hack' online dating. Further, while the internet has certainly helped to exacerbate this, the commoditisation of expectations is present in almost every aspect of today's romantic practices. One of the crucial elements of this commoditisation is that, as in the case of Martina, it instils in the subject a consumer-like mentality to always keep coming back, to keep looking for the next deal/best lover (see Slater, 2014).

Intimate subject

While Rupert describes thinking about his ideal loved one as 'a bit of daydreaming', Martina herself admits hesitating about her expectations every now and then. Meanwhile, in *Don Jon,* Jon meets and starts a relationship with

Esther, played by Julianne Moore. An older woman and a widow dealing with the loss of her family, she teaches Jon how to be sexually intimate with a woman without having to revert to the fantasy of porn. At the end of the movie, Jon and Esther have begun dating but without any compromise; neither wants to get married and Jon denies being in love in a 'mechanical' way – he simply feels he can get 'lost in her'. Many of the participants relished the fact that this acknowledgement of true intimacy was woven together with a long-standing trope that still resonates strongly: the reformation of a damaged lover.

Karen, a 39-year-old, divorced copywriter suggested in an interview:

> That girl was right [she refers to a participant in her group interview who expressed positive views about Esther and Jon], the best part of the film is when she teaches him to how to have sex ... women spend so much time having shit sex because we are taught by society that we can't speak about it or tell our boyfriends what we like because we will be shunned for it ... I may be a bit cheesy, but I think that one of the most beautiful things about falling in love is to see how you improve each other and that happens when you communicate and trust.

In another group interview, a participant claimed Jon's transformation was 'what you always wish for when you meet a hot but douche guy'. In a figure of love Barthes (1990) calls *rapture*, he writes that when falling in love we first fall in love with a *picture*. This picture is full of innocence, later tainted by the recognition of the other as different. I would add that an immense pleasure of love lies in how differences help to create a unique common world, as expressed by Karen. It isn't simply the fusing of two into one; it is also the reinvention of the two. That this transformation and desire for it come attached with the desire for complete intimacy is no coincidence. Shumway (2003) argues that:

> intimate relationships are valued because they cross the presumed boundary that separates self from others, allowing another to be 'most-within'. The problem with this formulation is not only that it assumes the alienated individual as its norm but also that the proposed antidote to this state is nothing more than its formal opposite. We still don't know in what having intimacy actually consists ... Intimacy sometimes seems to be mainly a kind of talk ... But more often, it seems to entail a kind of deep communication, one that requires talk but is not exhausted by it. Scarf appears to define intimacy as the condition of openness or freedom of self-expression, 'an individual's ability to talk about *who he really is*, and *to say what he wants and needs*, and *to be heard by the intimate partner*'.
>
> (Scarf, 2008, pp. 141–142, italics in original)

Intimacy then, is not just an open communication between romantic partners. It is a transcendental type of communication, where the relationship between self and other goes beyond language, entering a multi-levelled connection that includes affects, emotions and a belief in the possibility that has been constructed as the epitome of heterosexual romance in European and American culture: the fusion of two as one. Communication is a long-standing way of loving for women, and one (very) slowly gaining traction with middle-class men in some sociocultural milieux. However, in the sexual arena, the heteronormative patriarchal dictum that a woman's pleasure is subservient to that of the man's is very much alive both in film and in everyday life. Participants like Karen appreciate that in *Don Jon*, irrespective of other flaws of criticisms one may level, the recognition of a woman's sexual pleasure as equal is what leads to the redemption of the chauvinistic male lead – a recognition made possible by a dialogical intimacy we see them construct. Jon's and Esther's buddying sexual intimacy offers a glimpse of this; the redemption of the masculine that shuts down both his inner and the outer femininity. His failure to be human as a character is redeemed through a leap of faith into the frail humanity of Esther, whose communicative labour leads to the final sequence of the film, where he declares: 'It's like I know what she's thinking and I know what she's thinking. I don't know, it's a two-way thing, I fucking love it.' The sequence is accompanied with a montage during which the couple is seen talking and wandering in a plaza, eating, smiling, publicly displaying their affection and finally *making love*. It is relevant to note that none of my participants noticed the class traits and connotations of both characters and how problematic it is that the redeeming embodiment of intimacy and healthy relationships came from the upper-middle-class character towards the middle-low-class one. This may be because of the overtly outlandish characterisation of the leads and late introduction of Esther.

The shift from 'fucking' and 'having sex' to 'making love' highlights the transformation intimacy has had on Jon. This is what Karen's intervention points towards when she says that 'women spend so much time having shit sex because we are taught by society that we can't speak about it or tell our boyfriends what we like because we will be shunned for it', and though it cannot be reduced to just increased sexual intimacy, the role this plays should not be understated. Herein lies the intriguing relationship between sequences or elements of films we like or dislike. They trigger a way to articulate our romantic disappointments, frustrations, hopes and imagination by presenting a possible extrapolation that takes place nowhere in particular but reorganises, even if so briefly, our relationship between the romantic possible and the ideal.

In an environment where consumer and marketplace logics have inundated romantic love, to bet on intimacy is a risk that looks out of place. Yet, it persists. *Don Jon* sets itself up as a parody on one level and a drama of sorts on another, clearly delineating a before and an after for Jon, a moment where his obsession with pornography gives way to a sincere attempt at intimacy with another human being. This clear division between an unmoved, emotionally and sexually stunted Jon and a warmer, more humane one is a division unique to fictional texts. It provides a resolution to his inner conflict while at the same time introducing, in Esther, the recognition that conflicts and the unresolvable are a part of intimacy. Yet this jump is never as seamless off-screen. In a period of increased periods of personal, sensual and sexual experimentation before settling down with a romantic partner or as a single (Illouz, 2012; Slater, 2014), and when relationships are mostly individual contracts and promises of commitment, the path to romantic and self-fulfilment is fraught with anxiety and uncertainty. Further, it is trodden in many ways. The tension between ideals and yearning of intimacy and romantic love and the neo-liberal marketplace rationalisation of romantic actors is further complicated by the lack of a unified protocol of action; there is an uneasy privatised awkward, and many times rocky, socialisation of expectations, desires, hopes and ways of loving.

Thus, in the next section, I will explore in-depth the idea of romantic affordances.

Romantic affordances

In *The Ecological Approach to Visual Perception*, Jerome Gibson (1986), introduced the term *affordances* – in his theory of visual perception – to refer to the possibilities of action within an environment that were available to an actor, regardless of the actor's ability to recognise them. Since then, technologists, psychologists, cognitive scientists and philosophers have appropriated the concept in order to develop theories of perception, interaction and cognition. Ian Hutchby (2001), who draws on Gibson's original concept and develops it to draw middle ground between constructivist and technologically determinist positions in the sociology of technology, defines affordances as:

> functional and relational aspects which frame, while not determining, the possibilities for agentic action in relation to an object. In this way, technologies can be understood as artefacts which may be both shaped by and shaping of the practices humans use in interaction with, around and through them.
> (p. 444)

Brian Rappert (2003) has criticised the term for being too simple and general to explain the intricacies and more complicated relationships between technological artefacts and actors.[4] In this work, however, romantic affordance is understood more broadly as the interaction between a set of possible scripted, real and imagined romantic attitudes – as in Roland Barthes' (1990) figures of love – and the *environment*, here understood as the interplay of racial, classed, embodied and gendered factors that affect individual subjectivities. At the level of the scripted, which contains filmic texts, romantic affordances play out in two ways. The first is the ways in which the experience of the text and the medium can be appropriated for romantic endeavours, feeding into the level of the real. The second is the way in which the narrative or content of the text can be and is experienced as an imaginative resource or pressure for romantic endeavours, the level of the imagination. This is not to say that cultural scripts determine the other two attitudes; rather, it is the constant feedback back and forth between all three elements that constructs the affordance. Between these links there is a tension that arises not as a component of the affordance but as a by-product of an expectation about affordances. This is the mismatch between real experiences, the ideas and expectations one has of romance, and their expression mediated via a cultural text like a film. This tension expresses and reaffirms the uneasy relationship in romantic love that the imaginary and the real have, between fiction and practice, the liminal and the everyday. Affordances are easily expressed when a subject confronts a fictional text because the distance between the ideal and the practice is articulated via the fictional text. Films provide a plethora of moments where affordances are articulated, where a viewer can identify, distance, yearn or adopt other positions in regards to romantic love. Here, I make use of *Her* (2013), a film directed by Spike Jonze, and audiences' reactions to a sequence of this film to highlight how romantic affordances affect romantic love, both in the way it is represented and the way it is lived.

641

'641' references a sequence in *Her*, which I will get to imminently. *Her* (Jonze, 2013) depicts Theodore Wombly (played by Joaquin Phoenix), an introvert, writer, romantic and recent divorcee, as he struggles to get over his failed marriage with Catherine (played by Rooney Mara), his high-school sweetheart and fellow writer. Unable to cope with the fact that his marriage is over, Theodore refuses to sign the divorce papers. He purchases an operating system with an advanced artificial intelligence, which he calls Samantha, voiced by Scarlett Johansson. As Theodore and Samantha bond, he finally meets Catherine to finalise their divorce. With this out of the way, Theodore and Samantha form a romantic couple and try to bypass hurdles like Samantha's lack of a physical body and Theodore's fear of commitment. After a while, Samantha goes offline, much to Theodore's chagrin and panic. Samantha, shortly after meeting a virtual reconstruction of British philosopher Alan Watts, comes back online and announces to Theodore she has gone beyond the need of matter to update and process information. This step towards technological singularity prefaces, in the film, a unique way of announcing 'the end'. For some audiences, this was infuriating as it complicated, unnecessarily in their view, the falling out of love of Samantha and Theodore. For most others, it was a level above their understanding of technology. Further along the film, when Samantha confesses to maintaining contact with over 8,000 people/users and having fallen in love with 641 of them, that audiences grasped that was the end of their relationship. Theodore does not like this and reproaches her. The moment at which Theodore sits on a staircase and hears the number of times Samantha has fallen in love is a critical one.

'What do you reproach? 641 or Theodore's reproach?' asks a participant. Before I can come up with an answer, another participant asserts vigorously, 'the number'. Here I reproduce the extended group interview excerpt that followed this exchange between the participants:

SARAH: I get that she's a robot or something, but I would never go behind my hubby's back and talk to loads of strangers and 'fall' in love with them … if she's trying to be human and have a relationship with one, she should respect the fact he's exclusive to her.

FIONA: But we never see that they discuss that, or did they?
BENJAMIN: No, exclusivity in dating is not openly discussed in the film. Do you guys believe that relationships can only work if they are 'exclusive' or monogamous?
SARAH: I think, yes, anything else is a mistake. People don't have respect for other people and so they just jump from one person to another without thinking how much they are hurting them ... And I think society does nothing to stop teenagers from engaging in this and it creates a culture where the more partners you have the better.
JENNIFER: But if they never made it clear they were exclusive, why would she know what that means? I see it more as thing of being curious than of wanting to hurt Theodore ... I'd say they are both to blame if anything.
FIONA: Hmmm, yeah, I can see that. But she's always with him, and she can see through his glasses or something everywhere he is, all the time. She even asks about Amy and Theodore because she's the only woman she sees him with.
JENNIFER: Yeah, yeah ... don't know, I think women should be allowed to be as carefree as men when it comes to relationships, especially if both are ok with having other partners.
SARAH: I have tried being in an open relationship, and it is not for me. I don't think I'm particularly old fashioned or anything, but for me all it did was to fill me with anxiety and lots of questions ... we were never able to build the trust and intimacy you can when it is only the two of you.
MARTHA: I felt that when that scene happened [Theodore plumbing through the city and finally sitting on the stairs] a lot like that, he was hurt she didn't trust him, I think we can all relate to that moment you realise that.

Sarah, Fiona and Jennifer, European Caucasian women in their mid-thirties living in London and working either in the cultural industries or media and PR, exchange attitudes towards monogamy and the idea of multiple romantic partners that illustrate how complex and new this subject is in an open discussion. It is telling that Sandra speaks of intimacy in a broader sense to refer to the possibilities of connection between a dyad, as this connects to how the discourse of coupled intimacy (see Shumway, 2003; Sternberg, 2006) has been built but also to the triangular structure of romantic love. This structure, just like the discourse of intimacy, considers two subjects and a third *non-subject* as the pillars of the relationship; in romantic love, this third element is a hurdle, an obstacle, whereas in the discourse of intimacy it is 'relationship labour', be it emotional, communicative or physical. The bedrock of both discourses is monogamy as any disruption to their triangulation prefigures a complete reconsideration of the discourses themselves.

Thus, it is not hard to see how monogamy procures an ontological security for participants like Sarah as it grants a validation of the discourses she embodies. Further, when she expresses that 'People don't have respect for other people and so they just jump from one person to another without thinking how much they are hurting them' she is constructing polyamory as a solely sexual relationship. Further, she is making a pervasive binary division between love and sex. Paul

Johnson (2012) suggests that the discourse of compulsory monogamy has a connotation of 'virtuous sex' – because love is understood as the base from which sex happens – whereas non-monogamies 'do not'. In other words, in Sarah's discourse, the possibility of pluralistic sexual and love ethics is foreclosed.

Christian Klesse (2006, 2011) and others (Anapol, 2012; Barker, 2005; Schippers, 2016) have argued that this understanding of polyamory is part of a larger fear of three things: a 'devaluation' of the institution of marriage, an incremental difficulty in the building of trust, and an adverse effect in younger people – insofar as it would make them supposedly promiscuous. All three elements are articulated by Sarah. Interestingly, Klesse's work with bisexual and gay men in the UK argues that the discourses of polyamory espoused by his participants are: trust, communication, dedication, freedom, reciprocity, mutual ethical agreements and love. Jennifer's discourse about exclusivity, 'being carefree,' and consensus touches upon this. Interestingly, many of these elements form the axis on which coupled intimacy is built (Berlant, 1998, 2012b; Hatfield & Sprecher, 1986; Shumway, 2003). Klesse argues that this conceptualisation of polyamory, what Lano and Parry termed 'responsible non-monogamy', is an attempt to distance from more sexualised discourses of polyamory. Thus, even within discourses of polyamory, in an attempt at a hegemonic definition of it, the binary division between love and sex is still at play.

In addition to the excerpt above that touched on polyamory/non-monogamy, the field is divided across the group interviews and subsequent personal interviews I held. The attitudes revealed by the differing perspectives is revealing not just of the sexual progressiveness or conservatism of different audience members, their racial and class backgrounds, but also in attitudes and expectations towards the representation of human romantic affordances. For some, regardless of the impossibility of comparison, to 'love' 641 people is just ludicrous, even for an operating system. Participants are keenly aware of how silly they sound when they say it is 'too many' but they just 'feel' it is so. Few things are as embedded in the heteronormativity of romantic relationships as the number of one's romantic partners which has been fetishised in Western romantic films for decades. There's an exchange between two participants that helps to illustrate how pervasive and omnipresent this attitude is. Tove is a 27-year-old actress and Paul a 36-year-old web designer, both white and European:

TOVE: You know, one thing guys looove to come up over and over again is this stupid metaphor of the key and the lock.
BENJAMÍN: And that is?
TOVE: … that it is not the same a lock [metaphor for a vagina] that opens with every key [metaphor for a penis] that a key that opens every lock. It's so fucking disgusting, I hate it when somebody messages me that … and you can see it coming, but I can't stop falling for assholes.
PAUL: I don't see the second part, but what good is a lock that opens with everything? … I'm not saying girls shouldn't experiment or live how they want to, but you got to have some respect for yourself. For me there should be some self-restraint.

BENJAMIN: If I may, why do you assume there is a lack of control?
PAUL: It just looks awful … you know that girl in a bar that's so fucked you don't even want to talk to her? I feel something similar when I see girls making out with loads of guys or I know they've been around … I don't know, it's just a turn-off for me.

…

TOVE: … A key that is overused will break eventually …

Paul is an excellent case of how sexist attitudes can be latent but be brought to the fore at the slightest of triggers. The idea that past a certain accidental or arbitrary threshold of sexual partners and/or romantic interests a woman is 'devalued' is fairly common. There are two factors I would like to explore further: On the one hand, monogamy and romantic's love naturalisation of the romantic dyad; on the other, female purity and romantic worth. Analysing these elements is a fundamental step towards understanding how audiences appropriate representations of love for the construction of their own romantic identity.

While monogamy and social/kinship construction of human groups have been a long-standing interest of anthropologists (Goody, 1974, 2004; Levi-Strauss, 1971; Levine, 2008; Murray Schneider & Gough, 1974; Radcliffe-Brown & Forde, 1952), the cnonsensus is that polygamy is associated with status and wealth, and thus not as common as monogamy. Anthropological arguments, however, only reach into the efficacy and arbitrary modes of association in the different societies across the globe (Fuentes, 1998). They say little to nothing of romantic love between subjects. Romantic love is considered as a tool that foments and strengthens the desire of association, a purely utilitarian view of love. The implicit assumption, however, is that of serial monogamy. As Helen Fisher, a biological evolutionary anthropologist, writes:

> One can feel deep attachment for one individual *while* feeling romantic passion for someone else *while* feeling the sex drive for a range of others. The relative biological independence of these three mating drives may have evolved to enable ancestral men and women to opportunistically engage in monogamy and **adultery** simultaneously and/or sequentially
> (2006, p. 106; bold emphasis mine)

Fisher suggests that monogamy is not natural per se, but it is more efficient for human groups to organise and survive. More tellingly, instead of opting for the anthropological term of polygamy, Fisher opts to call the relationships 'adulterous', thus casting them as deviant. Furthermore, she highlights the singularity of the love drive, erasing the possibility of polyamorous sentiments. This heteronormative dictum reveals an ideological positioning that is not unique to Fisher. Indeed, much of the literature on romantic love explored in Chapter 2 dedicates very little or nothing to the possibility of polyamorous relationships. The idea of exclusivity, of the romantic relationship as a dyad, is so embedded in the discourse of romantic love that it is easy to forget that just as with any other theme, a romantic dyad is arbitrary and socially constructed. I would like to illustrate the manner in which this crops up with audiences via a brief excerpt from another group interview about *Her* that included Jason, a 37-year-old bisexual man who works in the fashion industry, and Janis, a 29-year-old woman working in retail:

JASON: I get that six hundred whatever [romantic partners] is a lot and makes it almost a joke to really consider ... one relationship is a lot of work, just imagine that many more ... though really, how many times have you not felt in that position where you think you have feelings for two or more people?
JANIS: A few times, but it wasn't like I loved both of them. I had feelings and I wasn't sure even if I wanted to have anything with either of them.
JASON: And how is that different from loving both of them?
JANIS: It *is* very different. If I had gone further than a few dates with either of them I definitely would have chosen one or the other. I think giving wings to somebody just to tell them you've chosen another person is a bit cruel.
BENJAMÍN: Do you feel it is impossible to reach a stage where you could have loved both of them or where you fall in love with two people?
JANIS: I don't know, perhaps you can, I don't think I can ... most of the time it turns out that you've been dating somebody for a while and then somebody shows up and turns your whole world around and you end up choosing between either the old and stable or the new and shining. I think being a bit jealous helps you prevent that ...
JASON: Yeah, but I think that it is possible to make it work. I also don't think I can, I'm too jealous, but I do know of somebody who is in two relationships and they are happy ... they know each other.

This scenario of the newcomer hijacking a pre-established relationship is a common trope of romantic films, with decades of films dedicated to it. Films like *In the Mood for Love* (Kar-Wai, 2000), *Closer* (Nichols, 2004), *An Affair to Remember* (McCarey, 1957), *Night and Day* (Akerman, 1991) and *Brief Encounter* (Lean, 1945) all explore this trope in different ways, approaching it and taking it to diverse conclusions. Thus, the trepidation of people like Janis is only understandable; few are the media representations where instead of fear and instability, a newcomer is presented as the missing piece of a relationship. Some participants in the group interviews expressed regrets when they found themselves in this scenario, as to whether they had made the right decision. Why is it that most of us, whether we consider ourselves to be possessive, jealous, 'naturally' monogamous or not, find it so difficult to conceive of the possibility of nurturing and maintaining multiple romantic relationships?

Psychological and biological literatures suggest monogamous dyads have to do with a biological reproductive drive that humans have little to no control over. Monogamy becomes a matter of reproductive security and group stability. There are many things wrong with this view. Not only does it contain an assumption of a biological imperative reigning supreme over the human psyche, it is as convenient as the desire to ignore the ever-diminishing social role played by marital relationships in many societies across the globe and, in this particular, in the West. Further, it ignores that monogamy and marriage are historical constructs made for profit (status and wealth) and economic stability in the West, and are not universal. Also, as feminist and queer scholars like Lauren Berlant (1997, 2001) and Eleanor Wilkinson (Wilkinson, 2013; Wilkinson & Bell, 2012) argue, in contemporary Western societies, where the social and economic stability provided by marriage has eroded, hetero-marital coupled love as an ideological discourse still works to monitor women's bodies, identities and sexualities. In film, this is largely present in the women's film genre, where two of the common features of the genre is the impossibility of the woman's happiness and also her submission to a man through marriage or her punishment for failing to adhere to do this (Gledhill, 1987; Kaplan, 2000).

A path to better understand and analyse the ideological entanglement between monogamy and romantic love lies in further research of the triangular structure of romantic love. As romantic films of the past 15 years show, writers and directors find themselves more and more pressured to find and write in the third element that disrupts the lover's path. Sexual orientation, through LGBTIQA cinema with films like *Shortbus* (Mitchell, 2006), *Sunday Bloody Sunday* (Schlesinger, 1971), *Me, You, Them* (Waddington, 2000) and *Wild Side* (Lifschitz, 2004),[5] to name just a few, has slowly risen as an important niche that challenges heteronormative assumptions about romantic love, positing other sexualities, other relationship patterns and their stigma, lived out both internally and socially throughout the plot. As cultural products that contribute to our understanding and relationship with romantic love, it is refreshing to see myriad innovative ways of approaching romantic love even to this day. For many reasons beyond the scope of this book, asking for head-on confrontation of monogamy which reveals it to be an entirely arbitrary element of our romantic relationships is, quite likely, a step too far in terms of what we can ask of our current mainstream cultural production. However, it is important to raise awareness, to understand that the belief in monogamy is not necessarily natural across eras, groups and all individuals, and that it is interconnected with almost every other facet of how we understand, feel and conduct ourselves romantically.

Numbers and female purity

Linked to heterosexuality and monogamy, the idea of romantic purity still plays a major role as a cultural trope in contemporary culture across the West and the Global South. It can be phrased more colloquially: the number. An idea so popular in pop culture, it already has an entire romantic comedy dedicated to it. In *What's Your Number?* (Mylod, 2011) a female protagonist, played by Anna Faris, struggles with herself after reading a woman's magazine column that suggests that those who have had over 20 sexual partners have problems finding a husband. Because her number is 19, she decides to not have sex with anybody else until finding 'the one', who ultimately comes along, and is played by Chris Evans. After a few mishaps and comedic moments, the two leads marry each other. In this film, the third element of the imaginary love triangle is the number of the woman's sexual partners. In other words, 'the number' of her sexual or romantic partners is the arbitrary threshold between her purity and her otherwise completely tarnished character. The burden put on women to maintain an ethereal and imposed sense of decorum, an otherworldly – and plenty of other times very much of this world – imposition on their sexual behaviour and desires, is an extremely resilient strand in contemporary romantic films. Set against the women's liberation movement and the struggles of feminism aimed at recuperating women's bodies and desires for themselves has created a lived-in, embodied paradox for many women when it comes to their sexual history (see Weitz & Kwan, 2013). This struggle is even translated to imaginary disembodied characters like Samantha. A clash between three participants partly exemplifies this in a discussion of the 'rule of three' in relationships:[6]

BIANCA: Even if you don't mention it, when you tell somebody, they are going to do the stupid math in their heads and judge you … it always happens.
PAULA: But you shouldn't tell them, nothing good ever comes out from somebody who cares about your number … I think's it's better to tell them what they want to hear … Samantha was a bit too honest, which is just weird, though she is a computer.
JAMIKA: If you have been a good woman you can be honest to your husband … where I come from [Jamaica] we believe that you should keep yourself to your man … Western women don't respect themselves or men … It's so different here … I don't think this movie is made for Jamaicans, we don't get it.
PAULA: I know very little about Jamaica but I don't really agree that it is about respect … my history is mine, like, as long as I'm not hurting anybody why do people feel they need to call me a slut, or a whore or make me feel bad because I like sex? … like, I'm not a bad person and it's my private life.
JAMIKA: I think that women here just have different values … like, in Jamaica we don't understand why a guy would be with a computer, that's wrong, he should be a man and be with a woman.
BENJAMIN: I think that's a fantastic aspect of the film, maybe not the liking of all, but let's pretend for now that Samantha was, let's say, a co-worker of flesh and bone. What would you make of their conversation if this were the case?
BIANCA: Creepy. [general laughter]
JAMIKA: But didn't he have the choice to choose Olivia Wilde? [who plays an unnamed blind date of Theodore] … I think a nice film would have him going back for Olivia after he learns the other girl is not serious about getting married.
PAULA: But we don't know if her character also has a big number.
BIANCA: Yeah … what I'm trying to say is, I think that if you were taught and believe that keeping yourself for your future husband and all that is like super-important for you then you should act like that and you will find a husband that is like-minded but if that's not where you're coming from, I

think it is really frustrating to fall for a guy and then when you have committed a lot into the relationship they jump with these double standards that you had no idea they were hiding all along.

Jamika is a 29-year-old Jamaican, mother of one, Catholic and newlywed. Paula and Bianca are both 26 and single, and work as restaurant managers somewhere undisclosed in Hackney. The latter described her civil status in a manner indicating a recent heartbreak. The double standard of the number is clearly expressed by the contrasting views held by Jamika, Paula and Bianca. Jamika's position vis-à-vis the film is one of cultural alienation whereby Jamaican values are opposed to Western values, or a perceived lack thereof. The teleology of relationships lie, in her view, in religious marriage. Jamika's discourse on honesty and respect is one where a perception of sexual purity acts as a gateway to self and social fulfilment. Religion, expressed as a cultural and racial difference, provides an explanatory rationale as to why 'the number' is such a powerful ideological policing device of sexuality and gender in some cultures of romantic love. It is because it contains expectations of motherhood, of sainthood, of woman-as-man's-partner and, as Jamika put it, of a 'good woman', amongst others that are simply inarticulate and contradictory for the vast majority of women, not even the most righteous and strict of followers can easily navigate the many prescriptions and rules of what it means to be a believer. Further, the idea of purity acts as a bargain chip, a commodity women offer to secure the company and marriage of a man. Here it is important to highlight that the idea of the number is not some unique phenomena, with many cultures demanding complete chastity from women in order for them to have any sort of social worth. In countries like China, India and Japan courtesan romantic films are a type of romance where a woman finds redemption of her 'forced' sexual and social situation by choosing the right, usually wealthy, man. Furthermore, in films like *Pretty Woman* (Marshall, 1990) and *What's Your Number?* (Mylod, 2011), a woman who is not 'pure' is redeemed when and if she finds the 'right' one, *and* if he chooses to accept her, despite her past. The common thread of these films, and of religious marriage, is how by submitting herself to marriage with a man, a woman is 'purified.'

In contrast, Paula's position comes from a secular ideology that attempts to demystify female sexuality as intrinsically associated with a reproductive drive, sanctioned through religious marriage. In support of Paula, though also recognising Jamika's position as a viable choice, Bianca elaborates something she does not say directly but can be recognised from her intervention. That is, that a woman's sexual life shouldn't be an intrinsic indicator of her personal and social worth. Further, both of them express a direct concern with the double standards they have and that women potentially face about their sexual lives. (This was also exemplified in the exchange above between Tove and Paul about the metaphor of the 'key and lock'.) Linked to this is one of the continuous dilemmas that the discourse of contemporary intimacy begets: Paula says 'Samantha was too honest' and that one 'shouldn't tell them' about the number of sexual partners. Paula does not make it explicit but it is possible to infer, just like with Bianca, that they have had personal negative experiences by being 'too honest'. Yet the discourse of intimacy claims relationships ought to be built on constant self-disclosure, trust and communication. Patriarchal demands pull women in incomprehensible directions and films like *What's Your Number?* reproduce them with little to no regard for the tensions and pulls on their real audiences. Even if it isn't the director's intension for *Her* to function as a pervasive, retrograde and conservative argument that seeks to police women's bodies and sexual desires, including it is received as a consenting nod to it. If a film, critically acclaimed for its screenplay and story, fails to treat such a delicate subject as the number of romantic and sexual partners with nuance and critical sensitivity, the picture is indeed bleak for what one may expect romantic films to do about it.

It should come as no surprise then that, as Bianca, Paula and a few others commented, they constantly lie about this number or they simply walk away from the date or romantic encounter the moment the other person asks about it. In this excerpt and the others above, the romantic affordances of honesty, communication, trust and female sexuality are intertwined with hegemonic and counter-hegemonic ideological discourses at every level (scripted, real and imagined). Ideology and pleasure thus cohabit in the contradictions, the strife for complexity in films. The negotiation between an ideological subject and the ideological text provides positions across a spectrum. Pleasure, ideology and subjective expression tend to find themselves at extreme positions of appraisal and critique. In other words, even if there are elements, figures of love, that create discomfort while watching the film, there are pleasures to be derived, borrowing from Barker and Brooks's (1998) use of the terms.

Conclusion

Monogamy and purity are thus two crucial elements which inflect at almost every level the romantic affordances of my participants and, I would guess, of millions others. Further, this inflection is also affected and negotiated by the tension between a marketplace logic of romantic search and the yearning for the promise of happiness and stability of romantic love and lived intimacy. This means that while there is still a hegemonic way to live out one's romantic self (hetero-marital romantic love), there are many paths either on the way to it or pushing for recognition as equally valid, fulfilling and worth walking.

I have outlined how different elements and sequences of films are read by 'intended' audiences and how they subsequently use these to construct their own romantic identities. Likewise, I have suggested several ways how representations of love articulate gender and class identities in my participants. Finally, through an exploration of responses to significant sequences in the chosen films, I have explored how conceptions of the self and an emotional-ideological engagement with these sequences can be expressed.

If I have avoided using the term 'romantic frustrations' or 'disappointments', this is because this term operates within romantic literature and film in such a fatalistic fashion. A 'romantic frustration' is absolutely closed, the resolution has already been reached, the solution to the frustration already known. Eva Illouz (2012) speaks of 'disappointed lives' to refer to the emotion an individual experiences acutely and chronically as the imagination of the future and the frustrations of the past and present (bad romantic experiences and the anodyne of the everyday) collide, making a convergence of the three impossible, and painful. This solution, like many romantic comedies falsely premise, is that 'nothing will ever change' in love. This formulation encounters a problem whereby it aims at a neat, modernistic separation of the forces that feed the romantic: the past, the real and the imaginary. It settles for a facile conclusion of perennial separation, and this is mostly to do with Illouz's failure to understand romantic love as more than a practice. A romantic affordance, it is my contention, recognises that romantic love is a practice, an idea, an affect and, above all, a tension between ideas, texts, frustrations, hopes and the everyday. Romantic love is not just lived in the real, it also inhabits the other two realms. That's what makes it so fascinating.

Notes

1 *Amour* won both the Palme d'Or and the Academy Award for Best Foreign Film in 2012. *Omar* won the Jury Prize of Cannes Festival in 2013. Films like *Weekend* and *Catfish* were hits with both the public and film critics. *Weekend*, made with a £120,000 budget, racked up over a million USD in the box office. In addition to this, it also won and was nominated for different awards at festivals like SXSW Film Festival, BFI London Film Festival and Frameline Film Festival. *Catfish*'s success led to a TV show. *Broken Circle Breakdown* was nominated for an Academy Award for Best Foreign Language Film and it won the 2013 LUX Prize. *Like Crazy* won the Jury's Grand Prize at the 2011 Sundance Film Festival.
2 Campbell's concept, though pioneering in name, bears little relationship to the concerns of my use here.
3 See https://www.wired.com/2014/01/how-to-hack-okcupid/ and https://www.npr.org/2014/04/25/301822006/can-you-use-algorithms-to-find-love
4 Another case of borrowing from Gibson's term can be found in Donald Norman's (1988) *The Design of Everyday Things*.
5 Though I mention works of fiction, there's also a growing body of documentaries exploring the same subjects. See, for example, *I Love You. And You. And You* (Friend, 2006), *Three of Hears: A Postmodern Family* (Kaplan, 2004) and *When Two Won't Do* (Finch & Marovitch, 2002).
6 The 'rule of three' as it is understood popularly is the division or multiplication one does when told the number of sexual partners of a person: divide by three the number a man tells you and multiply the number a woman tells you. This 'cultural rule of love' reveals the sexist and shaming tendencies of our romantic discourse of love.

References

Abu-Assad, H. (2013). Omar. Produced by Hany Abu-Assad, Waleed Zuaiter and David Gerson.
Akerman, C. (1991). Night and Day. Produced by Martine Marignac, Maurice Tinchant and Marilyn Watelet.
Anapol, D. (2012). *Polyamory in the 21st century: love and intimacy with multiple partners*. Rowman & Littlefield.

Atkinson, P., & Silverman, D. (1997). Kundera's immortality: the interview society and the invention of the self. *Qualitative Inquiry*, 3(3), 304–325. https://doi.org/10.1177/107780049700300304.

Barker, M. (2005). This is my partner, and this is my ... partner's partner: Constructing a polyamorous identity in a monogamous world. *Journal of Constructivist Psychology*, 18 (1), 75–88. https://doi.org/10.1080/10720530590523107.

Barker, M., & Brooks, K. (1998). *Knowing audiences: Judge Dredd, its friends, fans and foes*. University of Luton Press.

Barthes, R. (1990). *A lover's discourse: fragments*. Penguin.

Bauman, Z. (2003). *Liquid love: on the frailty of human bonds*. Polity Press.

Berlant, L. G. (1997). The queen of America goes to Washington city: essays on sex and citizenship. In *The queen of America goes to Washington city: essays on sex and citizenship* (pp. 1–221). https://doi.org/10.2307/2927393.

Berlant, L. G. (1998). Intimacy: a special issue. *Critical Inquiry*, 24(2), 281–288. https://doi.org/10.1086/448875.

Berlant, L. G. (2001). Love: a queer feeling. In T. Dean & C. Lane (eds), *Homosexuality and psychoanalysis* (pp. 431–452). University of Chicago Press.

Berlant, L. G. (2012). *Desire/love*. punctum books.

Campbell, C. (1987). *The romantic ethic and the spirit of modern consumerism*. Basil Blackwell.

Chekhov, A. (2010). El Beso. In *Cuentos imprescindibles* (pp. 91–111). DeBolsillo.

Clare, S. D. (2013). (Homo)normativity's romance: happiness and indigestion in Andrew Haigh's *Weekend*. *Continuum*, 27(6), 785–798. https://doi.org/10.1080/10304312.2013.794197.

DeVault, M. L., & Gross, G. (2012). Feminist qualitative interviewing: experience, talk, and knowledge. In S. N. Hesse-Biber (ed.), *Handbook of feminist research: theory and praxis* (pp. 206–236). SAGE. https://doi.org/10.4135/9781483384740.n11.

Doremus, D. (2011). *Like Crazy*. Paramount Vantage.

Doucet, A., & Mauthner, N. (2012). Qualitative interviewing and feminist research. In P. Alasuutari, L. Bickman, & J. Brannen (eds), *The SAGE handbook of social research methods* (pp. 328–343). SAGE. https://doi.org/10.4135/9781848608429.

Dröge, K., & Voirol, O. (2011). Online dating: the tensions between romantic love and economic rationalization. *Journal of Family Research*, 23(3), 337–357.

Evans, M. (2003). *Love: an unromantic discussion*. Polity Press.

Finch, D. & Marovitch, M. (2002). When Two Won't Do. Galafilm productions.

Finch, J. (1984). *It's great to have someone to talk to: the ethics and politics of interviewing women*. In C. Bell & H. Roberts (eds), *Social researching: politics, problems, practice* (pp. 70–87). Routledge & Kegan Paul.

Fisher, H. (2006). The drive to love: the neural mechanism for mate selection. In R. J. Sternberg & K. Weis (eds), *The new psychology of love* (pp. 87–115). Yale University Press.

Fontana, A., & Frey, J. H. (2008). *The interview: from a neutral stance to political involvement*. In N. K. Denzin & Y. S. Lincoln (eds), *The Sage handbook of qualitative Research* (pp. 695–727). SAGE.

Friend, L. (2006). I Love You. And You. And You. Firecracker Productions.

Fuentes, A. (1998). Re-evaluating primate monogamy. *American Anthropologist*, 100(4), 890–907. https://doi.org/10.1525/aa.1998.100.4.890.

García Guillem, S. (2015). The other in the mirror: 'Amour' by Michael Haneke. *Area Abierta*, 15(2), 19–34.

Gibson, J. J. (1986). *The ecological approach to visual perception*. Lawrence Erlbaum Associates.

Gledhill, C. (1987). Home is where the heart is: studies in melodrama and the woman's film. BFI Publishing.
Goody, J. (ed.). (1974). *The character of kinship*. Cambridge University Press. https://doi.org/10.1017/CBO9780511621697.
Goody, J. (2004). *Comparative studies in kinship*. Routledge.
Gordon-Levitt, J. (2013). Don Jon. Voltage Pictures, Hit Record Films and Ram Bergman Productions.
Gray, J. (2013). The immigrant. The Weinstein Company.
Haigh, A. (2011). Weekend. Peccadillo Pictures.
Haneke, M. (2012). Amour. Les Films du Losange.
Hatfield, E., & Sprecher, S. (1986). Measuring passionate love in intimate relationships. *Journal of Adolescence*, 9(4), 383–410. https://doi.org/10.1016/S0140-1971(86)80043-80044.
Hesse-Biber, S. N. (ed.). (2012). *Handbook of feminist research: theory and praxis*. SAGE.
Hutchby, I. (2001). Technologies, texts and affordances. *Sociology*, 35(2), 441–456. https://doi.org/10.1177/S0038038501000219.
Illouz, E. (1997). *Consuming the romantic utopia: love and the cultural contradictions of capitalism*. University of California Press.
Illouz, E. (2012). *Why love hurts: a sociological explanation*. Polity Press.
Johnson, P. (2012). *Love, heterosexuality, and society*. Routledge.
Jonze, S. (2013). Her. Annapurna Pictures.
Joost, H., & Schulman, A. (2010). Catfish. Universal Pictures.
Kaplan, E. A. (2000). *Feminism & Film*. Oxford University Press.
Kaplan, S. (2004). Three of Hearts: A Postmodern Family. Bravo Cable.
Kar-Wai, W. (2000). In the Mood for Love. Universal Pictures.
Kipnis, L. (2003). *Against love: a polemic*. Vintage Books.
Klesse, C. (2006). Polyamory and its 'others': contesting the terms of non-monogamy. *Sexualities*, 9(5), 565–583. https://doi.org/10.1177/1363460706069986.
Klesse, C. (2011). Notions of love in polyamory—elements in a discourse on multiple loving. *Laboratorium: Russian Review of Social Research*, 2, 4–25.
Kvale, S. (1996). *Interviews: an introduction to qualitative research interviewing*. SAGE.
Lean, D. (1945). Brief Encounter. Eagle Lion Distributors.
Levi-Strauss, C. (1971). *The elementary structures of kinship*. Beacon Press. https://doi.org/10.2307/2093974.
Levine, N. E. (2008). Alternative kinship, marriage, and reproduction. *Annual Review of Anthropology*, 37(1), 375–389. https://doi.org/10.1146/annurev.anthro.37.081407.085120.
Lifschitz, S. (2004). Wild Side. Peccadillo Pictures.
Madriz, E. (1998). Using focus groups with lower socioeconomic status Latina women. *Qualitative Inquiry*, 4(1), 114–128. https://doi.org/10.1177/107780049800400107.
Madriz, E. (2000). Focus groups in feminist research. In N. Denzin & Y. Lincoln (eds), *Handbook of qualitative research* (2nd edn) (pp. 835–850). SAGE.
Marshall, G. (1990). Pretty Woman. Buena Vista Pictures.
McCarey, L. (1957). An Affair to Remember. 20th Century Fox.
McKinlay, C. (2014). *Optimal Cupid: mastering the hidden logic of OkCupid*. CreateSpace.
Maclaran, P., Broderick, A., Theadopoulis, A., Goulding, C., & Saren, M. (2005). The commodification of romance? Developing relationships online. *Journal Finanza, Marketing e Produzione*, XXII(3), 41–47.
Mitchell, J. C. (2006). Shortbus. THINKfilm.
Murray Schneider, D., & Gough, K. (1974). *Matrilineal kinship*. University of California Press.

Mylod, M. (2011). What's your number? Regency Enterprises.
Nichols, M. (2004). Closer. Columbia Pictures.
Norman, D. (1988). *The Design of Everyday Things*. Currency & Doubleday.
Parameswaran, R. (2001). Feminist media ethnography in India: exploring power, gender, and culture in the field. *Qualitative Inquiry*, 7(1), 69–103. https://doi.org/10.1177/107780040100700104.
Radcliffe-Brown, A. R., & Forde, D. (1952). *African systems of kinship and marriage*. Oxford University Press.
Rappert, B. (2003). Technologies, texts and possibilities: a reply to Hutchby. *Sociology*, 37(3), 565–580. https://doi.org/10.1177/00380385030373010.
Reynolds, T. (2002). Re-thinking a black feminist standpoint. *Ethnic and Racial Studies*, 25(4), 591–606. https://doi.org/10.1080/01419870220136709.
Rosinski, M. P. (2015). Touching Nancy's ethics: death in Michael Haneke's *Amour*. *Studies in French Cinema*, 15(2), 180–196.
Scarf, M. (2008). *Intimate partners: patterns in love and marriage*. Ballantine Books.
Scheurich, J. J. (1995). A postmodernist critique of research interviewing. *International Journal of Qualitative Studies in Education*, 8(3), 239–252. https://doi.org/10.1080/0951839950080303.
Schippers, M. (2016). *Beyond monogamy: polyamory and the future of polyqueer sexualities*. New York University Press.
Schlesinger, J. (1971). Sunday Bloody Sunday. United Artists.
Shumway, D. R. (2003). *Modern love: romance, intimacy, and the marriage crisis*. New York University Press.
Silverman, D. (2014). *Interpreting qualitative data* (5th edn). SAGE.
Skeggs, B. (1997). *Formations of class and gender: becoming respectable*. SAGE.
Skeggs, B. (2001). Feminist ethnography. In P. Atkinson, A. Coffey, S. Delamont, J. Lofland, & L. Lofland (eds), *Handbook of ethnography* (pp. 426–442). SAGE. https://doi.org/10.4135/9781848608337.n29.
Slater, D. (2014). *A million first dates: solving the puzzle of online dating*. Current.
Sternberg, R. J. (2006). A duplex theory of love. In R. J. Sternberg & K. Weis (eds), *The new psychology of love* (pp. 184–199). Yale University Press.
Swanberg, J. (2006). LOL. Washington Square Films.
Thapar-Björkert, S., & Henry, M. (2004). Reassessing the research relationship: location, position and power in fieldwork accounts. *International Journal of Social Research Methodology*, 7(5), 363–381. https://doi.org/10.1080/1364557092000045294.
Van Groeningen, F. (2012). The Broken Circle Breakdown. Ruben Impens.
Waddington, A. (2000). Me, You, Them. Columbia TriStar Films.
Webb, A. (2014). *Data, a love story: how I cracked the online dating code to meet my match*. Plume.
Weitz, R., & Kwan, S. (2013). *The politics of women's bodies: sexuality, appearance, and behavior*. Oxford University Press.
Wilkinson, E. (2013). Learning to love again: 'broken families', citizenship and the state promotion of coupledom. *Geoforum*, 49, 206–213. https://doi.org/10.1016/j.geoforum.2013.02.012.
Wilkinson, E., & Bell, E. (2012). Ties that bind: on not seeing (or looking) beyond "the family." *Families, Relationships and Societies*, 1(3), 423–429.
Willig, C. (2014). Interpretation and analysis. In U. Flick (ed.), *SAGE Handbook of Qualitative Data Analysis* (pp. 136–149). SAGE. https://doi.org/http://dx.doi.org/10.4135/9781446282243.n10.

4 A class apart

Love, expectation, and the middle-class construction of self

Introduction

In this chapter, I will concentrate on the results of the group interviews that took two films as their subject: *Blue Valentine* (Cianfrance, 2010) and *Once* (Carney, 2007), though a few other films will be brought aboard to illustrate the discussion further. My aim is to elucidate the different connections and inflections of class and the different discourses of romantic love. Thus, I aim to underline how class is being represented in these two films, how the audiences' class positions influence their interpretations and how these interpretations are linked to their own romantic practices.

As discussed in Chapter 3, the choice of films is not arbitrary. Both produced outside of Hollywood and financed by independent and multiple sources, these films were both 'sleeper hits' – that is, produced for a minimal budget and exceeding the box-office performance originally expected. Both films received Academy Award nominations, were critically praised and received far wider attention than their initial marketing budget would have suggested possible. It is difficult to pinpoint a single precise cause for these unexpected successes, but unquestionably, as the responses from audiences below aim to show, the romantic plots of these films contributed a great deal to this success. However, as *Blue Valentine* is a modern 'woman's film', borrowing elements from the genre, and *Once* is a classic story of unrequited love set in a modern, globalised setting, it is not sufficient to suggest that the plot alone is enough to have guaranteed these films' success. I argue that it is the settings and contexts within which the films' characters enact the plots that contributed to their success and to making them modern classics.[1] In particular, the working-class backgrounds, situations and other socioeconomic elements explored grant these two films a privileged vantage point from which to contemplate romance and love as so many other romantic films will use an (upper-)middle-class setting that wilfully ignores the everyday and how class-ridden it is.

It is thus similarity in connections between socioeconomic context and romantic narrative that unites the themes of this chapter. In addition, an analysis of aesthetic aspects (shooting style, the 'realist' inclination of both films, score) will be used to highlight the main themes of this chapter. First, however, a small introduction/synopsis of both films will contextualise the discussion. After this, I will

DOI: 10.4324/9781003164289-5

move on to the audiences and their relationship with the films' characters, the audiences' ideas of the films as 'possible romances', concluding with how the audiences draw from the films to speak about romance in general.

Production and characteristics of *Blue Valentine* and *Once*

Blue Valentine (2010) was director Derek Cianfrance's second feature film, released ten years after his first film. Much of the film's promotion was done through the two leads and executive producers, Canadian heartthrob Ryan Gosling and Michelle Williams, who was nominated for a Golden Globe and an Academy Award for her role in this film.[2] This was Gosling's first performance in three years after his Academy Award nominated act in *Half Nelson*. The movie was part of Cannes, Sundance and Toronto's film festivals' official selection. Finally, the producers had to appeal against a NC-17 rating in the United States for an R rating, mainly because of a scene depicting cunnilingus.[3] This set of paratextual elements gave the film an aura even before its screening, via a pseudo-mirroring of some of the narrative elements of the film.

Blue Valentine's examination of a couple's crumbling relationship provides no silver lining. It does not solve a conflict, and even reassuring equilibrium sequences are clearly shown as a 'thing of the past'. This is not to say that it is unique, narratively speaking. While some are more tragic than others, recent Hollywood films such as *The Break Up* (Reed, 2006), *Atonement* (Wright, 2007), *Brokeback Mountain* (Lee, 2005), *(500) Days of Summer* (Webb, 2009), and *Revolutionary Road* (Mendes, 2009) all end with the lead couple's last moments as a couple. Unlike some of these examples, however, *Blue Valentine*'s most striking characteristic lies in its dramatic focus on the disintegration of a relationship in a *working-class* context.

Once, on the other hand, is an Irish production of less than US$150,000 shot entirely on a handicam. It tells a classic story of unrequited love. Set in Dublin, *Once* is a film that spent several years in development limbo as no funds were secured and once it received a green light, it was shot on a minimal budget with a skeleton crew.[4] Many shortcuts were taken to accommodate the minuscule budget, but the quirkiness of the production grants the film an aura of 'realness' that audiences appreciated and enjoyed. With minimal to no marketing, the film circulated at a couple of festivals, including Sundance, in 2007 before enjoying a limited release in the United States and a full one in Ireland. The film went on to make more than US$20 million in the box office, becoming 2007's sleeper hit and making it onto a plethora of critics' top ten of 2007. Its success was so unexpected and so astronomical that it has spun off a musical and the two leads have formed a band to continue making music.

As a narrative, *Once* is a platonic romantic story of boy meets girl, boy falls for girl and girl falls for boy, but for several reasons do not end up together. It is a musical, melodies playing a crucial role in advancing the narrative. The score was crafted by the leads, both professional musicians. It is a key element in the success of the film. Eschewing the flamboyance of previous musicals like *Moulin Rouge* (Luhrmann, 2001), *Chicago* (Marshall, 2002) and *Dreamgirls* (Condon, 2006), John

Carney opts for a low-key, fly-on-the-wall approach to the melodies of the film. Thanks to this and the choice to keep the leads anonymous, *Once* manages to provide an uplifting feeling of satisfaction to many audiences despite its unhappy ending.

The two films possess peculiar elements that allow them to stand out when compared to other contemporary romantic films and when examined by themselves. Signalling these here is of particular interest as they are traits of the film that audiences pointed out repeatedly as the 'extra' element which guided their viewing. In the case of *Blue Valentine*, the fragmented narrative and the stylistic decisions that accompany this fragmentation help to create two parallel aesthetic and affective frames. The past is always shot in handicam while most of the 'present' is shot from fixed cameras. This play between flow and static is symbolic of the couple's own stagnation. Furthermore, the sequences of the 'past', as they portray joyful, sometimes awkward, endearing moments, are juxtaposed against the dry background of the 'present' and the increasingly aggressive exchanges of the couple. The music played in the 'present' is always an allusion to the 'past' and helps to increase the feeling of detachment and erosion of the couple from their idyllic coupledom. In *Once*, the characters are nameless. This narrative device is used to heighten the idea that this is a universal, timeless romance. As a musical, the songs in the film are the vehicle through which the lovers disclose their feelings, ideas and frustrations. Furthermore, the film explores, through music, the language barrier between lovers: the male lead is Irish and the female lead is a Czech immigrant.[5] Shot on a shoestring budget, many of the locations are closed and the post-editing of film is minimal, lending the film a gritty aesthetic. These elements help to position audiences in relation to each film and suggest the elements they prioritised, dealt with in depth in the next section.

Of realism and 'not-meant-to-work' romances

In discussions of romantic films, some aspects are more salient than others. Music, for instance, and the way it carries certain critical events in the film, was mentioned by several audience groups while others named dialogue and what particularities it offers; but there is one aspect which is paramount to all viewers of a romantic film: the appropriateness and authenticity of the romance plot. The search for the authentic, the alikeness with what one would expect out of a romantic relationship, how well fitted its claims of truth are to the audience's emotional experiences are all part of the pleasure and of the code necessary to read this kind of films. While some audiences manifest a clear knowledge of how unrealistic the romantic ideas presented in romantic comedies are when compared to their lived experience, it is exactly this mismatch in which they may be seeking refuge.

Dealing specifically with romance, what looks real and feels real is derived not only from a rational standpoint but also an affective one. Furthermore, the realm of fantasy plays an equally important role in the consideration of the film and the pleasures audiences derive. This interplay between the fantastic, the ideal, the real and the past is what I have termed 'romantic affordance' and it is also what

Giddens (1992) refers to as the insertion of a 'narrative' in our romantic selves. It involves the managing of one own expectations regarding romance, an understanding of how things may work out and how maybe they never will.

So, how do real audiences experience this romantic affordance? Blair, a 31-year-old charity worker, suggests that it is not as simple as considering how truthful or emotionally real the love on screen is as:

> It's not like you don't know from the cover what type of film it's going to be ... this one is all dark and gloomy, of course you know you are going to watch a depressing film that probably is not going to end well ... but sometimes all you want to be taken away so you choose a film you know it's going to be perhaps cheesy but happy and nice.

Giselle, a 32-year-old PR and communications worker, also expressed:

GISELLE: I'm not saying the film is bad but it just doesn't have *the magic I want from a romantic film* ... this is a story I can totally imagine happening. I *prefer to escape* into a romantic film, even if for a bit, that ends in a happily-ever-after
BENJAMÍN: Can you tell me why that is?
GISELLE: Because I think we all want to believe in that love is still out there and that it will last ... you watch a film like this and you end up double-depressed [laughter](Emphasis added)

Richard, a 25-year-old student, said:

> I don't want to deny *the beauty of this film* because it kinda works as a cautionary tale of love but there's enough of that in most people's lives ... I think we watch romantic films *to feel like love and happiness are real*, that we are deserving of love.
>
> (Emphasis added)

These three participants are aware of the cinematic divide between the real and the realm of fantasy (see Kuhn, 1994; Stam, 2000; Thompson & Bordwell, 2009). They expect romantic filmic texts to create a distance between what they believe is possible in their own real lives and the imaginary – the realm in which fantasy and wish fulfilment about partners, intimacy and so on occurs. What they do not expect is for these films to shrink the imaginary, which is what a film like *Blue Valentine* aims to do. While it is irresponsible to caricature the consumption of 'chick flicks' and romantic comedies as simply an evasion of reality (or a desire to do so), people pursue their delight in these films for myriad reasons. As discussed by researchers like Ien Ang (1985), and Peter Evans and Celestino Deleyto (1998), the pursuit of an escape, the preference for fantasy over reality, constitutes *a mode of dealing with the limitations of the practical*. It permits uninhibited expression of a range of pleasures that women – and perhaps even men – do not have many, if any, other spaces to express. The consumption of this type of films goes beyond this, though. As Ferriss and

Young (2008) suggest, chick flicks also play a huge role in the construction and mediation of women's identity through ambivalent messages about commodity consumption, female friendship, female sexuality, family and reproduction.

Then what drives audiences towards more 'realistic' romances? I argue that audiences consume these films with a desire to gauge and compare the filmic romance to their own romantic experiences. This can be done as a form of escapism, or as a masochistic pleasure, but more importantly it is done to understand, cope and mediate one's own romantic reality. Again, here the idea of romantic affordance comes into play. As a tension between the lived experience, and the ideal, romances that strike a balance between fiction and the verisimilar heighten, depending on the audience, either the utopian or dystopian characteristics of romantic love.

Another form of understanding this constant comparison is through the consideration of what differentiates a film like *Blue Valentine* from romantic comedies like *No Strings Attached* (Reitman, 2011) and *Just Go with It* (Dugan, 2011). In the latter, the focus lies exclusively on the lead characters and the advancement of the romantic narrative; the hurdles along the road are apparently the result of failures of character that can be solved through the power of love and individual will; all of this is helped by the reduction of external variables that can affect the relationship. In *Blue Valentine*, the narrative is set against external elements that act as hurdles; the personality traits of each character are also affected by these elements and are not given a clear resolution (or even the hope of one) and the advancement of the romantic narrative is intertwined with the possibilities afforded (and curtailed) by multiple socioeconomic and cultural constraints in the environment. Thus, while one set of films deals with relationships between characters who are isolated binaries responding and reacting only to one another, films like *Blue Valentine* work as a reminder that the figurations of love experienced by people are limited and affected by the background setting in which they reside. In other words, structural constraints woven into these romantic narratives act as a form of realism that is actively sought out by some audiences.

The presence of these constraints engages different members of the audience in a consideration of the effect of what they perceive to be 'reality' on the romantic relationship on screen. This consideration is done through the audiences' own lived constraints. As Karen, a 32-year-old single mother, expressed:

> I think a film like this changes completely if you watch it without having kids … I could not stop thinking about what was going to happen to the child while if you watch the film, he is barely in three or like four scenes … I could not understand why more of the dialogue and plot of the movie didn't have to do with the child … I guess it's not a film for single mothers!

But while for Karen the child played a key role in disengaging her from the verisimilitude of the on-screen couple, for others, like Agnes, a 44-year-old stay-at-home mother of two, their limited means is a strong element of connection to the verisimilitude of the on-screen couple:

> I have been in both situations [she refers to giving an invitation to go away and being invited to do so] ... me and my husband don't get holidays and we can't afford another person to take care of my babies ... I have wanted to both get away and I have also gotten upset when my husband comes up with crazy ideas for us to have some fun ... I can see ourselves in that argument they have.

A shared experience and a perceived shared class background help Agnes validate the on-screen romance as 'real'. Beyond identifying with one or the other character, this participant expresses a commonality of relationship, of the possibilities and intricacies of romance on and off screen. Her comment, as well as Karen's, also contains a nod to two elements usually not present in romantic comedies, caregiving and *the asymmetrical distribution of gender roles* in many relationships. Contrary to the structuring in romantic comedies, where the setting's importance is erased by its lack of effect on the narrative, a romantic drama like *Blue Valentine* encourages the reading of the setting as paramount. In this case, the possibility of affording child care is treated as a class luxury that heavily determines the romantic possibilities of a couple. This is not unique to audiences of a working-class background, nor are the elements of the narrative always compared favourably or negatively in the same way by participants who shared something with the on-screen couple. Other single mothers did not put the emphasis Karen did on the child, with some focusing on the getaway and others on the absent father. Alex, a 39-year-old engineer, mentioned:

> I feel the film portrays one of those situations where romance and life get in the way and everything goes to shit ... it does make you think that we are very lucky with what we have and we shouldn't take it for granted ... I think part of what makes it so depressing is that sometimes, no matter how much or how little you have, it just doesn't work out ... I think that really hit me about the film.

Alex's contribution is one of several that highlighted, despite the recognition of the material constraints of the on-screen couple, that relationships are not stable even if these are not present. This idea regarding the contingent nature of relationships is one I will come back to. Thus, while class constraints and the socioeconomic background presented in the film are almost always at the forefront of readings of the film, or at least play a role in the overall interpretation of the narrative, audiences' pleasures and readings clearly go beyond these structural constraints. One of the elements that were salient in the audiences' reading of the film was the identification or detachment from the characters and their perceived traits. I suggest that the relationship the audience built and maintained with either or both characters is not isolated from their classed subjectivity. Rather, it is informed by it.

On characters of a romance and discourses of romance

'But they really didn't love one another' is one of the most common claims I hear about *Blue Valentine*'s on-screen couple. 'It simply was never meant to last' is the one

I have heard the most for the romance in *Once*. Why are these two responses the most common? Although an important aspect of the answer consists in pointing out how dominant frames and narratives tend to prevail over the course of the interpretation of a text (see Stam, 2000), it is equally relevant to signal that these answers point to two of the most prevalent discourses of love that we still manage in the everyday. One is the discourse of intimacy and the other of platonic love. Several participants claimed that the couple in *Blue Valentine*, Dean (Ryan Gosling) and Cindy (Michelle Williams), *simply never loved each other*, while others voiced the conviction that they were in fact *too different* for their romance to work regardless of their economic difficulties, that 'love was simply not enough'. This is in tune with the increasing recognition in narratives of love of the required emotional labour to make relationships work (see Bryson, 2014; Hakim, 2010; James, 1989; Schneebaum, 2014). Some audience members blamed 'an essential difference of characters' as to why love didn't suffice, while other audiences noted that Cindy and Dean *wanted different things* from the relationship that the other could not fulfil. Jenna, a 33-year-old retail worker, highlights the idea of intimacy and emotional labour:

> Maybe it is not fair to judge because it is only a film and you don't really have all the information, but from the film you could see that they never actually discussed their problems, they simply shouted and got drunk and thought forgetting about things would make them go away ... I felt they did love each other but that they fell apart because there was simply no communication, they *didn't work on their relationship like they should have*, like everyone does.
>
> (Emphasis added)

Ryan, a 36-year-old civil servant, mentioned:

> They were just so different. I think he never tried to be at her level ... I feel she always wanted to aspire to better things and work things through and was always so frustrated by his childish behaviour ... a relationship needs to *people who are willing to work at it* because you know, looks fade ...

The idea that only one or neither character 'worked' for it matches what Shumway (2003) has called the discourse of intimacy in film, or intimacy in the larger context (Giddens, 1992). Self-disclosure and self-interrogation are pivotal elements of intimacy in contemporary relationships, and presuppose a form of work or labour. What Jenna and Ryan point towards is that there is a high degree of incompatibility between romantic love as something that happens to us and intimacy, a discourse of relationships very much forged on the idea of constant, precarious labour. This labour inscribed in relationships is related to the gender roles of every relationship and the usually asymmetrical distribution of work between these roles. Cianfrance's decision to make a film with sparse dialogue punctuated by long moments of silence clearly accentuates the sense that no one is working at communication. But while much could be made of the director's decision to cut dialogue and focus on camera movement to generate certain affective states, it is the reading by the audiences which ultimately makes this such a pivotal point of discussion.

In *Blue Valentine*, the clash of personalities and subsequently of the relationship begins, of course, with the traits of each lead. Looking back towards the various theories of love considered in earlier chapters, Dean would seem to embody a discourse of love-as-passion that is incompatible with his social background and context as a blue-collar worker with a child. Love-as-passion is the discourse that posits the idea of love as an unavoidable force which overwhelms and dictates the actions of a helpless subject. It is tragic in nature; that is, the romantic relationship is always marked by the death of one or both lovers. Forces beyond the control of the lovers lead them to this end. Sometimes, part of the plot is the struggle against these forces (as in contemporary films like *Eternal Sunshine of the Spotless Mind* where absolute memory loss occurs or *Her* where one partner is non-human) or an embodiment of them. In comparison to this discourse, there is Cindy's (Michelle Williams) embodiment of a modern lower-middle-class individual: goal driven, college educated and aspiring subject of late capitalism to create the tension between the discourse of love-as-passion and that of a pragmatic, reflexive, class-bound therapeutic love (intimacy). What is tragic about Dean and his *dramatis personae* is his lack of reflexivity, his inability to go beyond his particular romantic discourse, his failure to transform and adapt to the demands of Cindy's therapeutic love discourse, which is more attuned to the demands of late capitalism in relation to the romantic couple (see Illouz, 1997; Berlant, 2008). This failure is the epitome of his romantic frustration and, ultimately, of his position as a working-class subject with no intention or opportunity to go beyond his own social position. As another participant in my group interviews, Leslie, a 23-year-old student, commented:

> I think they would have broken up because they never loved each other … infatuation, yeah, they had a crush on each other but Cindy is too different to Dean … I mean, she goes to school, wants to become a doctor and is nice … *Dean is the kind of guy you just have fun with, you don't build a future with* … I mean, he only likes to drink beer.
>
> (Emphasis added)

Beer drinking, a mark of Dean's working-class status, is pinpointed as a trait mismatched with aspirational middle-class traits. To Leslie this gap seems unbridgeable, and is seen as a commanding factor in why the couple's relationship ends so miserably.

This sense of 'doomed to fail' from the start, which the film's chronological and narrative structure delays deliberately, is considered by over 18 of my participants as the element which 'completes' the film. In other words, the idea that some couples are 'destined' to fail reassures audiences that their own romantic choices have either been justified or that their mistakes are attributable to factors outside their control. Beyond this reassurance, however, lies an extremely ingrained idea that is never made explicit but surfaces when audiences relate their own failed romantic experiences with the one portrayed by

Blue Valentine. It is the idea that a successful couple is one where both parties come from a similar socioeconomic background and share similar cultural and class values. Two excerpts in particular illustrate this. First, Sylvia, a 46-year-old woman (profession undisclosed):

> I was once with a rich man ... like really rich. And he bought me things, beautiful things, but he was evil and mean. He had no love to give, he always thought money and material things would buy him love. But I may be poor and I can't say those times were not very good to me, but my mom raised me with morals and money can't buy happiness ... I see what happens to them like a similar thing, not with rich guy, but because *he's poor and a bum and she's a nice lady* ... I think she made the same mistake I made. She went for the good-looking guy who was not right for her instead of going with the other guy who seemed nicer and better for her.
>
> (Emphasis added)

And Fred, a 39-year-old music producer:

> My relationship of a couple of years ago was with this woman who was really interesting and we clicked right away ... but after a while you start to notice things, like they don't say 'thank you' to the cashier or that they don't eat your food as if it is valued ... and I can understand why it took the girl in the film so many years to do something about it ... you really want to believe that things can work, with a chat you can make them change and be better but you really can't ... I know it is harsh, but I say it because I lived it, *relationships don't work if the two are not like ... similar in some things ... if they do not share the same values and manners* ... it's a thing of how you were raised I think.
>
> (Emphasis added)

These two participants emphasise the differences in class mentality that underpin the view that romantic love is not the great democratic tool of the twentieth century as Giddens makes it out to be (Giddens, 1992). Rather, through dating and marked class ethos, possibilities of social mobility and 'pure relationships' are hindered and stymied at every corner. Few families and individuals will be overtly classist or segregationist in their romantic pursuit, of course, but even if they have not had an inter-class romance failure, the majority (22/28)[6] maintained that romances such as Cindy and Dean's fail because they 'do not like the same things'. These participants averred that in their own relationships they always sought that minimum (classed cultural) common ground on which to build it. It is possible, then, to argue that both discourses of love work twofold ideologically both for the audiences and in the film. On the one hand, in 'cross-class' romances the narrative works towards a resolution where class differences are dissolved through the power of love (Sharot, 2010; Shary, 2011). In these kind of romances, a common plot twist includes the revelation that the lover of lower class origin is wealthy or will inherit great wealth. Or, as in *Pretty Woman* (1990), the male 'rescues' the working-class female from her impoverished condition. In the case of *Blue Valentine*, redemption through love is not reached because Dean's active embrace of his status as a working-class male hopeless romantic eliminates the possibility of him adapting to the dominant discourse of love, Cindy's largely feminine therapeutic/intimate love (see Berlant, 2012; Giddens, 1992; Illouz, 1997; Shumway, 2003). Thus, pure romantic love as an ideal is shown not just to be out of touch with the requirements of an aspirational subject of late capitalism, but also to be a reactionary, flawed escapist reaction to the material conditions that surround Dean.

In this manner, *Blue Valentine* complicates the idea of love as something people can establish a dialogue about and through which they can work out wider social structural issues. It showcases how differences in the adoption of a given discourse of love and relationships are part of the larger uneven distribution of cultural competences and capital in our society. While playing it out as a clash of discourses, romantic love highlights the middle-class underpinnings of the putatively feminist discourse of intimacy, its implied subjectivity compliant to the demands of late consumer capitalism. Furthermore, during the first altercation in the motel, Dean claims he's providing for the family and angrily shouts to Cindy that he's at a loss as to what else could be asked of him. At this moment, Dean is shown to be out of synch with the times, invoking a classic gender-role distribution of the family that underscores his underprivileged position and heightens the middle-class milieu from which Cindy comes.

The film also borrows certain elements of the women's films: out of wedlock pregnancy, the woman's loss, her resignation to romantic failure, silent suffering, missed opportunities and a sombre, disillusioned ending. But unlike some of the characters in women's films of decades past who were strong-willed and assertive (*Jezebel, All about Eve, Gone with the Wind*), Cindy's development is shrouded in an anxiety over her feelings and her own actions. It is only at the end when she explodes and finishes her relationship with Dean that we see any sign of her assertiveness. This indecisiveness is undoubtedly related to her potential economic precariousness and position as a single mother. Furthermore, her portrayal as being 'overly concerned' with the material aspects of the relationship had the effect for audiences I talked to, that her character development came off as slightly 'bossy', 'rigid', 'neurotic' and 'too dependent'. Natalie, a 37-year-old manager, highlights this:

> One of the things I found most irritating about Cindy was her constant nagging of money and stuff. I mean, she couldn't have been so blind to not know what she was getting into ... or maybe that's the message of the film [giggle] ... I think she had a problem with letting go and accepting where she was ... I'm not sure how much of that is Dean's fault though.

Sophie, a 38-year-old media worker, also saw Cindy in this light:

> Maybe I'm too soft, but I see in Cindy the problem of too many women who decide to carry on a pregnancy when they are absolutely not ready or even sure of what they want. I think part of the film is to show that Cindy

couldn't make her mind up about what she wanted and then, when she does realise that she wants something better, she finds that now she has to think for two and can't figure out how to get herself out of the mess she's gotten herself into.

The 'mess' that Sophie alludes to and her manic behaviour are characteristic of the lack of upward social mobility that was expected of Cindy. Though Sophie and Natalie differ in their appreciation of Cindy's position, both of their interventions highlight that Cindy's position is one where romance necessarily must give way to material concerns over caregiving and provision. This displacement is not only opposed to romance but, in the case of Natalie, paves the way to the idea that Cindy's position ought to be one of resignation. Sophie's more empathetic outlook, given her acknowledgement of the child, is one that understands the precarious position of single parenthood while recognising one of the main problems of contemporary relationships, their contingency. The contingency is expressed through the growing frustration and dissatisfaction Cindy expresses towards Dean, their inability to communicate and her estrangement from the same romantic quirks that were shown to initially win her over. Cindy's subjectivity and romantic possibilities are juxtaposed with her duty to her family. Thus, her failure in romance is translated and equated to her failure as a wife. However, unlike in classic woman's films and melodramas, she is joined in this failure by Dean, who is neither virtuous nor victorious in any shape or form at the end of the film. Furthermore, as I have argued above, Dean's romantic persona is out of tune with the contemporary requirements of intimacy. Thus, romantic and personal failure in *Blue Valentine* aims to highlight the porousness and fragility of contemporary relationships. This is compounded by the link the film establishes between the seemingly incompatible classed romantic ethos of Cindy and Dean.

Platonic love in the era of globalisation

If *Blue Valentine* works on the idea of irresolvable, essential differences between two individuals of different class backgrounds, *Once* (Carney, 2007) works on several fronts underlining or erasing these differences. Although the film overflows with elements of a working-class romance for several participants, these are secondary to the storyline of a platonic romance also 'destined to fail' from the beginning, if for entirely different reasons. Busking in Dublin, living in a cramped apartment where your neighbours use your living room to watch TV, the lack of money to use a studio, working as a hoover repairman are irrelevant when speaking of the romance between the 'Guy' (Glen Hansard) and the 'Girl' (Markéta Irglová). Instead, audiences appear to read the film as a 'pure relationship', even despite a recognition of the socioeconomic constraints that make the relationship impossible. Beatrice, a 29-year-old teacher, mentioned:

> I just think that the important thing of the film is that no matter where you are and what you have, you can always have true love come to

you ... It is ok if it doesn't last forever or if like it doesn't go all the way even for a bit... to know you had it once makes it all worth it, that's what *Once* is all about for me, *love can be found and be perfect no matter what is around you.*

While in ironic contrast to readings of *Blue Valentine*, such a beautiful reading of the film clearly resonates with many participants and the idea of love as available to all is one only a cynic would try to belittle. Not only that, but it is in line with Lauren Berlant (2001), who argued that, ultimately, love 'is a scene of optimism for change, for transformational environment' (p. 448). Furthermore, other participants considered that there was a unique beauty to a love that could not last for reasons beyond the control of the couple. Its preordained demise was a necessary factor, as otherwise this romance would simply have been an ordinary 'getaway' romance. As Mary, a 33-year-old nurse, said:

> Sometimes it doesn't have to last for it to be the best thing that happened to you ... I love my husband very much, but I have never loved anyone like I loved this guy I was with for five months when I was living in Berlin ... *sometimes it just doesn't last or is not meant to happen.*
>
> (Emphasis added)

Diane, a 41-year-old business woman, shared this view:

> I am not sure the setting is necessary ... I can picture this, and perhaps it is because I have watched way too many films, on a sort of Victorian upper-class setting or like a really posh romance as well ... I think they didn't work out because sometimes the time simply is not appropriate, or because *you simply are not meant to be with that person* and that's why you have to cherish it you know.
>
> (Emphasis added)

What is striking about participations like Diane's and Mary's (and those from at least 11 others who participated) is that in the recognition of the contingency of contemporary relationships, they focus on the inevitability of finitude in romance. This idea is a long-standing trope related to romantic love, its association with tragedy, instability and ephemerality. Their positions romanticise the finitude of romance in a positive manner; this contingency provides a sense, in the case of Mary, that in romantic relationships there is usually an ongoing tension between intensity and longevity. This is the tension between Eros and Agape, where the latter contains and sublimates the erotic energy through marriage and devotion. Certainly, privileging an untimely meeting over the constraints of a working-class context gives the filmic narrative a glint of romanticism, a big part of its appeal, but also helps to reinforce a problematic connection between romantic agency, class and gendered subjectivities.

In *Once* the idea of a 'fateful, platonic encounter' is one that attempts to sanitise the lived experience and practice of romance that is constrained by the intersectionality of the subjectivities involved. The idea that love is possible no matter what the setting is only made possible in the film because of all the socioeconomic constraints the lovers face and are unable to overcome. In addition, this is tied to an ideological reinforcement of hegemonic scripts of motherhood, duty and domesticity.

The film doubly plays on this tension by having both lead characters also involved in another, stable relationship. The Guy has recently broken up with his girlfriend, though he hopes to reunite with her by travelling to London. The Girl, on the other hand, is married. In the resolution of the film, the Guy calls his ex-girlfriend, who is seemingly happy at his arrival in London. The Girl is reunited with her estranged husband. This reunion is foreshadowed in the film when the Guy tries to persuade the Girl to spend his last night in Dublin with her. She reveals that she has been in contact with her husband and though verbally agreeing to meet with the Guy before he moves to London, she stands him up. The film portrays a liminal romance, one that must eventually give way to the routine of sanctioned sustainable relationships.

This narrative decision to have the Girl be a married woman who decides to stick with her estranged husband is ideologically significant. E. Ann Kaplan (2000) argues that in Hollywood representations of mothering, 'The work of the film is to reinscribe the Mother in the position patriarchy desires for her and, in doing so, teach the female audience the dangers of stepping out of the given position' (p. 468). While *Once* is not a mainstream Hollywood production, it does make use of the trope of motherhood to maintain the Platonism and contingency of the romance. While it is possible to recognise the utopian dimension of the romance as the participants above do, it is important to highlight that narratively it makes use of the trope of motherhood in a reactionary way, reinforcing ideas of 'womanly duty' and 'virtuosity' for the Girl while letting the Guy be the adventurous male.

This interplay between class and gender roles is better highlighted by the readings of the film that expressed discontent with the romance between the Guy and the Girl. In between comments about how 'clean' the lovers were for the situation they were in, how soft spoken and calm they remained despite their seemingly desperate context and how 'beautiful' they are to be playing working-class characters, participants voiced two main discontents with the film: first, they did not find it believable that, in the twenty-first century, a woman would stay in a loveless marriage over the opportunity of a fresh start somewhere else; and second, that a working-class, immigrant woman with children and a family to look for would allow herself this game of courtship and flirtation with the Guy is inconceivable or morally condemnable for others. As Natasha, a 42-year-old married retail worker, expressed:

> She's a bit irresponsible flirting around like that … I loved the music and their [the lovers'] chemistry but I think when you marry somebody you need to remove yourself from these situations. You can tell she was lonely and all but then I think she should have moved back to her husband.

Sidney, a 29-year-old single manager, said:

> I don't think you should stay in a loveless marriage, no matter the distance or what's in the middle. I think women should be more proactive in what they want ... I get that this story is like a break from the routine and that's why it's so idealistic, but I think nowadays you can create your own romance.

These two contrasting positions highlight the uneasy gendered relationship between family, duty and romance. Just as with Cindy in *Blue Valentine*, the romantic subjectivity of the Girl is judged in the context of her position as a wife and a mother. Their romantic agency is undercut by their motherhood. This, as Christine Gledhill (1987) argues, is part of the construction of female subjectivity as belonging to domestic spaces, to family life. But whereas *Blue Valentine* is interested in showcasing the fragility of these spaces and this life, *Once* invites the consideration of female virtue and adultery. The film, at the same time, connects these with a classed ethic. As authors like Eva Illouz (1997) and Elizabeth Povinelli (2006) have pointed out, the discourse of romantic love over social duty has a distinctly middle-class ethos to it. This ethos contains a detachment from economic necessities, practicalities and realities, such as child-raising. Thus, it is possible to consider that the differing positions which Sidney and Natasha take up with regards to the Girl are representative of two different classed subjectivities and attitudes towards romantic love.

Romantic agency and the aspirational characteristic of the romantic here are a temporary escape the Girl encounters in her situation as a working-class single parent. The dilemma faced by the Girl, whether to make this temporary situation permanent or not, invokes both the middle-class sensibility of the 'pure relationship' and the working-class duty to the family. In addition, the ideological notion of woman's dependency, portrayed as loyalty and virtue, on a man is also brought into play.

Of course, romantic aspirations and familial duties are not necessarily classed as opposites in general. In the film, however, the Girl's romantic escape is an escape from her working-class condition. This is so because by allowing her both the free time to record music *and* the money to do so, the film places her outside her role of a working-class wife and mother and into that of a sexualised woman. This liminal moment, reminiscent of narratives in Bollywood films (Derné, 2000; Banaji, 2006) and in particular of the sequence in *English-Vinglish* when a kind housewife passes her English test and says goodbye to her delightful French admirer, once over, is ultimately vindicated by her 'virtuous' decision to stand by her family. This vindication is possible because the romantic escape is completely platonic and any attempt at its consummation is turned down by the Girl herself. Thus, the *de-sexualisation* of the romance is an ideological reinforcement of the film's hegemonic portrayal of female romantic subjectivity as always subsidiary to other duties.

In the next two sections, I will further analyse audience responses to the studio rental, a pivotal element of *Once*, and the motel sequence in *Blue*

Valentine, as two sequences that highlight the classed relationship between audiences and romantic narratives.

A studio for love

Once, as a romantic film, asks for a certain suspension of disbelief. Many romantic films ask of their viewer to believe in the possibility of love despite all odds. Somewhat ironically, one of the aspects that plays into the perception of verisimilitude in a romantic film, then, is what those odds are. For participants of my project who came from a working-class background, there were certain elements of the film that broke such suspension of disbelief. First, Lauren, a 49-year-old unemployed woman, intervened:

> She's very pretty ... but you never see her frustrated or rushing to work to feed her children. They run around and make a lot of noise but she just smiles ... I have three children and I just can't believe all you do is smile when you know you have no money and you have to work for money ... [after being asked what would make her more believable] I would be crying a lot and angry, I think the film has to show her crying and frustrated that she's in that situation, it's just not for me.

Rob, a 38-year-old handyman, said:

> I'm too cynical for this, you know what I mean? ... A bloke and a lass broke as hell singing and shit like everything's fine, who believes this? ... I get that it is a film but I've been in that situation, that's not when you meet your soulmate, you're out there looking for a job.

Lauren and Rob's suspension of disbelief is broken because the aestheticised portrayal of a working-class romance is at odds with their own experiences. In Lauren's comment, the busy routine of a single parent, something she identifies with, and, in synch with Rob, the constant concern with money are two key elements that are completely mispresented by *Once*. Her remarks about the smiling is poignant in that it disconcerts her, while highlighting the distance to her reaction to a similar situation. Their critique stems from a personal understanding of the concerns with money and time that the protagonists ought to be living out. Their identification with the characters or the film as a narrative starts with a class position before a romantic one. These interventions highlight not just how an audience's class background affects readings of the film, but also how the film's idealisation of working-class conditions works to undermine the negative affects that come with an intersectional experience of love.

In addition to this, at least ten other participants, Rob included, expressed an incredulous curiosity over how much exactly it would cost to rent a studio in Dublin and to get a sample from it. For them, the gesture from the Girl seemed far from believable. Participants objected to that kind of money being spent for a complete stranger, as it would mean not being able to feed her own children or herself with the amount of money they thought she was making. In the film, the Girl announces to the Guy that she can help him rent a studio to record his EP and get him to London. In the film, it is revealed that a studio rental for a weekend costs £2,000, partially paid through a bank loan they secure. They go on a hunt for other street buskers to set up a band to play the songs they have been recording throughout the movie. The song the newly formed band plays for him quickly surprises a begrudging studio manager. The band is shown enjoying themselves, for several sessions, alongside rejuvenated studio managers, eager to listen to them. During this sequence the Girl reveals her love for the Guy, but says so in Czech and declines to translate what she has told him.

As Raquel, a 33-year-old single mother and part-time charity worker, said:

RAQUEL: I find it just a wee bit too hard to believe that a Girl who lives in really harsh conditions goes out of her way to pay for a studio and all the stuff ... I get that it is a film, but this kind of indie films aim to feel 'possible', 'real'. You know what I mean?
BENJAMÍN: Yes, and what do you think it's not making it feel that way for you in the film?
RAQUEL: That I understand that she's falling for him and she wants to help him, but you know, she's poor and also a single parent, no matter how much she thinks he's the one ... I think that the moment she sees that a studio costs like a grand she'd say no ... She has a child to look after and her flat could use so many repairs.

Raquel's point about the lack of verisimilitude is one that speaks of her own class expectations and the limitation of the romantic possibilities for her. In other words, love does not conquer all, at least not for those of low- or no-income positions. Even though the studio rental was facilitated through a bank loan, a plot device to enable the suspension of disbelief and the continuity of the romance, this still needs to be paid back somehow. This is compounded by the fact that the Girl is a flower seller, a low-income profession in general. This highlights that the platonic characterisation of this romance finds itself being questioned by the participant's own class condition and lived experience.

These elements provide an overview of how viewers' class affects their readings of a romantic narrative. While the 'reality effect' of a film, especially films predominantly consumed and targeted at women, is not necessarily the most important aspect a viewer will take from it, it is crucial to the overall experience of the romance. The 'emotional realism' of the film, as Ien Ang (1985) called it, is just as important for many audiences, just like the music and the dialogue play a pivotal role for the enjoyment, identification and feeling of 'closeness' a romantic film can generate. What is unique about the relationship between the verisimilitude of the filmic text and the class element is how it can cut across more isolated pleasures derived from the text (e.g. a line from a romantic moment, a song, a given figure of love) to affect the overall pleasure from the film. This trait is not unique to class, as gender, race, religion and family are all elements that constitute a subject's identity and thus modify her/his entry point into the film. In the following section, I will suggest further how personal romantic experiences and ideas on love and family are a particular trait that also impinge on a subject's reading and allow a flexibility of attachment and enjoyment of the narrative unique to romantic films.

A motel or the classed rules of the game

In a key romantic sequence from *Blue Valentine*, Cindy and Dean finally reach a motel and start to drink vodka while beginning yet another argument. The next time they are shown in the motel they are slow dancing to 'their song' and kissing. The sequence ends with Dean trying almost forcefully to have intercourse with Cindy, who is too drunk to give consent. When he realises this, he storms off from the motel. Formed of three different scenes that are juxtaposed with moments in the second timeline of the film, the motel events are the defining plot twist of the film. This sequence is the moment where the erosion of love and the disintegration of the couple are played out dialogically, through arguments and failed attempts at romantic intimacy, and symbolically through failed sexual intercourse.

This sequence also contains an intertwining of class and romantic elements that the participants discussed extensively. First, there was a polarisation on who was 'right' in the argument the on-screen couple were having. Group participants from working-class backgrounds argued that the escapade at the motel was not the time to be discussing the problems they had in the house. Leslie, a 23-year-old student who comes from a rural area and a humble background (as she herself put it), mentioned:

> I was kind of relating to the guy, who's enjoying life ... she was kind of bossy, very depressed, I mean after the marriage ... I try to enjoy but she was always disrupting ... drag me back to the reality and you should do all these things and you have to live up to your potential and the guy says, for what? For money? ... And the first thing she asks is, where is the fridge? Dunno, just relax!

While Leslie had some problems articulating her discomfort and frustration with Cindy's attitude, partly because English is not her native language, her reading is clearly one that favours a romantic ethos over pragmatic concerns. Another participant, Margot, a 37-year-old retail worker, mentioned:

> Cindy was a bit of a stuck-up snob you know what I mean? ... She couldn't deal with the fact she's poor and was taking it out on Dean ... Sure he drinks but all men do, that's just what they do. At least he was trying to make them both happy well knowing what they have.

These two observations highlight in a more critical way what Sophie (Cindy couldn't make her mind up about what she wanted and then ...) and Natalie (I think she had a problem with letting go and accepting where she was ...) expressed. Cindy's downward mobility, or at least the constant frustration of her middle-class aspirational ethos, is at odds with Dean's romantic attempts as they reinforce it. However, their focus is a positive one on the confrontation of one's situation and trying to have a respite of it. But while these participants see Dean's romanticism positively, other participants instead voiced their appreciation of Cindy's 'down-to-earth' approach, some highlighting the 'tackiness' and 'immaturity' of such a weekend getaway.

Compare to this the exchange two other participants had over the same event. Christine, 34, and Tracy, 37, work in the cultural industries, are college educated and from middle-class backgrounds:

CHRISTINE: I'm slightly appalled someone has the nerve to ask of this woman to just enjoy the night ... I know it is fiction and I should not get so upset over it but he did not even consult her, he's really forcing her to do what he wants, without any consideration to how she might feel ... so of course she's going to explode with a few drinks, she must be exhausted of being treated like a child ...
TRACY: I agree, you can't expect a woman to thank you every time you want to have a romantic moment simply because you are a man who's 'making an effort'. I think the real effort would have been for him to try and connect with her, see why she's so frustrated ... maybe even promise her that he'll try to get a better job. Or that he will help more with chores.
CHRISTINE: Yeah, I think it is easy to get carried away with the smooth character he is when young, seeing the motel as a follow-up on that ... I too like when my hubby surprises me with something romantic, but I'm not going to be happy if we leave for the weekend leaving the flat a mess. I still have to come back on Monday to tidy up. That wouldn't leave my mind all weekend.

This exchange suggests how timing and consideration for the romantic other in a relationship form part of a different romantic ethos in contrast with Dean's perhaps rather self-centred romanticism. A more pragmatic point of view, in line with love-as-intimacy's dialogical logic, is displayed here. The separation between the romantic moment and the everyday is, if not directly, highlighted by these two women as an essential component of carrying out one's romantic life. Thus, in their view, the failure of the motel as a romantic location is entrenched in Dean's inability to connect to his beloved, a blindness intrinsic to romanticism, and his failure to discern the relationship between romance and his beloved as a persona apart from himself.

This tension between those subjects who claim that Cindy needed to relax and those who disliked Dean's non-pragmatic attitude reveal a tension between two poles of contemporary romantic love: the platonic–romantic and the pragmatic–intimacy sides. Here it is important to remember how in *Once* the platonic nature of the romance is enabled by a precarious globalisation and its effects on migrants. This sets the stage for a romance that is impossible by a turn of events that speak more of a conservative, patriarchal ideology of motherhood and marriage than of the seemingly progressive and utopian dimension of romantic love initially portrayed. So, while platonic escapades are indeed usually enabled by setting up the romance with a set of situations, problems and situations to overcome, in *Once* the realisation of the escape is impossible as the narrative sets the Girl in an untenable position.

In *Blue Valentine*, the escape sequence isn't about making the platonic turn into a romance, but rather how the lack of romance highlights the lack of compatibility between platonic–romantic ideas and the (emotional) labour of intimacy as classed romantic discourses. Thus, while *Once* posits that regardless of the discourse of love, or one's own class position, the womanly duty to her family and the outwardly exploration of the male are 'unbreakable' ideological dictums. In *Blue Valentine*, what's at stake is the flexibility and knowledge of knowing when to adopt the 'appropriate' romantic discourse. The idea of 'appropriateness' reveals a class divide in such flexibility. In *Blue Valentine*, it would be unfair to characterise so strictly one character as more working class than the other. What I find more relevant is that the reading and the priorities audiences give to the sequence, as well as to what one chooses as preferable over the other in Cindy and Dean's situation, does have a distinct class separation that needs to be addressed. A weekend getaway can be a perfectly romantic and adequate way to release the tension between the couple, but, as Judith, a 29-year-old student from a relatively well-off background, explained:

> It was all icky and like, very anti-romantic or something ... the lights, the bed with this fake panel board, the metallic decorations, it is one of those places you really can't think of as romantic to save your marriage ... I don't expect like castles and jets or anything like that, but a more romantic place would have been nicer, like a nice park to camp in or something, I don't know of places in America but there has to be something better ... I think then Cindy would have relaxed more or something.

In addition to this, Mark, 35, an art director and graduate of Oxford University, suggested this in another group interview:

> I find the biggest mistake from Dean's side is his wilful denial of what has just happened around him. His wife gets angry with him for eating like a child and his response is to answer by going back to the past, by acting even more like a kid. Maybe, had he cleaned up and then surprised Cindy with the motel, it would have been well received. But presenting it just after she's done the cleaning is really poor timing.

Mark and Judith exemplify the difference between the priorities expressed by the working-class participants and those of middle-class or wealthier backgrounds. The latter focus on the *timing* of the getaway while the former focus on the *intention* of it. This is explained by the scarcity of such events (or lack thereof) of such events in the participants' own romantic lives. Furthermore, going one night to a 'cheap sex motel' reserved with a coupon to get drunk and make love, is a planned activity that sounds cheap, uninspired and lacking the romantic flair of the spontaneous date. Thus, Dean's working-class choice becomes salient because the motel as an escape conflicts with a middle-class ideal of 'appropriateness of the occasion', the idea that depending on the activity the couple desires to engage in, there should be an expenditure of money appropriate to it. This does not mean, as Illouz (1997) argues, that it necessarily entails spending any money at all, but rather it is about a concern for the context, the place and the uniqueness of the occasion. The creation of a romantic experience she argues, requires certain cultural capital, certain knowledge of one's own class sensibility and the aspirational trait of romance. The problem becomes then not the idea but the execution. This mismatch between an expected getaway from the depiction in the film is clear in Judith's words when she refers to the decoration of the motel and its non-conduciveness for romance. For her a 'more romantic place' is a rural one: a park or a camp. These spaces are usually preferred by the middle and upper classes, Illouz argues, as they present an escape from the urban noise and consumerist capitalist offers otherwise in place. Furthermore, privileging these spaces in the articulation of a romantic identity is directly related to the ironic detachment of the 'romantic cliché'. This entails a construction, through a middle-class romantic ethos, of these places as hierarchically superior to dates that involve an onerous spending.

In other words, while the first liminoid moment is something we are all entitled to, the second brings up the question of who and how one can 'relax' from reality, from everyday life and enjoy a romantic moment. The film poses this question to audiences and in doing so it brings forth links between social class and romantic love. A middle-class pathos – and the practices that ignite it – clashes with the motel as a clearly marked working-class setting. It disrupts the ideal spatial dimension of romanticism, of the possibility of escaping reality because the very setting in which it is based only highlights the inescapability of their working-class background. In turn, this creates a displacement with the audiences' possibilities and expectations of romance. The following excerpts highlight the expectations of the second moment. Tracy, a 37-year-old designer, expressed:

> I think the fact he proposes *going away with a coupon I just find awful*. If they are so skint then if you really are to go out, then you should make it really special. A motel coupon is not something I can imagine any woman getting excited for.
>
> (Emphasis added)

Giulia, a 22-year-old hospitality worker, mentioned:

> *It's just not romantic*, you know? If I'm going on a date with my boyfriend, it's a deal breaker if I feel or can see he's being a bit lazy and takes me somewhere cheap ... That's how Cindy feels with Dean, it's like when they were young he tried so hard and now a cheap motel, it's very disappointing.
>
> (Emphasis added)

Finally, Ryan, a 36-year-old civil servant, quipped:

> What bugs me is: why not stay at home? You can have a great time without spending any money if you just make an effort for the other person ... his lack of effort of any kind really bothers me. [laugh]

Tracy was one of several who mentioned the coupon, a plot device the film uses to enable the romantic escape for this impoverished couple. For Tracy, the problem lies in Dean's lack of subtlety, which undercuts the romantic intention. For all three participants Dean's laziness is a symbol of how his youthful romanticism is out of touch with his adult working-class positionality. A coupon normally isn't an item reserved to the working classes to enter commodified romantic love. In the film, however it does act to highlight the precarious conditions of the couple. Furthermore, for Tracy and Giulia, the fact remains that presenting the possibility of a romantic escape through a coupon diminishes the 'magic' of such an event, and is a damning sign of romantic laziness. Their interventions reinforce a tension between emotional and economic labour in the making of romantic moments. This tension is part of a romantic ethos that assumes knowledge of the saturated cultural images and situations of romance. With this knowledge, or cultural competence, the subject acts romantically. Eva Illouz (1997) argues that given different education levels and economic capital, middle and upper classes not only create a distance and a self-conscious *ethos* with the most repeated situations, experiences and places but also that part of this ethos involves learning how to conceal the commoditisation of romance. Thus, Dean's bluntness is a transgression due to lack of knowledge of the rules of romance and its commoditised practices. But while for Tracy and Giulia there's a direct correlation between the liminoid romantic and spending money, Ryan advocates an opposition between the two, privileging the domestic space. Again, this flexibility between the domestic–outer spaces and spending or not spending of money is part of the middle-class romantic ethos that possesses the flexibility of navigating these decisions more easily than those of lower socioeconomic backgrounds.

Blue Valentine is a romantic drama that emphasises this tension between class, the commoditisation of romance and the know-how it expects of its players both in the narrative and in its audiences. The coupon, the motel, the rural setting and the juxtaposition of two timelines work to deliver the opposition between two discourses of love: romantic love and intimacy. In the film and beyond it, class plays a clear role in underlining the expected emotional and economic labour behind both discourses, with attention to how romantic love is ill-suited to the self-disclosure, dialogical and aspirational qualities to which contemporary relationships must be attuned. Yet, the manner in which the case of *Once* highlights romantic love, with a touch of contemporary platonic love, still plays a crucial role in maintaining a utopian and possibly transgressive view of love in capitalist society. In the case of *Once* any putative transgressive undertones are undermined – although not erased, if one accepts Banaji's point that endings do not entirely undo the ideological work of the rest of a film

(2006: 169) – by its reactionary ending. In the next chapter, I will shift attention from readings of class to audience responses about gendered positions in interpersonal relationships in *Blue Valentine* and *(500) Days of Summer* to understand how these construct gender roles and subjectivities and how audiences read them vis-à-vis their own.

Notes

1 In the case of *Once* it is also necessary to mention the importance of the music for the audiences to relate to and create intimate connections with the film.
2 See https://en.wikipedia.org/wiki/Academy_Award_for_Best_Actress
3 See http://news.moviefone.com/2010/12/08/blue-valentine-rating-nc-17/
4 See http://variety.com/2007/film/news/once-upon-a-time-2-1117968768/
5 For a fascinating book on migrants and their search for intimacy and love, see Bloch (2017).
6 This is the total number of participants that watched *Blue Valentine* with me.

References

Ang, I. (1985). *Watching Dallas: soap opera and the melodramatic imagination*. Methuen.
Banaji, S. (2006). *Reading "Bollywood" the young audience and Hindi films*. Palgrave Macmillan.
Berlant, L. G. (2001). Love: a queer feeling. In T. Dean & C. Lane (eds), *Homosexuality and psychoanalysis* (pp. 431–452). University of Chicago Press.
Berlant, L. (2008). *The female complaint*. Duke University Press.
Berlant, L. G. (2012). *Desire/love*. punctum books.
Bloch, A. (2017). *Sex, love, and migration: postsocialism, modernity, and intimacy from Istanbul to the Arctic*. Cornell University Press.
Bryson, V. (2014). Time to love. In A. Jónasdóttir & A. Fergusson (eds), *Love: a question for feminism in the 21st century* (pp. 113–126). Routledge.
Carney, J. (2007). *Once*. Icon Film Distribution
Cianfrance, D. (2010). *Blue Valentine*. The Weinstein Company.
Condon, B. (2006). Dreamgirls. Paramount Pictures.
Derné, S. (2000). *Movies, masculinity, and modernity: an ethnography of men's filmgoing in India*. Greenwood Press.
Dugan, D. (2011). Just Go with It. Columbia Pictures.
Evans, P., & Deleyto, C. (1998). *Terms of endearment: Hollywood romantic comedy of the 1980s and 1990s* (ed. P. W. Evans & C. Deleyto). Edinburgh University Press.
Ferriss, S., & Young, M. (eds.). (2008). *Chick flicks: contemporary women at the movies*. Routledge.
Giddens, A. (1992). *The transformation of intimacy: sexuality, love and eroticism in modern societies*. Polity Press.
Gledhill, C. (1987). *Home is where the heart is: studies in melodrama and the woman's film*. BFI Publishing.
Hakim, C. (2010). Erotic capital. *European Sociological Review*, 26(5), 499–518. https://doi.org/10.1093/esr/jcq014.
Illouz, E. (1997). *Consuming the romantic utopi : love and the cultural contradictions of capitalism*. University of California Press.
James, N. (1989). Emotional labour: skill and work in the social regulation of feelings. *The Sociological Review*, 37(1), 15–42. https://doi.org/10.1111/j.1467-954X.1989.tb00019.x.

Kaplan, A. E. (2000). The case of the missing mother: maternal issues in Vidor's *Stella Dallas*. In E. A. Kaplan (ed.), *Feminism and Film* (pp. 466–479). Oxford University Press.
Kuhn, A. (1994). *Women's pictures: feminism and cinema* (2nd edn). Verso.
Lee, A. (2005). Brokeback Mountain. Focus Features.
Luhrmann, B. (2001). Moulin Rouge. 20th Century Fox.
Marshall, R. (2002). Chicago. Miramax Films.
Mendes, S. (2009). Revolutionary Road. Universal International Pictures.
Povinelli, E. (2006). *The empire of love: toward a theory of intimacy, genealogy, and carnality*. Duke University Press.
Reed, P. (2006). The Break Up. Universal Pictures.
Reitman, I. (2011). No Strings Attached. Paramount Pictures.
Schneebaum, A. (2014). All in the family: patriarchy, capitalism, and love. In A. Jónasdóttir & A. Ferguson (eds), *Love: a question for feminism in the 21st century* (pp. 127–140). Routledge.
Sharot, S. (2010). Class rise as a reward for disinterested love: cross-class romance films, 1915–28. *Journal of Popular Culture*, 43(3), 583–599.
Shary, T. (2011). Buying me love: 1980s class-clash teen romances. *The Journal of Popular Culture*, 44(3), 563–582. https://doi.org/10.1111/j.1540-5931.2011.00849.x.
Shumway, D. R. (2003). *Modern love: romance, intimacy, and the marriage crisis*. New York University Press.
Stam, R. (2000). *Film theory*. Blackwell.
Thompson, K., & Bordwell, D. (2009). *Film history: an introduction* (3rd edn). McGraw-Hill Higher Education.
Webb, M. (2009). *(500) Days of Summer*. Fox Searchlight Pictures.
Wright, J. (2007). Atonement. Focus Features.

5 Of happy endings and new men

> Something might happen and a structure might shift its symbolisations. That is the hope of love, the *Eternal Sunshine* to which you just have to say 'ok' to walking awkwardly and falling down on the ice. The truth is closer to *Amores Perros*, in which love wounds so badly that all you can do is walk away.
>
> (Lauren Berlant, 2012[1])

> How can you trust your feelings, when they can disappear just like that?
>
> (Cindy, *Blue Valentine*)

Introduction

Complementing Chapter 5's focus on class by telescoping in on gendered positions within relationships, here I analyse group interview data to understand how masculinities play out at the intersection of representation and the everyday for audiences of these films. In the previous chapter, I showed how one's own class background shapes the personal romantic affinities one looks for in a partner as well as the value judgement of certain romantic activities. I also suggest that the interconnection between romantic love (or lack thereof) and technology should be understood in the larger context of the impact of neoliberal reforms on younger adults instead of assuming a facile attitude that the introduction of technology means the death of romantic love. When recruitment for group interviews began, I had anticipated that the system I'd drawn up, which allowed volunteers to participate in whatever group interview session and on whichever film they preferred, would lead to imbalanced participation towards some and against some films. However, I had not anticipated the extent to which this happened. For *Once*, the release of its corresponding stage musical adaptation helped tremendously to boost its appeal. The proximity of *Her*'s release to the date of my research (and the very convenient DVD release for my fieldwork) gave me more participants than I could have hoped for. On the other hand, *Don Jon*, with its lukewarm popular reception and lacklustre advertisement,[2] and *Blue Valentine* (Cianfrance, 2010) received almost no interest for group interviews at first. Above all of them stood *(500) Days of Summer* (Webb, 2009), with dozens of volunteers for group interviews.

DOI: 10.4324/9781003164289-6

Arguably the most intensely resonant, and with a longer lasting half-life in popular culture, *(500) Days of Summer* was also the only film where seven interview participants had seen the whole film previously. The well-attended group interviews for *(500) Days of Summer* also helped me to fill the last focus groups for *Blue Valentine* by advertising it to my participants as a 'slightly darker version' of *(500) Days of Summer* (henceforth *(500) DoS*).

Blue Valentine and *(500) DoS* share striking similarities: the male lead is a hopeless, naive romantic; the female lead is either unsure of her feelings or appears never to have loved the man (depending on individual viewers' perceptions); time, in the form of flashbacks or non-linear time jumps, is an important narrative device; music is used to foreshadow events in both films; neither film is a clear-cut love story – one is a story of the erosion of love and relationships and the other a story about love; both films borrow elements from melodrama and women's films; neither film has a categorically happy ending (though *Blue Valentine*'s is clearly more bleak); and both films have been critically noted for their presumed realism.

There are, however, some key differences: *(500) DoS* operates with an omniscient narrator and within the first three minutes it announces that it is *not a love story*, thus inviting some viewers to take a contrarian position and declare that it is. *Blue Valentine* foreshadows its own unhappy ending in some ways, but only unveils the particular type of unhappiness at the climax of the film. In *(500) DoS*, the ending hints that love and relationships are still possible, despite cynicism, the conditions of urban modernity and the film's own unsuccessful romance. *Blue Valentine* refuses such a redeeming thread. Another way of understanding this crucial difference is through the notion of sub-genric conventions: *(500) DoS* is a romantic comedy and *Blue Valentine* is a romantic drama. *(500) DoS* uses self-consciously complex cinematographic and screenplay elements to drive forward the plot (e.g. split screen, a musical scene, black-and-white scenes), while *Blue Valentine*'s style is more akin to *cinéma verité*. Finally, class – and class conflict – is a crucial aspect of *Blue Valentine*'s narrative, whereas *(500) DoS*'s narrative is not concerned with it at all.

With these parallels between the two films established, I will scrutinise how the representation and reception of white straight masculinities, femininities and relationships in these two films constructs a possible lens through which to re-examine ideas about romantic films in the post-classical era of Hollywood. Fuelled by the empirical work, my central argument is that although neither film provides a fully anti-hegemonic discourse with regards to modernity, heterosexual relationships and love, they owe a large amount of their popularity and critical acclaim to a more nuanced form of representation of gender and relationships in romantic films than previously available. In line with this, I suggest that in contemporary urban Euro-American life, more than ever, failure and pain take on a particular contemporary normative form in our experience of romance both in real life and on-screen. This is connected to melodrama, the women's film and their link with contemporary romantic comedies and to newer subgenres like the 'bromance', 'beta male' comedies and the anxious romance. These newer subgenres, as John Alberti suggests (2013a, 2013b), are embedded in the larger context of a crisis of masculinity, and the romantic comedy's genre shift of attention to the role of men in it.

'How many times can you fall in love before you can't anymore?'

It is in the context of this crisis of (Western), white, straight masculinity, in part caused by greater visibility of queer and female sensibilities (Connell, 2006; Deleyto, 2003), that the two most popular romantic comedy(-dramas) of the 2000s in North American independent cinema have been produced, namely *Eternal Sunshine of the Spotless Mind* (Gondry, 2004) and *(500) Days of Summer* (2009). Released in 2004, *Eternal Sunshine of the Spotless Mind*, captured audiences and critics for its mixture of science fiction, romance and comedy. The similarities outlined at the beginning of this chapter between *(500) DoS* and *Blue Valentine* can easily be stretched to Michel Gondry's directorial debut. Their success – and *Blue Valentine*'s critical acclaim – stems, I argue, from their disruption of the traditional teleology of romantic comedies of heterosexual couple love and a fluid representation of both masculine and feminine identities. To a certain extent this challenges heteronormative constructions and readings of masculine and feminine identities and coupledom. *Eternal Sunshine of the Spotless Mind* deals with the relationship break-up of the central couple, who have both undergone a procedure to completely erase all memories of each other.

The film which unfolds counter-chronologically finishes with the following dialogue that takes place in a hallway outside the male lead's apartment:

JOEL: I can't see anything that I don't like about you.
CLEMENTINE: But you will! You know … you will think of things and I will get bored with you and feel trapped because that's what happens with me.
JOEL: Ok. (shrugs shoulders)
CLEMENTINE: Ok.
BOTH: (laughter and tears)

In the context of a film which is all about the pain of memory that necessitates a violent erasure of each character's other half from psychic existence, it would be facile to read this as just a reaffirmation of heterosexual couple love as the ultimate form of love, a staple device of romantic comedies. A more productive way of reading this type of ending lies also in the recognition of the fragile nature of romantic love both always and specifically in the contemporary world. The characters laugh and cry at the same time, pleasure and pain both conveyed as they embark on a new attempt. The mistakes, the details that led them adrift in the first place have been pointed out to the audience throughout the film and they are highlighted in the recording that plays at the end. In this recording, Joel (Jim Carrey) lists a good number of things he disliked about Clementine (Kate Winslet) and their relationship. Of course, the film has also showed the positive lifeworld of the relationship, the intimacy. This ambivalence plays on the audience's own state of belief regarding love and relationships.

In a similar vein, *Beginners* by Mike Mills (2011) portrays two leads who are both dealing with father and intimacy issues. The film tells us from the beginning that the male lead's father has died after living his last few years having come out as gay. The female lead lives a semi-nomadic existence, seemingly afraid to get too attached to anything or anybody. The couple separates shortly after moving in together because neither is shown to be able to cope with living as a couple. However, it is the on-screen death of the male lead's father that triggers the reunion of the lovers.[3] In the final scene, sitting side by side, the male lead asks: 'What happens now?', and the female lead replies: 'I don't know'; he continues: 'How does that work?' They smile while looking at each other and the screen cuts to black. The film does not resolve the issues of either lead, though symbolically they are now shown to be capable of doing this for themselves. This ambiguity is unlike the characteristics usually associated with romantic love. The ending, as it ought to be expected, should either sanction or champion the heterosexual union. Here, however, there is a high degree of uncertainty regarding the future of the couple. As with *Eternal Sunshine of the Spotless Mind*, romantic love no longer is a warranty of narrative suture. In the next section, I analyse *Blue Valentine* (2010), focusing on the link between these three narratives and what the endings represent as a shift in contemporary romantic love.

And then it ends

Blue Valentine portrays the potentially 'tragic' ending of this recognition of human frailty and relationship finitude. This is greatly to do with the fact that the film is not a comedy; instead it borrows heavily from the woman's film and melodramatic conventions to draw out a narrative of disillusionment and erosion of a relationship.

In *Blue Valentine*, the sequences that take place in the past are only used to heighten the emotional hook of the impending and foreseeable finale. In the final sequence, Dean angrily walks into Cindy's workplace. He confronts her about why she left him in the motel. She responds that she no longer loves or feels anything for him. He proceeds to punch a doctor and to scream in rage at Cindy. They have one final discussion, where Dean walks away from Cindy, who is left in the company of her father and her child. A marriage broken, fireworks in the background, Dean walks away as Cindy travels back to her father's house with her daughter in her arms. The dissolution of this marriage signals the failure of romantic love, intimacy and the frailty of contemporary relationships. Certainly, Cindy's return to her father's home can be read in a sort of psychoanalytic fashion as her ultimate return to the 'benevolent' father and her unavoidable submission to patriarchal authority through her recognition, as it is common in the woman's film, of the impossibility of female happiness. However, I find the reading of Matthew, a 35-year-old charity worker, worth considering:

But even if she goes back to that horrible dad, I'm not saying he's all of a sudden all great, but that at least shows for me that he's going to be there for her ... also, she's a nurse and even got offered a nicer job, he's [Dean's] just a drunk who's alone ... Divorce isn't pretty, but I take from the film that she's going to be fine, I think my feeling for Dean is that even though he's not really a great guy, he's screwed up the one thing he had.

In this interpretation, it isn't so much a question of happiness, but rather of who is seemingly going to be less affected by divorce. The recognition of potentiality is one that is highlighted in different aspects of all these films and picked up in group interviews. While Matthew's interpretation of the sequence wasn't the dominant one in his group, he wasn't alone in feeling the potential for the female character to be successful. His glimmer of optimism is rooted in an attitude to relationships and love as cyclical in contemporary societies, not as one-time events. Anishka, a 31-year-old 'new mum', was also cautiously optimistic, albeit for different reasons:

ANISHKA: It is depressing to watch but I think it's because it hits on that thought that the whole idea of one partner for life is bollocks ... I like the fact the film puts this in your face but just sort of leaves it there.
BENJAMÍN: What do you mean by that?
ANISHKA: Well, you know like in *Brokeback Mountain* Jack dies and in ... yeah *Closer*, they all turn out to be psychopaths ... here it's just like what happens, they were in love and had a kid and then it became really toxic so they split up, no big twist ... plus you know, there's always someone else out there!
Finally, Aba, a 32-year-old second-generation Ghanaian-English woman who works in retail, contributed this fascinating reading of *Blue Valentine*:

ABA: I can't stop thinking of what my mum would think of this film.
BENJAMÍN: Why is that?
ABA: Because I wonder if she would have even considered the divorce ... for her that is not a possibility, she's always saying to me: Why don't you try to accept ____ [her partner's name, unintelligible] flaws and get married? In Ghana if a woman fails in her marriage, it's the ultimate crime ... For me the thing is, I don't have a problem with being single or having just a boyfriend or whatever, you get used to both.
BENJAMÍN: And marriage?
ABA: I don't really see the point of it ... They sell you that it is this huge thing that makes your life better and it isn't like that anymore. I think it can work for some people, but at least for me to be able to survive now, you have to be ok with being by yourself.

Aba's brief reflexion of how generational and cultural change and migration can affect attitudes towards marriage and relationships is poignant on several levels. In recognising her mother's reduction of her worth to that conferred by marriage, she recognises the social and cultural power this institution still holds for millions of people; something not unique, of course, to Ghana. For women like her mother, it bestows on them status and security of being. Aba's commentary also provides an insight into a different ideological perspective regarding gender roles and attitudes.[4] Unfortunately, a more in-depth analysis of her reflection is outside the scope of this book.

These three excerpts show a rich spectrum of negotiations over the value of marriage and its representation. More precisely, they represent a sympathetic critique of a particular representation of it that is in tune with the contemporary sensibility towards romantic relationships. Aba's perspective, echoed by 19 other participants during my fieldwork (roughly one-quarter of my interviewees), is not one of cynicism towards marriage, relationships or love as it might initially appear. Rather, Aba's claim about resilience during singlehood being a necessary quality to cope with contemporary life is one that seeks to dissolve the ideological opposition between relationships and singlehood and to live them as a continuum. This acceptance should not be understood as an absolute, as anyone who's been heartbroken can surely understand. Instead, it conceives and welcomes singlehood as an integral, if at some points painful, part of one's life; not as a failure that needs to be corrected, which is the view of so many 1980s and 1990s Hollywood films and of Aba's mother. Matthew expresses a belief based around economic rationality whereby the end of marriage is not seen as a fatalistic flaw of the inadequacy of either lover but simply a possible outcome. Anishka's participation exalts the realism of this and further adds, optimistically so, that after a divorce, rather than the stigma, new romantic possibilities await. These two participants did not mention whether they had gone through a divorce or if they are single parents. The hardships, the stigma, the pain of break-ups and single parenting is not something I wish to minimise or ridicule. But these optimistic outlooks and Aba's seemingly 'cynical' view do contain a shift in attitudes and expectations towards relationships, singlehood and their representations.

This recognition is based around the fact that *Blue Valentine* is a film that openly acknowledges what every other film discussed in this chapter gives a subtle nod to – something not lost on most of the audiences that participated – that relationships end. For reasons of generic convention all the other films give an optimistic nod to the heterosexual couple, whereas *Blue Valentine* is interested in exploring how to represent this in one of its most common manifestations, divorce. Granted the film itself never actually depicts the legal procedure, but the final exchanges, which are intertwined with flashbacks of their wedding day, and the film's theme song, 'You always hurt the ones you love', are symbolically figurative of this.

That relationships end or might end sounds like a banal assessment when extrapolated to the real world, but in the teleology of romantic films, this is, if not necessarily novel nor widespread, clearly gaining traction given the response all these films have received, critically and popularly. Woody Allen's films – particularly his productions in the late 1970s and early 1980s – and other 'nervous romances' of the 1970s had already explored this. However, there are two clear distinctions between the 'nervous romances' and the films I have brought up thus far. As Evans & Deleyto (1998) suggests, the former 'explore the tensions between a narrative structure still based on erotic love leading to regeneration and transcendence and a modern experience of sexuality as a culturally prestigious channel of access to the contemporary project of self-identity' (p. 144). In other words, these films are positioned in a cultural environment where sexual liberation and the women's movement began to carve a dent in the social and personal promises of marriage through love (Illouz, 2012). Yet marriage and remarriage figure prominently and are causes of anxiety, regret and pain. They either stand in the way of the self-fulfilment and self-realisation of the main characters or, in the case of remarriage, become the path to them. Thus, marriage, given the time, still played a pivotal part in the resolution of the conflict in these films. Not only that, Allen's treatment of it is riddled with irony, sarcasm and a permanent link to sexuality. It is possible, then, to posit that these films position the end of a marriage as a possible path of regeneration towards another. As Frank Krutnik (1990) highlights:

> Although such films [nervous romances] are at pains to stress modernity, their impetus is more headily nostalgic. They capitalize upon a desire to slip back into a fantasied past of secure options and a less chaotic sexual menu which can be regulated by and through heterosexual monogamy. Even while acknowledging the contemporary breakdown of marriage, these films manifest a yearning for rules, norms, and boundaries within which The Couple can come, and stay, together; within which both inter- and intrasubjective relations can be safely regulated.
>
> (p. 69)

This is not the case in the films mentioned thus far nor in the readings expressed above. As mentioned before, these are films soaked in melodrama and woman's film iconography but with a recognition of uncertainty and frailty without leading to the resolution of both internal and interpersonal conflicts. Furthermore, in the case of *Blue Valentine*, there is no clear focus on one of the protagonists as romantic comedies tend to have, and concern is shifted from one character and their relationship with the loved other to the relationship itself. However, heterosexuality, monogamy and 'The Couple' are still affirmed and never questioned.

What ties all these films together, and their tapping into a contemporary romantic sensibility, can be understood by way of Anthony Giddens' (1992) idea of 'confluent love'. Opposed to romantic love, Giddens suggests that nowadays

> ideals of romantic love tend to fragment under the pressure of female sexual emancipation and autonomy ... romantic love depends upon projective identification, the projective identification of *amour passion*, as the means whereby prospective partners become attracted and then bound to one another ... Opening oneself out to the other, the condition of what I shall call *confluent love*, is in some ways the opposite of projective

identification ... Confluent love is active, contingent love, and therefore jars with the 'for-ever', 'one-and-only' qualities of the romantic love complex ... The more confluent love becomes consolidated as a real possibility, the more the finding of a 'special person' recedes and the more it is the 'special relationship' that counts.

(pp. 61–62)

As I mentioned in the first chapter, Giddens argues that relationships have become contingent, uprooted from the social ties of before and a constant process of self-disclosure and self-interrogation. In other words, Giddens argues that relationships have become a never-ending communication process.

The weakness of the concept is that it sets a demarcation all too clear between discourses of *amour passion*, romantic love and companionate love while ignoring that intimacy conflates and incorporates many of the elements of these other types of love. This can be identified in the conception of the lover as a rational choice individual that can, somehow, not fall for 'projective identification'. Thus, Giddens obviates the fact that for many people, if not all, the 'special relationship' is to be built or is special precisely because they have found a (maybe) 'special person', maybe in a 'special moment', maybe in a 'special place'. Even if the elements are mundane from outside the relationship, a 'special relationship' will construct and be constructed by a narrative of singularity. Of course, this is not an absolute of all relationships and all peoples.[5] The strength of the concept lies, in my view, in its emphasis on the rejection of the 'forever' element of romantic love, that tragic quality that has long been embedded in both Western and Global South cultural repertoires and which plays a crucial role in the ideologically re-affirmative character of romantic comedies. That is one side of what is novel in these films and is attuned to contemporary expectations and experiences of love and relationships. When speaking of *Blue Valentine* and *(500) DoS*, Jan, a 37-year-old media worker, summarised his reading of both films thus:

They are films about people who just fail in love and relationships and that makes them honest and appealing for people today ... They have problems like everybody and they tried to work them out ... they are of different like relationships, one is not too serious and the other is a marriage but I find that at the end of the day, both show that disappointment we have all become so used to.

Isabelle, a 45-year-old woman (profession undisclosed), said of *Blue Valentine*:

They tried and failed. It sucks but I'm sure that they will either get back together for the girl or find somebody else. *There's always somebody else outside. I don't know a single person in my life that has just had just one boyfriend.*
(Emphasis added)

These ideas resonated and were echoed by most of my participants, especially the younger ones. Without fully subscribing to the idea that these characters 'just' fail in love (social class and its affective accoutrements play an important role in *Blue Valentine*), the pervading affect of today's 'single lover' is not of enthusiasm towards exploration but rather of expectation of disappointment. As several authors have argued, in contemporary societies the erosion of the social and individual promises of marriage has meant that settling down with a family (maybe through marriage) is delayed, in favour of an increased period of sexual, sensual and romantic experimentation (Beck & Beck-Gernsheim, 1995; Giddens, 1992; Illouz, 1997, 2012). This erosion of certainty is coupled, I reiterate, with increased economic pressures and lower standards of living available to young people and, as argued in Chapter 4, with an increased disillusionment of the promises of relationships, monogamy and marriage. My participant Anishka and her expression 'there's always someone else out there!' (see earlier in section) encapsulates the zeitgeist of our times. This attitude of sexual exploration and stalling has been derided as narcissistic, consumerist-driven and egocentric (see Badiou, 2009; Bauman, 2003; Beck & Beck-Gernsheim, 1995). These authors oppose to this l,ove an agapic, public love that purportedly doesn't shy away from risks, is open and looks to the transformative experience of an encounter with difference. These critiques come from established authors who have experienced love, sexuality and relationships long before the cultural effects of neoliberal economic and social reforms could be felt so they should be taken with more than a grain of salt. I would contend that while it is undeniable that the search for love is now fraught with economic calculations, some of them frivolous and callous, it hasn't been emptied of the yearning, the longing, the hopes, the desire to love. What this means is that even if the discourse of marriage, romantic love and relationships is unavoidably linked to that of neoliberal economic logics, it has not (yet, at least) been completely formed or devoured by them.

The films mentioned here recognise and explore this new environment of romantic love and relationships without reverting to facile equations to the Greek myth of Narcissus. They do so by showcasing moments where the couples speak of their former partners, of their wildest sexual adventures, of why these relationships failed. The exploration is there, marriage is marginalised and the happily ever after is rejected or is shown to be fickle and uncertain (in *Blue Valentine*'s case, there's no uplifting remarriage or self-exploration). These films do not tap into a crisis of marriage but rather into a generalised feeling of *angst* towards the frailty of contemporary relationships. This is what is contained in that statement of 'relationships end' of these films as well as in the audiences who recognise and live this.

The expectations of what relationships ought to offer become even more diffused and ambiguous. The search for romantic fulfilment is threaded with a vague sense of purpose; we no longer know exactly what it is that relationships do for us. That doesn't mean that people aren't looking for them; they simply do not provide the emotional and personal safety they warranted a few decades ago. Thus, the relevant shift these films offer from previous decades is an acceptance of this *angst* as a normative aspect of relationships and love nowadays, not a tragic one.

Of course, it must be noted that although these three films, *Eternal Sunshine of the Spotless Mind*, *Beginners* and *Blue Valentine*, do deal with the ambiguity and possible fractures of relationships and love, they do so in a middle-class, urban, white, straight, mostly monogamous environment for an audience arguably of a similar milieu. Any consideration of what anti-hegemonic narrative possibilities are being explored through these fractures is severely limited by its appeal to the hegemonic identity of Western societies. Furthermore, these changes and shifts do not affect men and women equally. Most still do benefit men.[6] It is also important to recognise that feminist scholars and/or artists have, for decades now, challenged and critiqued the primacy of the heterosexual couple as an ideological tool that privileges a very narrow perspective on love and intimacy (Bell & Binnie, 2000; Berlant, 2012; Comer, 1974; Johnson, 2012; Jonasdottir, 1991; Jonasdottir & Ferguson, 2014; Wilkinson 2012, 2013; Wilkinson and Bell, 2012). Coupled with these critiques, there is an increasingly large number of films dealing with other forms of romantic relationships that deal with non-monogamous and/or LGBTQ relationships, though these remain largely contained within film festival circuits of distribution or go straight to DVD release. These two elements, feminist critiques and Queer cinema, have been deconstructing, representing and reflecting on the instability and frailty of the contemporary heterosexual couple far longer than Hollywood, Bollywood or independent productions portraying a heterosexual couple.

Beyond the happily ever after

If these films play on the ambivalence, ambiguity and the frailty of contemporary relationships to shape their open endings, though (except for *Blue Valentine*) ultimately celebrating the possibility of romantic love and happy endings without stamping them as a definite, *(500) DoS* does so poignantly throughout but closes it off with a conservative, almost insignificant twist of the genre's canonical ending. Starting with the narrator's declaration that it is 'not a love story', the film foreshadows doubt and impending doom for the relationship. Yet, in the same monologue, it also says it is a story about: 'Boy meets girl. Boy falls in love. Girl doesn't.' Thus, the film consciously proclaims a contradiction of classic genre conventions. It follows the formula of destined heterosexual encounter but will not, seemingly, end in a positive reaffirmation of the romantic couple. As Chelsea, a 29-year-old fashion designer mentioned about that moment in the film:

> I remember that was what got me really intrigued about the film when it was released. Because you would see the rest of the trailer and it looked like another common romantic film ... I think it was very clever because it really made you think: are they going to break up? Do they end up together? It makes you want to see what's going to happen.

What Chelsea expresses here and others agreed on is that the film's opening statement intentionally belies the teleology of coupledom that audiences will watch for the next 90 minutes. At the same time, Chelsea and other participants expressed their belief in a 'traditional' ending, where Tom (Joseph Gordon Levitt) somehow woos back Summer (Zooey Deschanel). The film never completely closes off the possibility of the 'promised' heterosexual couple and their 'happily ever after' up until the revelation of Summer's engagement to another man. This invitation to doubt and wish for one's preferred ending is one of the lasting appeals of the film. *(500) DoS* speaks also of a shift in the representation and course of a relationship in a romantic film. Whereas classical and even post-classical films dealt with marriage in one way or another, *(500) DoS* announces from the onset the ambivalence and ambiguity of contemporary relationships. While films before, like *Say Anything* (Crowe, 1989)[7] and *My Best Friend's Wedding* (Hogan, 1997), have ignored the idea of marriage as the happily ever after, they replace this, as mentioned above, with friendship (Deleyto, 2003). In *(500) DoS*, marriage only appears to signal the ultimate division of the initial couple. Whereas Summer finds a classic happy ending, Tom encounters a far more common urbanite ending of the contemporary relationship: singlehood. This state Tom finds himself in is shown to be transitory, though, as in the last sequence of the film he meets a new girl, this time called Autumn. Thus, both Tom's and Summer's fate are decidedly a triumph of the heterosexual couple, and of serial monogamy, and on one level a reaffirmation of the superiority of these tropes. Contrary to *Eternal Sunshine of the Spotless Mind* and *Beginners* where the couple's relationship cracks have been exposed and left unresolved, *(500) DoS* places a symbolic emphasis of 'new opportunities' instead of 'second chances'.

In order to find resolution from grief, Tom has to endure one final meeting with Summer. This move heightens the *leitmotif* of the film: romantic relationships as a cyclic phenomenon of euphoria, pain, uncertainty, self-healing and hope. This alone is nothing new in romance films. The idea of 'conflict resolution' can be understood in this manner. Where *Eternal Sunshine* and *Beginners* end in a tenuous and ambiguous middle ground, and *Blue Valentine* on a clear low, *(500) DoS* scrambles these high and lows through a clever screenplay and by way of announcing the resolution of the conflict at the beginning of the film. This paves the way for a development of how the broken cycle of a couple can turn into the beginning of other fresh cycles. Furthermore, in allowing Summer's wedding and second relationship to play out on the fringes of the narrative, Tom's wounded heart is returned to normal, and the film opens the possibility of different readings of her persona as not necessarily ending up submitting to patriarchal logics or authority. Nora, a 31-year-old musician from London, drew attention to this point:

NORA: I don't really see her as ending as just a housewife like Nicola [another participant] does.
BEN: Why is that?
NORA: Well it may sound silly but in the end you see her dressed like she were working in the city.
BEN: But couldn't that be because she married a wealthy man?
NORA: Yes, sure but it's not only that. I see her as very independent and though she admits she had doubts with Tom, she's mature enough to let

him know she doesn't want anything serious. I feel she's a good model for girls who tend to get stuck with guys who don't make them happy or whatever simply because society has taught us that that's what women have to do.

Nora's focus lies in the agency and assertiveness of Summer. These are traits usually given to male characters in romantic films. Furthermore, by portraying her as active in her romantic decisions, Summer undermines the trope of the helpless woman of many romantic films. Finally, it is Summer who restores Tom's belief in romantic love and relationships, thus acting as both the subject of loss and the catalyst of reaffirmation. This marks a departure from the tenor of Kathleen Rowe's argument that 'melodramatised males of the post-classical romantic comedy use their feminisation to bolster their own authority, which they then invoke to "instruct" women about relationships, romance and femininity itself' (p. 187). Summer heals Tom of the cynicism that has flooded him after breaking up with her.

The appeal of Summer for participants like Nora lies in a reading that understands the most common trope of romantic films as a deeply patriarchal and ideological one: 'putting women in their place.' In a sense, what *(500) DoS* provides in this reading is that Summer has done what she's done from her own volition. Not only that, but the wisdom of romantic love and active searching, roles usually reserved for the male characters, are embodied by Summer. Jeanine and Sandra, a couple in their mid-thirties, and Clara, a 26-year-old student, on the other hand, read Summer's character and role differently:

JEANINE: I think if you get married so soon after breaking up with somebody then you never loved them anyway and it makes me think that person would only get married because they think they have to ... I felt it odd to have her marry just like that, I don't believe it.
SANDRA: I didn't like the fact she ends up married ... for me it destroys the whole idea of the film that she could be fine on her own.
CLARA: Summer is a free spirit and quirky, that doesn't mean that she can't fall in love with someone and marry them but it feels forced you know, it doesn't go at all with the rest of the film ... I think she looked a bit miserable.

These comments illustrate the different subject positions that Summer-as-woman occupies vis-à-vis my participants. Whereas Nora's reading decidedly focuses on Summer's quasi-feminist agency without challenging her decision to become a wife, many other participants were far more ambivalent about her decisions. In the case of Sandra, the classic heterosexual and arguably consumption-based hegemonic ending is seen as out of place for a film that sought not only to reverse the gendered roles of romantic characters but also to explore the frailty of contemporary relationships. Jeanine and Sandra's suspension of disbelief is stretched too far with the resolution of Summer's character.

This discomfort and/or disbelief, I suggest, has to do both with marriage as her 'fate' and with the regression to a classical romantic narrative, even if it is disjointed into two couples instead of resolved either by an affirmation of the original couple or the individual search of self-fulfilment as it was the case with the 'nervous romances'. In other words, the seemingly ambiguous future of the relationship foreshadowed in the beginning of the film is a discursive mismatch with the bland, classic ending of the film. Janice Radway's (1984) analysis of romance novel provides an eloquent way to understand this:

> By perpetuating the exclusive division of the world into the familiar categories of the public and the private, the romance continues to justify the social placement of women that has led to the very discontent that is the source of their desire to read romances. In continuing to relegate women to the arena of domestic, purely personal relations, the romance fails to pose other, more radical questions. Because the romance finally leaves unchallenged the male right to the public spheres of work, politics, and power, because it refurbishes the institution of marriage by suggesting how it might be viewed continuously as a courtship, because it represents real female needs within the story and then depicts their satisfaction by traditional heterosexual relations, the romance avoids questioning the institutionalized basis of patriarchal control over women even as it serves as a locus of protest against some of its emotional consequences.
>
> (p. 217)

The director's decision to marginalise Summer to two sequences – an engagement party, where she's barely visible, and a brief meeting in the park – only heightens the final, necessary arguably neoliberal masculinisation of Tom in order to enter a new cycle of romantic love. He quits his job as a sentimental greeting card writer and starts to fill out his architect portfolio. He dresses up and opts to look for a professional job, applying and interviewing. For a brief period, he embodies the classical male lead of romantic comedies: cynical, pragmatic, active and independent. This journey is also a restoration of his middle-class aspirational ethos, which paves the way for the consolidation of classic masculinity. This reaffirmation is incomplete, as he is 'lacking' in the romantic sphere, and the final ingredient comes through Summer, after he has regained public spaces and his personal life as his own. In the final scene, Tom takes on the active role of the pursuer, asking for the name of Autumn, thus completing his return to an active masculinity. Again, however, I stress that Summer's character wasn't viewed negatively by my participants for marrying; and several defended this representation of her as 'positive', 'empowering' and/or 'refreshing'. Borrowing from psychoanalytic approaches to cinema and spectatorship, here the concept of 'masochistic aesthetic', as initially put forward by Gilles Deleuze and developed by several film scholars (Del Río, 2008; Nichols, 1981; Rowe, 1995; Studlar, 1985), provides an initial insight into both the discomfort of my participants and the overall success of the film without fully embracing it.

In masochism, pleasure in the pre-Oedipal stage is located in an all-powerful mother. This mother figure is plentiful. Masochism then implies the denial of phallic power and of the father and its replacement by the mother, to whom the masochist submits. This does not position the woman as conveying a lack, but rather exalts her as whole and thus invokes a desire to merge with her. In other words, this theory of masochism plays on the ambivalent forces of desire and rejection of the male, with feminine identity as a threat to the stability of the former. In romantic comedies, Del Río (2008) suggests, the 'nonphallic sexuality of masochism has to be abandoned and the divested romantic hero, once familiarized with the feminine, has to be empowered' (p. 83). While I do not contend that *(500) DoS* represents a fully masochistic aesthetic, I do find that the final abandonment of Summer and her femininity qua 'unruly woman' partially accounts for the contrasting readings of my participants. At the same time, it is Tom's feminised masculinity that provides much of the pleasure for most of my participants, both men and women. Next, I elucidate why.

Anxiety and masculinity

Recently, in romantic comedies the main focus has become the place of men in the genre, with the main question: 'Why are men in romantic comedies?' (Alberti 2013b). This question, in turn, is anchored in the disruption generated by what Connell (2006) terms 'heterosexual sensitivity' in definitions of masculinity. As Connell suggests, this sensitivity that some men have developed is greatly indebted to the struggles of feminism, women's liberation movements and their questioning of patriarchy and fixed gender roles. This heterosexual sensitivity constitutes a destabilising point of classic alpha masculinity with the introduction of feminine concerns and the consideration of the masculine as lacking and thus also in process.

Such an undermining and questioning of classic heterosexual masculinity entails that masculinity is no longer defined in isolation but, rather, in relationship with the feminine. The dialogue that ensues is not entirely symmetrical or horizontal, but its recognition is part of a continued attempt by both men and women – not all of the men and not all of the women, of course – to envision new possibilities of gender politics and gender identity.

Connell (2000) highlights that masculinity then finds itself torn between an opening to the feminine and an aggressive backlash towards an atavistic, immanent masculine. In romantic comedies, this is expressed in a renewed interest in the exploration of possible and new configurations of masculinity that are responsive to the larger cultural struggles of gender identity and relationships like in the films here discussed. At the same time, a regressive counter-production is in full motion as well in a film like *The Ugly Truth* that contains a hyper-masculinised, virile male (see Alberti 2013b for an analysis of this film's portrayal of masculinity) or in the 'bromance' subgenre where the anxieties of a crisis-ridden middle-class masculinity are expressed through misogyny, gross-out humour and the subordination of the female in almost every respect. What it means to be a man and what it means to be a man in or looking for a relationship is what is at stake in male-centred romantic comedies. From this perspective, Tom is not so much of a man, but a man-boy who is in dire need of a sentimental education. What is interesting in this process in the film is that the recuperation of his feminised self, not the championing of a classic masculinity, enabled by Summer, is the final ingredient in his journey. During the final discussion, the roles have been reversed, Tom is cynical and claims all that he previously believed in, namely fate, love, relationships, are 'bullshit'. Summer replies to a cynical Tom that he wasn't wrong about these things, 'it just wasn't me that you were right about'. This triggers the final scene of the film, where Tom meets Autumn. Summer then redeems the destined meeting of the lovers, a fundamental pillar of romantic love, and the cycle may begin anew.

I argue that Tom's final emotional recovery constitutes an attempt at a reconfiguration of a representation of a hegemonic (romantic) masculinity that seeks to involve traits usually associated with the feminine, like idealisation, emotions and confession as a challenge to a macho-masculinity that derides such traits. Connell initially defined hegemonic masculinity as 'the configuration of gender practice which embodies the currently accepted answer to the problem of the legitimacy of patriarchy, which guarantees the dominant position of men and the subordination of women' (p. 77). Connell herself and others (Christensen & Jensen, 2014; Demetriou, 2001) have critiqued the concept, arguing for the inclusion of considerations of intersectionality, power relations – between men and other men, and men and women – historical and social contexts. In short, the concept of hegemonic masculinity cannot be understood monolithically, in absolute terms of mass domination, but must be seen as an ongoing process of winning consent to a bundle of tropes, ideals, practices, identities and beliefs. In what follows I will outline a few aspects of Tom's feminised masculinity as presented in the film and how they are perceived, read and identified by my participants.

At the beginning of the film, the narrator informs the audience that Tom believes he won't be happy until finding 'the one', a belief stemming from his cultural consumption of British music (the mise-en-scène points to bands like Joy Division and The Smiths) and a 'gross misreading' of the film *The Graduate*. Summer is introduced as sceptical of this with the experience of divorced parents to bolster her scepticism. This opening exposition sets up the gender-role reversal as one of idealisation of romantic love and of its failure. When asked about Tom, participants across different group interviews maintained:

JEANINE: I felt it [of love] was a very real portrayal, because he's not afraid to show his feelings and in the film they show all the things that go through his head and stuff … Tom for me is like my soulmate of how I fall in love … that scene that puts 'expectations' and 'reality' side by side is pretty much me every time I have a crush … I think it sums up that he's shy, a bit insecure and always wondering what he did wrong, those are things girls do way more than guys.
MARK: I loved the dancing scene, I think it was a great way to show that happiness you feel when you've just met someone … I haven't danced but

I do remember walking down Stoke Newington Road smiling to everyone when [his partner's name] and I had just been on like our second date.

MARTHA: The feeling I get watching the movie again after so long is that like Tom is a bit girly … from the way he's shown crying, he's the one who gets really upset when Summer breaks it up and he's the one who's shown all mopey … isn't that the way girls act on romcoms?

BENJAMÍN: Usually, yes, what do you think of having a guy do that in the film?

MARTHA: I guess it's ok, but I personally do not like men like that.

BENJAMÍN: Why?

MARTHA: It kinda irritates me, you know? I like it when guys just mark their territory and confidence is just sexy.

BIANCA: JGL is amazing in here, his acting really makes you believe his pain, he not only shows his feelings, I feel he's actually feeling them … I think many women now prefer someone with at least a bit of a feminine side because it makes relationships better.

BENJAMÍN: How so?

BIANCA: I think because men like these are more understanding of women and how we feel … yeah, and it makes communication easier, if he never shows emotions, it just becomes a huge wall you can't jump [over].

EMMA: that expectation and reality split screen is just genius. I loved that they show a guy also does something I think goes through women's head all the time when we are crushing on somebody … oh and those bits with all the films they are replaying.<line space>

HENDRIK: Tom is in a journey to learn to stop idealising women and all the film within film scenes show us that … it's kind of like an internal monologue he has to the tone of other films … the film presents him as believing in love instead of being cynical and all macho and I think that's what makes it so real for me, the fact he cries, gets depressed and all the things that come with falling in love and heartbreak, that's something everyone can relate to and it's very honest.

These excerpts encapsulate the most significant aspects of Tom's persona. Beginning with Martha ('Tom's a bit girly …'), nine other participants voiced a similar discontent with Tom's feminised masculinity. Another participant, Lucille, a 35-year-old professional working in media, claimed he was not 'husband material' and suggested he 'should have stopped whining, manned up and get the girl'. These readings of Tom suggest that not only is a feminised masculinity competing against a more classically virile alpha masculinity, showing emotions is seen as emasculating. As Connell suggests (2006), 'the project of having an open, non-assertive self risks having no self at all' (p. 136). On the other hand, positive perspectives of this feminisation constantly marked one of the two the most iconic sequences of the film: a dance parade Tom does on his way to work after being with Summer (Mark: 'it was a great way to show that happiness you feel when you've just met someone …') – a homage to *Ferris Bueller's Day Off* (Hughes, 1986) – and a split screen of 'expectations vs reality' of a party, hosted by Summer, Tom attends after they break up (Jeanine: 'that scene that puts "expectations" and "reality" side by side is pretty much me every time I have a crush.' Emma: '… is just genius'). The plot twist contained in the latter is that this party turns out to be Summer's engagement, the reality side, compared with a rekindling of the romance between the two in the expectations side.

Romantic affordances consist of practices, affects, ideas, tensions between the everyday and ideal, hopes and frustrations of the lover. The relationship between the imaginary, the past and the real is full of mismatching scenarios that feed into one another. In these two scenes, fictional character Tom's romantic imagination clouds his perspective on the cinematic 'real'. Particularly during the dance sequence, his lack of awareness of the rules of romance are highlighted when he expresses the bliss of his new romance in such an over-the-top manner that it undercuts the moment in the previous scene where they have sex for the first time, and Summer tells him she wants to keep it casual. This is reminiscent of Dean in *Blue Valentine*, who, because of his persona as a hopeless romantic, is not only youthful, but also doomed to fail. But whereas in *Blue Valentine* the possibility of learning is closed, Tom's naiveté only requires mending. The dance sequence then represents the lover's romantic idealisation of the loved one, one cut off from 'the real' and which the film is gently satirising. The split-screen scene furthers this, in such a way that it not only forecloses the imaginary, but also the romantic.

Here is where Tom's feminised persona shifts to a classic masculinity of pragmatism, cynicism and disbelief in romantic love and relationships. Again, *Annie Hall* (Allen, 1977) used a similar device during the scene where Alvy and Annie discuss with the psychiatrist their relationship and sex life. But whereas in *Annie Hall* it is a mismatch of perspectives and sexuality is a primary concern, *(500) DoS* makes full use of the internal monologue that is in constant motion in the lover's head and the overarching theme is romantic love. This is evident in the connection participants like Jeanine ('Tom for me is like my soulmate of how I fall in love … that scene that puts "expectations" and "reality" side by side is pretty much me every time I have a crush') and Emma ('I loved that they show a guy also does something I think goes through women's head all the time when we are crushing on somebody') make with Tom's idealisation of romance. These participants positively highlight that what they think is a woman's way of behaving during romance is showcased through the ruminations of a man. Furthermore, as Hendrik ('Tom is in a journey …') and Bianca's ('… he not only shows his feelings, I feel he's actually feeling them …') complementary interventions suggest, Tom's journey, through his shortcomings and failures, provides a glimpse at a romantic naiveté that is not usually portrayed through a male character. The appeal for audiences of these two sequences that highlight Tom as idealistic, naive, emotional, romantically ignorant and heartbroken is that they are portrayed from the point of view of Tom's psyche, heightening the connection to one's own personal romantic failures and excesses. This is evident in the connection Hendrik finds with the character, as it is in the vulnerability of Tom that he pins his enjoyment of the film. Bianca highlights that a feminised Tom/man is better suited for relationships as they are more open to intimate communication.

This is not to say that this narrative champions completely progressive and gender equal values, as evidenced in its ending. Rather, the fragmented narrative creates a possible semiotic interpretation of these traits as 'transcending' genders, if ever so briefly.

In the past 30 years, romantic comedies have represented female characters as the ones prone to such idealisation whereas men are seen, at least initially, as more pragmatic and *in the know* of dating and relationship rules (Alberti, 2013b; Evans & Deleyto, 1998) like in *Bridget Jones* (Maguire, 2001), *Green Card* (Weir, 1990), *Pretty Woman* (Marshall, 1990), *You've Got Mail* (Ephron, 1998) and *Sleepless in Seattle* (Ephron, 1993). In films like *Forgetting Sarah Marshall* (Stoller, 2008), *Roxanne* (Schepisi, 1987), *Say Anything* (Crowe, 1989) and *She's Out of My League* (Smith, 2010), where the male lead is portrayed as the idealising one or clumsy one, this idealisation or ineptitude in love is forged as the impasse he must overcome in order to be with the loved one. Thus, whether through physical, mental or emotional tests, the male lead must prove himself masculine enough. Kathleen Rowe (1995) argues that:

> the intermingling of romantic comedy and melodrama evident in these films should come as no surprise, given the thematic and structural similarities between the two genres. Linked by common ideologies of gender, romantic comedy and melodrama are, after all, the primary narrative forms available for telling the stories of women's lives ... What is more surprising, however – and disturbing – is the increasing use of melodrama to tell the story of men's lives and male suffering – and to tell it straight. Underlying the seemingly innocuous fantasies of these recent comedies is another, darker scenario that recasts the story of the struggle for women's rights into a melodrama of male victims and female villains. This scenario not only recuperates areas of culture traditionally associated with femininity to use *against* women, but, as a conceptual structure, it also extends well beyond the local Cineplex.
>
> (p. 185)

Rowe speaks of films she terms as 'post-classical romantic comedies' – films of the late 1970s up until the early 1990s – where men's romantic path was at the expense of the women around them like in *Pretty Woman*. For her, the use of melodramatic elements in romantic comedies not only permits the male to be feminised, it bestows on him the 'authority' to instruct women about romantic love, relationships and femininity. While this position was tenable for what she terms as post-classical romantic comedies, I would argue that *(500) DoS* and the other romantic comedies discussed here present a slightly different environment of gender roles in the genre. I concede that like in Rowe's analysis, in *(500) DoS* Tom's centrality turns the possibility of learning/teaching into one where masculinity is transcendental and femininity immanent, fixed if only because Summer's change of heart in regards to marriage and love, because it happens off-screen, is perfunctory and subservient of Tom's. The recuperation of masculinity is at the expense of the fixation of femininity. This fixed characteristic of femininity reifies a heteronormative view of femininity subservient to patriarchal authority. However, as I argued above, participants of my project expressed disbelief and discomfort at the ending of Summer's story. Yet, they also appreciated her maturity, strong will and self-assured nature.

The problem with Rowe's analysis of the shift in romantic comedies is that it fixates the spectator in a single-sex parallel gender identification, leaving no space for multiple identifications and positions. I contend that the feminised man of the romantic comedies discussed here is a form of hegemonic heterosexual sensitive masculinity – competing for hegemonic position – that has appropriated certain traits associated with femininity, but not at the expense of the woman. This competition and appropriation are brought about by a heterosexual sensitivity of some men. In romance, this is expressed in the recognition that the demands of contemporary intimacy also apply to men. It is because these demands are novel to men but a long-standing demand of women that romantic comedies have been centred around men's journeys. I will illustrate the difference between my contention with *(500) DoS* and Rowe's critique of 'post-classical romantic comedies' through a cursory comparison with the role women play in beta-male and bromance Apatow-style of romantic comedies. In *Knocked Up* (Apatow, 2007), the two women (Katherine Heigl and Leslie Mann) are frustrated, domineering, career-minded professionals. The men (Seth Rogen and Paul Rudd) are laid-back, weed-smoking unambitious young adults looking to escape the controlling ways of the women. During an escapade to Las Vegas – triggered by the break-up of both couples – and while during the influence of psychedelic mushrooms, the men decide to ask for forgiveness in their respective relationships. One of them is turned down (Seth Rogen). After a discussion with his father, he 'becomes' a man. This involves changing jobs, organising his apartment to make room for the baby and solving the problems that present themselves during the delivery of the baby. During this time, his ex-partner is refused entry to a nightclub because of her pregnancy. The male-centred focus, the marginalisation of the female and some of the narrative elements that signal the male lead's growth are repeated in both *Knocked Up* and *(500) DoS*. There are, however, substantive differences: the female lead of *Knocked Up* ends up moving in with the male and their new-born. This is after slowly realising that she belongs in a household with him and the baby. Furthermore, in the climax of the film, she apologises for not recognising that he's *truly* a man and the right one for her. Second, the growth of the male lead is enabled here by a larger patriarchal authority, the father of the male lead. The ending of the film highlights the male lead's newly found aggressive, assertive masculinity to which the women declare to be impressed by. The script of *Knocked Up* is, despite its gimmick of the 'average Joe getting the beautiful woman', a classic script of subordinating the feminine to the authoritarian patriarch. The male lead here showcases none of the feminine traits audiences praised about Tom in *(500) DoS*. Rather, the emphasis of this character lies in his ability to provide for his new family. This idea of man-as-provider is exactly the type of hegemonic masculinity that reinforces the idea that a man's role in a romantic relationship is to provide for his 'dependants' and nothing else. This, in turn, reinforces the idea of caregiving and domesticity as the role of women. *(500) DoS* provides, instead, the possibility of considering a new type of masculinity that does not necessarily have to be portrayed as superior to the feminine.

Not only that, but as Connell (1998) suggests, borrowing from Gramsci, it is possible for hegemony to be a positive force. Gramsci recognised that hegemony is never complete because the alliances that made it possible in the first place were under constant threat of being replaced by others. In the context of masculinity and romantic comedies, John Alberti (2013b) suggests that such a reconfiguration is taking place. He points out, in line with David Shumway (2003), that in the romantic comedies of the 1970s, the common thread of gender roles would be the male search for his own recognition of his need of intimacy while the female searches for autonomy. In contemporary romantic comedies, the marginalisation of the female could be read as a triumph of the recognition of her autonomy. This would be too early of a call, as films like *Knocked Up* (2007) would be eager to remind us. Rather, the continued focus on this new project of masculinity highlights how problematic it has become. Intimacy as a discourse of relationships that gives primacy to a deep, constant self-disclosure is, as Lauren Berlant (1998, 2000, 2007, 2008) suggests, a discourse of and on the feminine. She suggests that 'to rethink intimacy is to appraise how we have been and how we live and how we might imagine lives that make more sense than the ones so many are living' (2000, p. 6).

So, on the one hand, the incursion of intimacy signals the potential for more egalitarian relationships. On the other, it contains the destabilisation of the masculine by adding a feminine element to it. This double openness of intimacy requires men to learn and adapt scripts of self-disclosure and emotional attachment that have long been associated with femininity while recognising the irreducible character of those he's intimate with. No longer is it certain *he* will get the girl. This contrasts with the alpha male of classic romantic comedies, whose laconic character was part of his rugged charm, which serve to mythologise the idea of fixed gender separation in the genre (women talk, men do). In contemporary romantic comedies, the question of a woman's autonomy is sidestepped in many ways, though the films here discussed do provide female character with different degrees of such, and the problem has become that, as Berlant (2000) says, 'virtually no one knows how to do intimacy' (p. 2). Romantic comedies in the 1970s, 1980s and 1990s did not know either, but championed the idea that *as long as you communicated, somehow*, it would be possible to get to marriage or self-fulfilment. The films discussed here, I argue, portray some limits of communication, of intimacy. They do so by presenting characters who are oblivious to the rules. The anxiety and instability that not knowing produces takes on the form of misogyny, homophobia, male anxiety and other ideologies of discrimination in bromances and beta-male comedies (see Alberti, 2013a, 2013b; Deleyto, 2003; Greven, 2011). Furthermore, women and their struggles continue to be marginalised in favour of showcasing male anxiety. However, in their flawed way, romantic comedies can also portray that the ambivalence and ambiguity of intimacy is a journey not just of women. Thus, while I recognise the gender asymmetry still pervading the genre of romantic comedies, representations of masculinities like that of Tom or the other male leads can be helpful to construct less toxic notions of masculinity and relationships.

Notes

1 Taken from https://supervalentthought.com/2012/06/03/the-book-of-love-is-sad-and-boring-no-one-can-lift-the-damn-thing/
2 Taken from https://www.rottentomatoes.com/m/don_jon and http://www.boxofficemojo.com/movies/?page=intl&id=donjon.htm
3 The film also makes use of different timelines as a screenplay and narrative device. That is why we only see this death towards the end of the film.
4 It also reinforces the responsibility of this project to nuance, contextualise and circumscribe claims.
5 Giddens' concept (and my critique and use of it) is from and to a Western, urban, literate society. In many parts of the world, marriage still operates as a social contract and relationships are closely monitored, controlled and enforced by familial (kinship), societal, economic, and religious factors, affiliations and institutions.
6 This is so because even though women have gained much ground towards self-determination, they continue to be pegged down to their relationship with men, defined (at least partially) by it. Men, on the other hand, enjoy the flexibility of being celebrated either by their success elsewhere and by either their dedication to a relationship or lack thereof.
7 *Clueless* (Heckerling, 1995), another teenage romantic comedy, does end up in a wedding, but not the main character's one. Though remaining single, Alicia Silverstone's character ends up sharing a kiss with her romantic interest.

References

Alberti, J. (2013a). "I love you, man": bromances, the construction of masculinity, and the continuing evolution of the romantic comedy. *Quarterly Review of Film and Video*, 30, 159–172.
Alberti, J. (2013b). *Masculinity in the contemporary romantic comedy: gender as genre*. Routledge.
Apatow, J. (2007). Knocked Up. Universal Pictures.
Bauman, Z. (2003). *Liquid love: on the frailty of human bonds*. Polity Press.
Beck, U., & Beck-Gernsheim, E. (1995). *The normal chaos of love*. Polity Press.
Bell, D., & Binnie, J. (2000). *The sexual citizen: queer politics and beyond*. Polity Press.
Berlant, L. G. (1998). Intimacy: a special issue. *Critical Inquiry*, 24(2), 281–288. https://doi.org/10.1086/448875.
Berlant, L. G. (2000). *Intimacy*. University of Chicago Press.
Berlant, L. G. (2007). Nearly utopian, nearly normal: post-Fordist affect in La Promesse and Roset...: EBSCOhost. *Public Culture*, 19(2), 273–301.
Berlant, L. G. (2008). *The female complaint: the unfinished business of sentimentality in American culture*. Duke University Press.
Berlant, L. G. (2012). *Desire/love*. punctum books.
Christensen, A.-D., & Jensen, S. Q. (2014). Combining hegemonic masculinity and intersectionality. *NORMA: Nordic Journal for Masculinity Studies*, 9(1), 60–75. https://doi.org/10.1080/18902138.2014.892289.

Cianfrance, D. (2010). *Blue Valentine*. The Weinstein Company.
Comer, L. (1974). *Wedlocked women*. Feminist Books.
Connell, R. W. (1998). R. W. Connell's 'Masculinities': reply. *Gender and Society*, 12(4), 474–477. http://www.jstor.org.gate3.library.lse.ac.uk/stable/190181?seq=3#page_scan_tab_contents.
Connell, R. W. (2000). *The men and the boys*. Polity Press.
Connell, R. W. (2006). *Masculinities*. Polity Press.
Crowe, C. (1989). Say Anything. 20th Century Fox.
Del Río, E. (2008). *Deleuze and the cinemas of performance: powers of affection*. Edinburgh University Press.
Deleyto, C. (2003). Between friends: love and friendship in contemporary romantic comedy. *Screen*, 44(2), 167–182.
Demetriou, D. Z. (2001). Connell' s concept of hegemonic masculinity: a critique. *Theory and Society*, 30(3), 337–361. https://doi.org/10.1023/A:1017596718715.
Ephron, N. (1993). *Sleepless in Seattle*. TriStar Pictures.
Ephron, N. (1998). *You've Got Mail*. Warner Bros. Pictures.
Evans, P., & Deleyto, C. (1998). *Terms of endearment: Hollywood romantic comedy of the 1980s and 1990s* (ed. P. W. Evans & C. Deleyto). Edinburgh University Press.
Giddens, A. (1992). *The transformation of intimacy: sexuality, love and eroticism in modern societies*. Polity Press.
Gondry, M. (2004). Eternal Sunshine of the Spotless Mind. Focus Features.
Greven, D. (2011). *Manhood in Hollywood from Bush to Bush*. University of Texas Press.
Heckerling, A. (1995). Clueless. Paramount Pictures.
Hogan, P. J. (1997). My Best Friend's Wedding. TriStar Pictures.
Hughes, P. (1986). Ferris Bueller's Day Off. Paramount Pictures.
Illouz, E. (1997). *Consuming the romantic utopia: love and the cultural contradictions of capitalism*. University of California Press.
Illouz, E. (2012). *Why love hurts: a sociological explanation*. Polity.
Johnson, P. (2012). *Love, heterosexuality, and society*. Routledge.
Jonasdottir, A. (1991). *Love power and political interests: towards a theory of patriarchy in contemporary Western societies*. University of Örebro.
Jonasdottir, A., &Ferguson, A. (2014). *Love: a question for feminism in the twenty-first century*. Routledge.
Krutnik, F. (1990). The faint aroma of performing seals: the "nervous" romance and the comedy of the sexes. *Velvet Light Trap: A Critical Journal of Film & Television*, 26, 57–72.
Maguire, S. (2001). Bridget Jones. Miramax Films.
Marshall, G. (1990). Pretty Woman. Buena Vista Pictures.
Mills, M. (2011). Beginners. Focus Features.
Nichols, B. (1981). *Ideology and the image*. Indiana University Press.
Radway, J. (1984). *Reading the romance: women, patriarchy and popular literature*. Verso.
Rowe, K. (1995). Melodrama and men in post-classical romantic comedy. In P. Kirkham & J. Thumim (eds), *Me, Jane: masculinity, movies, and women* (pp. 184–194). St. Martin's Press.
Schepisi, F. (1987). Roxanne. Columbia Pictures.
Shumway, D. R. (2003). *Modern love: romance, intimacy, and the marriage crisis*. New York University Press.
Smith, J. F. (2010). She's Out of My League. Paramount Pictures.
Stoller, N. (2008). Forgetting Sarah Marshall. Apatow Productions.

Studlar, G. (1985). Visual pleasure and the masochistic aesthetic. *Journal of Film and Video*, 37(2), 5–26.
Webb, M. (2009). *(500) Days of Summer*. Fox Searchlight Pictures.
Weir, P. (1990). Green Card. Buena Vista Pictures.
Wilkinson, E. (2012). Ties that blind: on not seeing (or looking) beyond 'the family.' In S. Hines & Y. Taylor (eds), *Sexualities: past reflections, future directions*. Palgrave Macmillan.
Wilkinson, E. (2013). Learning to love again: 'broken families', citizenship and the state promotion of coupledom. *Geoforum*, *49*, 206–213. https://doi.org/10.1016/j.geoforum.2013.02.012.
Wilkinson, E., & Bell, E. (2012). Ties that bind: on not seeing (or looking) beyond "the family." *Families, Relationships and Societies*, *1*(3), 423–429.

6 Conclusion

Introduction

One of the earliest problems I encountered in this project was that the initial formalistic conceptual framework I adopted was an ill-fit for the real-life exchanges I was having with interview participants, and failed to account for their emotional, narrative and personal investment in the films. The distance between my readings and theirs stemmed largely from the fact that I, like many textual analysts, was *overvaluing the role and symbolism of certain cinematic features*, taking them not necessarily for granted, but at least as 'obvious' to the assumed gaze (of all spectators). Of course, many audience participants are aware of symbolic elements in films and in their relationship with formal and technical characteristics. But I naively – or perhaps arrogantly, as many film studies scholars and textual analysts tend to do – assumed that this technical and formal knowledge would easily be translated and understood in terms of ideology, pleasure and realism. Had I stuck with my initial readings and compared them to the audiences' with more weight given to mine as the analyst, the analysis could easily have devolved into a hierarchic diatribe about who's 'right and aware' and who is an 'ideological dupe', or into banal commentary on the ideological regressiveness of contemporary romance. This would have been disastrous for a detailed piece of audience research in the 2010s; but it would also have shown up fault lines in textual analysis that many choose never to consider. Thus, while the textual analysis of films plays a big role in the findings herein presented, the role of audiences helping me shape such analysis cannot be overstated.

As such, three overarching ideas guided the project. On the one hand, I have loosely borrowed inspiration from Roland Barthes' *figures of love* (1990) to articulate the conceptual framework and the methodology. On the other hand, it has elucidated both continuities and changes in discourses of romantic love, focusing on the (re)production of hegemonic positions and interstices of contestation in areas such as gender, sexuality, social class, technology, intimacy and the body. Drawing inspiration from previous film audience research (Austin, 2002; Banaji, 2006; Iglesias Prieto, 2004), the films discussed here were selected based on their central themes on screen as well as their cultural half-life off screen. Finally, there is no easy, uni-directional relationship of meaning-making from the films to the audiences (and back), thus necessitating a recursive approach that accounted for the

DOI: 10.4324/9781003164289-7

potential 'messiness' of belief, interpretation, action and behaviour. Thus, I have been mainly concerned with how romantic aspirations, idea and behaviours in films are negotiated, articulated, contested and appropriated by the audiences for their own romantic identities, with an emphasis on gender and class.

With this in mind, I will weave the guiding principles of this book with the general findings as to consider the impact of the former on the latter. Then, I will summarise the findings of the book and draw some logical theoretical conclusions about the links between contemporary romantic films, class, gender, commoditisation and technology. Finally, I want to end with a personal and intellectual reflection of what I hope to have achieved, considering ways forward for future research.

While reviewing the many perspectives that have theorised and thought of romantic love, I argued that I found, and still find, the Marxist feminist conceptualisation of romantic love the most relevant to understand the changes and continuities of romantic love nowadays. As I argued in the first chapter,

> the starting point of the conceptualisation of romantic love here is the understanding that patriarchal, hetero-marital couple romantic love is the hegemonic ideology of love ... This ideology contains a gendered and class division of roles that has been constructed to privilege men's position subordinating and sub-valuing women, their emotions, care-giving, roles and demands. At the same time, the concept recognises the utopian, positive dimension that the pursuit of such romantic love holds for many women (and men). A feminist conceptualisation of love understands the ambivalence, potentially divergent, fragmentary and intersectional experience of this hegemonic romantic love and the counter-hegemonies that feminist and queer theories have pushed forward, theoretically and practically.
>
> (p. 45)

How, then, does this fit with researching love through its figures? I contend it fits rather well. To further highlight this, I will briefly discuss one of the most important figures of love, the happy ending. I argued that the burgeoning of an uncertain, ambiguous ending in some films and its normative reception from audiences speaks to the increased romantic *angst* in contemporary Western societies. From a biological-evolutionary point of view, where reproduction is viewed as the single most salient end-goal of all interpersonal associations, this angst makes little or no sense. Then, why is it that the 'happy ending' plays such a pivotal role to understand the romantic zeitgeist? Ideas are interesting things. They either adapt to the times or are bound to perish, only to be found in arcane volumes buried deep in libraries. Romantic love today demands an impossible task: the spontaneity of the first look and the meant-to-be story with an increasing rationalisation of emotional bonds. Films have always found ways to provide solutions to these impossible demands. Historically, the two solutions were happy marriage or tragic singlehood. Thus, while the prevalence of marriage as a hegemonic discursive element of romantic love is undeniable, both in cinema and for its audiences, the chink in its armour speaks of the many social changes that have become commonplace in romantic love. In an environment where romantic failures are more common than successes, the experience of singlehood (tragic or otherwise) is slowly losing some of its stigma.[1] Further, the frustrations of many women to deal with emotionally stunted men beget the questioning of the idea of a relationship. Finally, some people also wonder if other non-monogamous affective structures might better suit their needs and desires. On the other, I emphasise that the normativity of angst that surrounds romantic love is one very much still riddled with the yearning of the stable embrace of love. In my own words, 'even if the discourse of marriage, romantic love and relationships is unavoidably linked to that of neoliberal economic logics, it has not (yet, at least) been completely formed or devoured by them'. Thus, a part of ourselves wants the comfort of the happy ending, while the other is painfully aware of its difficulty. That's why ambiguous endings resonate so much with today's romantic audiences.

Unpacking further this example and extrapolating to the rest of the figures analysed herein, the use of this concept to break down film narratives has been advantageous on several grounds. As the work of Banaji (2006, 2007), Austin (2002), Barker (Barker & Austin, 2000; Barker & Brooks, 1998) and Iglesias-Prieto (2004) demonstrates, *audiences do not read the film as a unified and ideologically totalising whole*. Rather, pleasure, ideology, realism and fantasy are articulated through different aspects of a subject's intersectionality in competing, contradictory and, at times, ambiguous ways. Foregrounding one sequence or element of a film over another involves the fragmentation of the narrative. In so doing, it is possible to envision how different theoretical concerns, such as gender roles, class and gender identities, play out metonymically in these elements. Thus, choosing to base the study around fragments of the films as absorbed and reacted to by audiences also permits and eases the search for patterns and similarities in the discourses. However, this also means that other elements both in films and in a subject's intersectionality are overshadowed. This, of course, entails that any findings must be circumscribed and clearly delineate their limitations. The first and most striking substantive absence in this book is that of race. I recognise that an over-emphasis on gender and class is not enough to account for this absence. Neither is it enough to call for future research to be more attentive, theoretically, methodologically and analytically, to this axis. It is also necessary, as I have attempted, to highlight racialised perspectives on the topics discussed, where race can be seen playing a crucial role in the articulation of positions vis-à-vis a specific figure of love. Another element I have not dealt with is religion and its influence in the practice of romantic love, particularly given the religious-political conservative backlash against gender equality in many regions of the Global South.[2] A third element to which I would like to call attention for future research are rural areas. In the following paragraphs, I will outline other limitations as a way to recognise the circumscription of its findings.

Any qualitative research project that draws on one geographic area to produce data and knowledge (the borough of Hackney, East London, in this case) is susceptible to paying more attention to some subjects and neglecting others. One of the potential skews of this is an overrepresentation of a certain type of participant, something I tried to balance as much as possible by attempting to attract participants from different races, sexualities, professions, ages, class backgrounds and so on. Regardless, women's participation rates were higher than those of men. This would represent a major problem if I had, at any point, assumed that the findings are generalisable and representative of social demographics. However, that was never the intent of the project. Instead, I consider the subjectivities of the sampled audience as indicative of wider patterns in viewing and interpretation. The third, overarching point of consideration, is that choosing certain films, in this case independent films with more leeway in narrative terms than their big budget studio counterparts, also affects the figures of love discussed and *how* they are discussed.

In line with this, what other possible figures of love, pertinent to our contemporary socioeconomic, politic and cultural juncture, has this project not examined at length? And, how appropriate are films as vehicles to discuss these? Two topics missing here are sexual violence and gender inequality in emotional labour and care-giving (Marino, 2019). Given recent films such as *The Salesman* (Farhadi, 2016), *Elle* (Verhoeven, 2016), *Room* (Abrahamson, 2015), *Spotlight* (McCarthy, 2015) and *Nocturnal Animals* (Ford, 2016) as well as actors Casey Affleck's and Nate Parker's now publicised cases of sexual assault, I believe there is further exploration of nuanced and sensitive depictions of sexual violence to be done (see Bonino, 2019). To my reader, I provocatively ask: In the past five years, how many films have you watched that feature a complex character who is a single parent or a non-white gay woman or both? I highlight these two topics out of many to signal that the topics discussed here are not exhaustive of romantic love, intimacy and relationships and neither are the films. Further, the positions expressed by my participants are also contingent, primarily, on geographical proximity and schedule availability. None of this invalidates the findings of this study; it merely points to necessary circumscription in order to make sense of what has been achieved and what are possible divergent or similar paths forward. With this in mind, I move to the summary of the findings.

Affordances, expectations and commodified reality

When it comes to dating, the online world, far from being a place full of new possibilities, reproduces many of the sexist, racist and classist behaviours found elsewhere (Chappetta & Barth, 2016; Hall et al., 2010; Kaufmann, 2012; McGrath et al., 2016; Maclaran et al., 2005; Ong & Wang, 2015; Simanowski, 2016; Sweeney & Borden, 2009). The online, an arena full of promises, clashes with centuries and decades of romantic ideas, desires, prejudices, patriarchal practices and more. And even in a film like *Her*, a story about technology, love and loneliness gives way to discussions centuries old regarding female sexuality. I found that while the idea of love at first sight is still very much alive in my participants' online romantic activities, it is counteracted by mistrust or wariness some of my participants appeared to have about the *online* as a novel way of meeting one's romantic partner. The online does seem to have the potential to strengthen some women's control of their romantic identities, events and pace in online dating given the possibilities of becoming active pursuers of their romantic engagements.

Moreover, because the landscape of online dating is still fraught with incredibly sexist attitudes, many women develop tactics to navigate this hostile environment. These tactics range from time-management to visual cues to help them decide who to talk to and who to ignore. One of the main reasons these tactics are developed is because female sexuality is still highly surveilled, controlled and censored. I reflected on the practice of hooking up and its implications for demands made with regards to female chastity. Contrary to what one might expect, gender and age played no role in who espoused progressive or retrograde positions on women's sexuality and right to hook up. Significantly, while hooking up is a subject that the majority of participants link to online dating, recent films that touch on this topic, independent of establishing such a link, do not attempt to demonise or berate women's sexuality. Further, I highlighted the case of Esther in *Don Jon*, who was praised for her sexuality and the film's open depiction of it. Thus, using the concept of romantic affordances, I have argued that while the representations of female sexuality in romantic films , in the context of independent North American cinema, attempt representation in progressive ways, this progressive representation is not always received and articulated positively (or in liberal ways) by the audiences of these films. The frequent negative reception was related to two elements this project could not, for reasons already explained, delve deeper into: religion and race. It remains to be seen how this debate plays out in different contexts, cinematically and sample wise. This leads me to the conclusion that the siloed ideological attitudes and values within communities regarding romance, femininity and sexuality require sustained challenge alongside those coming from (mainstream or alternative) filmic and other media representation.

Commoditisation of love and self

In online dating, as Dröge and Voirol (2011) suggest:

> By the way they present the profiles of potential partners in exactly the same manner as items on eBay, Amazon or other shopping sites, with their complex search forms that allow to define the own preferences in mate selection with a precision unknown before, with the tools they offer to evaluate one's own market value and to enhance this value if possible – with all these elements borrowed from modern forms of consumerism and the economic sphere, they suggest a subject position which is very close to what we have outlined above as the main characteristics of a calculating subject in the realm of the market. It is the position of an economic agent who compares offers on a level of equivalence and tries to maximize his own interests. At the same time, it is the position of a self-marketing 'supplier' in a very competitive 'economy of attention'.
>
> (p. 346)

This form of commoditised self on offer and being 'browsed' is frowned upon because it is seen to be embedded in neoliberal economic and cultural logics. Supposedly, following the long-standing criticism of love as proposed by Plato, this involves the love of certain features and not of the person as a 'whole', heightened by the fact that in online dating, according to authors such as Zygmunt Bauman (2003), discarding and choosing new lovers becomes the 'norm', instead of building stable, deep relationships with *one* whole Other. This is a position that easily conflates the contemporary romantic landscape with an assumed narcissistic, object-loving tendency, and obviates the shifts in economic, professional, personal and economic conditions of romantic love, intimacy and relationships in the past few decades. As Lauren Berlant (2012) argues, 'The reduction of life's legitimate possibility to one plot is the source of romantic love's terrorizing, coercive, shaming, manipulative, or just diminishing effects – on the imagination as well as on practice' (p. 87). I have demonstrated that for many young people in contemporary East London, engaging in relationships is at odds with their economic survival and professional development; this makes the idea of a stable relationship, and its consumerist corollaries like a suburban house, car and children, not just unattainable but even undesirable. The conditions, attitudes and behaviours towards online dating are perhaps not identical across London let alone the rest of the England, Europe and the world, given that East London primarily attracts young people into the arts, media and cultural industries while also containing working-class whites and diasporas from the Caribbean, the Middle East and South East Asia. Thus, economic conditions can be seen to inflect both outcomes and desires significantly, even as certain films pose certain outcomes as desirable. At the same time, I recognise that this change has included, as Anthony Giddens (1992) and others argue (Bell & Binnie, 2000; Berlant, 2001; Johnson, 2012; Wilkinson & Bell, 2012), increased periods of sexual, sensuous and personal experimentation that are and should be understood as *modalities* of love. Crucially, this does not mean, despite the encroachment of economic rationality and neoliberal logics on romantic love, that the yearning and search for love and 'the One' has diminished compared to nostalgia-laden past decades; rather, there is an increased recognition of its difficulty.

Classed love

One of the main findings I have illustrated is the still strong link between social class and romantic love. To highlight this, I analysed several sequences, in particular from *Blue Valentine* and *Once*. The first sequence is the studio rental in *Once*. In this sequence, the Girl, a Czech immigrant in Dublin who sells flowers, helps the Guy secure a weekend in a music studio to record a demo, paying £2,000 for it. In addition, she helps him build a band and practise his compositions. I argued, in line with Banaji's (2006) findings, that working-class audiences' responses to this sequence, as in the case of *Blue Valentine*, are informed first by their classed subjectivity before their gendered or romantic one. In so doing, the possibilities of emotional realism and pleasure are, at that moment, negatively affected and limited by class knowledge, which breaks the possibility for suspension of disbelief. Further, in this sequence, the platonic and idealistic romance of the film undermines the grim negative affects of an intersectional experience of love: to be poor in contemporary London or Dublin is to eschew even the possibility of grand romantic gestures such as that made by Girl.

Second, I focused on the motel getaway sequence in *Blue Valentine*. In this film, the main characters, Dean and Cindy, are embodiments of two classed discourses of love: one of youthful, working-class romantic love and the other of pragmatic, middle-class, adult intimacy. I argued that the sequence of the motel getaway brings to the fore the tension between economic and emotional labour in contemporary relationships. This is largely because the discourse of romantic love is at odds with the dialogic, aspirational and self-disclosing practices of contemporary discourses of intimacy. This tension is part of the larger cultural competences subjects require in order to act romantically *appropriately* (see Illouz, 1997, 2012). In the context of both *Blue Valentine* and its audiences, the main romantic practice is that of dating, which follows one overarching rule: that of the liminoid moment. In other words, a romantic act is felt and considered as such as long as it separates the lovers from their everyday and from their material conditions. Because the motel getaway is clearly a working-class romantic proposal that fails to achieve such distancing and in fact plunges Cindy and Dean deeper into their class antagonism, audiences' responses to this sequence are, I argue, class-informed. These responses position them vis-à-vis the perceived *lack of appropriateness* of the motel getaway where their own romantic cultural competences are the main axis from which they read Dean's working-class romanticism, emotionally and economically. This works both amongst audiences, and in the represented world of the film, to dispel the idea that cross-class romantic love conquers all. Having a romantic partner from the working classes is, in this case, almost as much of a barrier to long-term love as having a partner who drinks or is unfaithful.

Teleology of romance?

Alongside the previous finding, I have argued that North American romantic films have undergone two major narrative and ideological shifts. One of the main shifts I identified is a concern with the representation of masculinities. The second is the increased popularity of the ambiguous/unhappy ending. This, I argued, is closely related to a suffused, normative anxiety over the teleology of romantic love, intimacy and relationships and the social and individual promises they used to hold. These cannot be disconnected from the economic and cultural effects of neoliberal policies and logics. Yet it is important to note that the effects these have had in East London and on its inhabitants are most likely not identical to those in Barcelona or Mumbai. As I have mentioned in Chapter 4, attitudes towards marriage have been steadily changing in Britain,[3] and for many young people, relationships are at odds with their economic survival and professional development. Further, I have highlighted that, compared with the nervous romances of the 1970s where marriage and self-fulfilment still held a pivotal role in maintaining the utopian dimension of romance, contemporary North American romantic narratives have, in some cases, ditched the end goal of marriage. This can be explained by the fact that marriage, in the West, has gradually lost its significance as a social mobility tool for many, becoming rather a way of sustaining and reinforcing the status quo.[4] Rather, the reality effect of these narratives lies in their meandering exploration of *romantic anxiety* itself, sometimes leading even to a withholding of any concrete promise of long-term stability or resolution. This anxiety is rooted in a deep questioning of what it is that relationships offer. I demonstrated this in Chapter 6, analysing the endings of some of the most successful North American romantic films of the past years, including *Eternal Sunshine of the Spotless Mind* and highlighting the 'extreme' case of *Blue Valentine*. The latter's ending and the audiences' reception and articulation of it speak to the contrast between the erstwhile 'crisis of marriage' argued to have fuelled the romances of the 1970s and 1980s to the diminished expectations and connections between romantic love and marriage in the twenty-first century, insofar as East London is concerned. Whether this is tenable in more progressive or conservative areas of England and elsewhere, particularly in the Global South, is something that remains to be explored.

This is tempered by wildly successful utopian platonic romantic films such as *Once* and in a film like *(500) Days of Summer*, where both the anxiety and the utopia coexist. These two films, though containing reactionary endings, maintain the possibility of the utopian and potentially transgressive characteristics of love in late capitalist societies. I argue that these two contrasting narrative themes of utopia and transgression constitute the main, though clearly not the only, reasons why audiences still watch North American romantic films. Further, while the settings have changed, imaginative utopia and ideological transgression are constitutive elements of the success of contemporary romantic films, which can be traced back as far as a tale like Romeo and Juliet. Importantly, the emotional realism and the verisimilar in the films – expressed through the recognition of the contingency and frailty of romantic love – coexist with the genre's ultimate affirmation of romantic love. This, however, as I have argued in all chapters, is still confined to hetero-normative-coupled romantic love within circumscribed class and racial boundaries, with little to no envisioning of other modalities of love or society.

Masculinities

As I mentioned above, in the past years, North American romantic films as a genre have become increasingly (pre)occupied with the question: what role do men play in relationships? – as opposed, I suggest, to a question that vexed a whole genre of melodramas in the 1950s – what role can and do women and relationships play in changing or taming masculinity? – (Alberti 2013a, 2013b; Greven, 2011). Early in the 2000s, Deleyto (2003) identified that *friendship* had become a possible alternative to the heterosexual romantic couple, suggesting this was to do with the loss of vitality of heterosexual desire. Following this, two responses to this have been the subgenre of 'bromances' and 'beta-male comedies' pioneered in Hollywood by Judd Apatow with films like *The 40-Year-Old Virgin* (2005) and *Superbad*

(2007). In the bromance, the heterosexual couple and their journey are replaced by a male couple that share a 'homo-confused' bond that mixes homophilia, homophobia, misogyny and the male's journey to recover his *maleness* in order to enter a viable heterosexual relationship. The 'beta-male comedies' emphasise the male's journey towards a hegemonic masculinity, dealing on the way with the dangerous femininity, and homoerotism that melodramatises him and threatens his sexuality. In these subgenres, women tend to be marginalised and, in a sense, masculinised and misogynised.

In this context of masculinity in crisis, I explored the appeal for audiences of *(500) Days of Summer* (2009), focusing on its portrayal of masculinity. I argued that despite the film's reactionary ending and the male-centred approach to the narrative, Summer's agency was praised by some participants, with others denouncing her ending as a wife, which they viewed as a mismatch with the seemingly ambiguous future foreshadowed early in the film. The character of Tom, who starts as an idealistic romantic and becomes cynical after his break-up, recovers his feminised (and classed) masculinity thanks to a final meeting with Summer. I have argued that this journey and the representation of Tom's masculinity highlights two crucial differences to other feminised masculinities. First, Tom's feminised persona, which I linked to Connell's (2006) concept of 'heterosexual sensitivity', is one that highlights that the demands of intimacy – self-interrogation, self-disclosure, and emotional communication – are no longer made on women alone, but also apply to men, at least in urban metropolises in the contemporary West. This, in turn, reinforces the anxiety, frailty and uncertainty of contemporary romances I mentioned in the section above, because in its recognition of the limits of intimacy, male heterosexual desire is no longer assured as sufficient to ensure romantic success. Thus, I have argued that this specific representation of a feminised masculinity attempts to compete for a hegemonic position of masculinity but that, in contrast to previous versions of feminised masculinity, it is not deployed at the expense of female characters and woman per se (see Rowe, 1995). This is important because, as Connell (2006) and a romantic film like *The Ugly Truth* (2009) suggest, alongside this sensitivity, there is also an ideological and discursive backlash against feminised masculinities, and an expressed longing for hyper-masculine virile masculinities.

Achievements and ways forward

I analysed five contemporary North American romantic films and their audiences through group and individual interviews in the working-class but recently gentrified borough of Hackney, London. By choosing films which were critically and popularly acclaimed, I sought to explore not just the reasons for their success, but also what precisely their resonance is with the audiences' romantic identities, affects and experiences. In order to nuance my analysis, I tried to diversify the sample of those interviewed as much as possible, though as expected, the majority of participants were women. Through discourse analysis, I highlighted patterns, continuities and changes in both representation and reception of romantic love narratives. Significantly, one of the ways forward to complement this research is to balance, contrast and compare how the findings presented herein differ from those of films produced in different sociopolitical and cultural contexts, cinematographically, geopolitically and romantically, and to compare the readings and values of audiences that articulate their romantic identities alongside them. Another way forward would be to explore how audiences elsewhere – in rural areas, outside the UK and outside Europe – respond to the kinds of North American cinematic representations of romantic love that I have captured in this book.

I sought to emphasise the importance of the socioeconomic and cultural contexts of romantic love in which these films were made and in which audiences' read and articulated their responses. One of the implications of this is the necessity to mitigate critiques of the apparently hegemonic commoditisation of romantic love and self with an understanding that people, especially younger people, navigate a romantic, economic and social environment where the promises of romantic love continuously erode and are questioned on many levels. Part of this questioning involves a widening of the modalities of love. My contribution in this regard has been to further elucidate how the ideological hegemony of heteromarital coupled romantic love is both contested and reproduced in cinematic representations and through audiences' readings. In this push and pull, I have emphasised the progressive possibilities envisioned in Anglophone popular cinema while recognising that in many regards it is still a highly conservative medium. It is in this recognition that one of the most intriguing possible ways forward opens up. Plenty of literature attests to the fact that in order to speak about romantic love, intimacy and relationships cinema is not necessary. However, as I argue, cinema provides a powerful medium through which to articulate rich discussions of different figures of love and their ideological baggage. Thus, in further research about romantic love and in educational or vocational discussions of passion, romance, relationships and sexuality, I would strongly suggest using people's responses and positionings vis-à-vis sequences alongside sequences from popular, independent and arthouse films outside the North American circuit of production and reception, which openly contest the arbitrariness of monogamy, the hierarchies of love and other topics.

Further, by pursuing an empirical analysis of ideologies and discourses of romantic love and its main medium of representation, cinema, I have shown that if one is to pursue any form of intellectual and emotional engagement with love, it is of paramount importance to go beyond armchair analysis and to engage with the ways in which people practise, feel and think about it. As I accrued more and more perspectives on love, intimacy and relationships, it became clearer to me that the allure of positions – both lay and scholarly – that berate contemporary romantic love (and surreptitiously champion marriage as *the* way of love) lies in their absence of practical relevance or context. Perhaps not coincidentally, most of these treatises have been written by men. One, written by Laura Kipnis (2003), stands out in her recognition of its provocative perspective to encourage empirical and impassioned research to balance hers. It's far too easy to believe 'Others' are too confounded by the neoliberal, competitive and measure-driven economic and cultural logics of late-stage capitalism to 'truly' experience love. What's unbelievably hard is to continue believing in something that requires so much rethinking, reconsideration and reflecting on its promises so that its allure is kept alive while its coercive powers wane.

Notes

1 Recent studies suggest that single women report higher levels of happiness than those in a relationship while studies have shown for a while that married men are happier than single men. See https://www.theguardian.com/lifeandstyle/2019/may/25/women-happier-without-children-or-a-spouse-happiness-experthttps://www.businessinsider.com/why-single-is-better-according-to-science-2018-2?utm_content=bufferdbf8a&utm_medium=social&utm_source=facebook.com&utm_campaign=buffer-biuk&r=UK&IR=T, https:// www.economist.com/special-report/2017/11/23/the-state-of-marriage-as-an-institution
2 See https://www.nytimes.com/2017/03/20/world/asia/duterte-same-sex-marriage-philippines.html, http://larepublica.pe/impresa/sociedad/842614-un-intenso-debate-ideologia-de-genero-o-educacion-integral, and http://www.eltiempo.com/politica/proceso-de-paz/equidad-e-ideologia-de-genero-en-el-acuerdo-de-paz-34069
3 http://www.bsa.natcen.ac.uk/latest-report/british-social-attitudes-30/personal-relationships/marriage-matters.aspx
4 See https://www.economist.com/special-report/2017/11/23/the-state-of-marriage-as-an-institution

References

Abrahamson, L. (2015). Room. A24.
Austin, T. (2002). *Hollywood, hype and audiences: selling and watching popular film in the 1990s*. Manchester University Press.
Banaji, S. (2006). *Reading "Bollywood" the young audience and Hindi films*. Palgrave Macmillan.
Barker, M., & Austin, T. (2000). *From Antz to Titanic: reinventing film analysis*. Pluto Press.
Barker, M., & Brooks, K. (1998). *Knowing audiences: Judge Dredd, its friends, fans and foes*. University of Luton Press.
Barthes, R. (1990). *A lover's discourse: fragments*. Penguin.
Bauman, Z. (2003). *Liquid love: on the frailty of human bonds*. Polity Press.
Bell, D., & Binnie, J. (2000). *The sexual citizen: queer politics and beyond*. Polity Press.
Berlant, L. G. (2001). Love: a queer feeling. In T. Dean & C. Lane (eds), *Homosexuality and Psychoanalysis* (pp. 431–452). University of Chicago Press.
Berlant, L. G. (2012). *Desire/love*. punctum books.
Bonino, S. (2019). *Nature and culture in intimate partner violence: sex, love and equality*. Routledge.
Chappetta, K. C., & Barth, J. M. (2016). How gender role stereotypes affect attraction in an online dating scenario. *Computers in Human Behavior*, 63, 738–746. https://doi.org/10.1016/j.chb.2016.06.006.
Connell, R. W. (2006). *Masculinities*. Polity Press.

Deleyto, C. (2003). *Between friends: love and friendship in contemporary romantic comedy.* Screen, 44(2), 167–182.
Dröge, K., & Voirol, O. (2011). Online dating: the tensions between romantic love and economic rationalization. *Journal of Family Research, 23*(3), 337–357.
Farhadi, A. (2016). The Salesman. Memento Film Distribution.
Ford, T. (2016). Nocturnal Animals. Focus Features.
Giddens, A. (1992). *The transformation of intimacy: sexuality, love and eroticism in modern societies.* Polity Press.
Greven, D. (2011). *Manhood in Hollywood from Bush to Bush.* University of Texas Press.
Hall, J. A., Park, N., Song, H., & Cody, M. J. (2010). Strategic misrepresentation in online dating: The effects of gender, self-monitoring, and personality traits. *Journal of Social and Personal Relationships*, 27(1), 117–135. https://doi.org/10.1177/0265407509349633.
Iglesias Prieto, N. (2004). Gazes and cinematic readings of gender: danzon and its relationship to its audience. *Discourse*, 26(1 & 2), 173–193.
Illouz, E. (1997). *Consuming the romantic utopia: love and the cultural contradictions of capitalism.* University of California Press.
Illouz, E. (2012). *Why love hurts: a sociological explanation.* Polity Press.
Johnson, P. (2012). *Love, heterosexuality, and society.* Routledge.
Kaufmann, J.-C. (2012). *Love online.* Polity Press.
Kipnis, L. (2003). *Against love: a polemic.*
Maclaran, P., Broderick, A., Theadopoulis, A., Goulding, C., & Saren, M. (2005). The commodification of romance? Developing relationships online. *Journal Finanza, Marketing e Produzione*, XXII(3), 41–47.
Marino, P. (2019). *The philosophy of sex: an opinionated introduction.* Routledge.
McCarthy, T. (2015). Spotlight. Open Road.
McGrath, A. R., Tsunokai, G. T., Schultz, M., Kavanagh, J., & Tarrence, J. A. (2016). Differing shades of colour: online dating preferences of biracial individuals. *Ethnic and Racial Studies*, 39(11), 1920–1942. https://doi.org/10.1080/01419870.2015.1131313.
Ong, D., & Wang, J. (2015). Income attraction: an online dating field experiment. *Journal of Economic Behavior & Organization*, 111, 13–22. https://doi.org/10.1016/j.jebo.2014.12.011.
Rowe, K. (1995). Melodrama and men in post-classical romantic comedy. In P. Kirkham & J. Thumim (eds), *Me, Jane: masculinity, movies, and women* (pp. 184–194). St. Martin's Press.
Simanowski, R. (2016). *Data love: the seduction and betrayal of digital technologies.* Columbia University Press.
Sweeney, K. A., & Borden, A. L. (2009). Crossing the line online: racial preference of internet daters. *Marriage & Family Review*, 45(6–8),740–760. https://doi.org/10.1080/01494920903224335.
Verhoeven, P. (2016). Elle. SBS Distribution.
Wilkinson, E., & Bell, E. (2012). Ties that bind: on not seeing (or looking) beyond "the family." *Families, Relationships and Societies*, 1(3), 423–429.

Index

active audience, notion of 68–69
active masculinity 139
Adams, P. 23
affordances 91, 153–154; component of 90–91; definition of 90
agape 18, 24, 32–33, 35–36
Ahmed, S. 26
Alasuutari, P. 57
Alberti, J. 64, 146
alienation 2, 20–22, 24, 98
All about Love (2000) 29–30
Allen, R. C. 43
Allen, W. 43
aloneness 21–22
A Lover's Discourse: Fragments (Barthes) 2, 16
Althusser, L. 38–40
altruism 27
Amazon 84, 154
ambiguity 26, 41, 130, 135–137, 146
ambivalence 26, 36–37, 45, 60, 84, 136–137, 146, 151
amour passion 32–33, 133–134
anger 26
Ang, I. 40, 60, 66, 107, 119
anthropological arguments 94
anthropology of conflict 1
anti-hegemonic discourse 128
anxiety 33, 90, 140–147
anxious romances 64
Apatow, J. 63, 145, 157–158
appropriateness 106, 122–123, 156
Aristotle 56
articulation of identity 57
The Art of Loving (Fromm) 20–21
assertive masculinity 145
atomisation 17
attachment love 18

audience research: new orientations in 68–69; new (studies of) romance 69–72
audiences 44, 53–57, 69; emotional and affective participation 8; emotional experiences 106; empirical interest in 53; identification 70; incorporation/resistance paradigm and ethnographic turn 57–59; interpretation 8, 70; interviews of 4; pleasures 70; relationship with romantic media 64; romantic 2, 7–8, 64–68, 158; today's 72–74; women's films and melodrama to bromance 59–64
Aumont, J. 55
Austin, T. 4, 53, 69–70

Badiou, A. 22–24
Bakhtin, M. 42
Banaji, S. 53, 62, 70–71, 155–156
Barker, M. 8–9, 37
Barthes, R. 16, 42, 88, 150; list of fragments 16–17
Baudry, J. L. 38
Bauman, Z. 22–23, 35, 83, 155
Beauvoir, S. de 27–28
Beck-Gernsheim, E. 23
Beck, U. 23
beliefs: druidic 30; messiness of 150–151; in romantic love and relationships 138; in traditional ending 136–137
Berlant, L. 26–27, 146, 155
Berscheid, E. 17–18
beta-male comedies 157–158
Bhabha, H. 41
Blue Valentine (Cianfrance) 9, 104, 109–110, 122, 127–128, 130–136, 143, 155–156; interpersonal relationships in 125; production and characteristics of 105–106; readings of 115; romantic

drama 124; romantic sequence from 120
Borda, O. F. 6
Bourdieu, P. 7, 34, 67
Bowlby, J. 17
British cultural studies 40, 57
British masculinity 3
bromances 157–158; discrimination in 146; subgenre 140
Brooks, P. 40, 59
Butler, J. 41

capitalism 3; ideological thought on 22
care 21
Carr, D. 37
categorisation 17
catharsis 7
Cavell, S. 41–42
celluloid love 16–18 *see also* love; romantic love; eros and Plato 19–22; feminist and queer theories on 25–30; foundational myth of romantic love 30–32; Gramsci and counter-hegemony 39–40; historical and sociological approaches to 30; ideology 37–39; intimacy in contemporary sociological approaches 32–34; liminality and ideology 40–44; narcissism, identification and difference 22–25; projective identification 36–37; psychoanalytic theory and eros 18; romantic identity 35–36; self-commoditised love 34–35
censorship, of verisimilitude 56–57
characters: development 113; female 144; male 138; re-affirmative 134; relationships between 108; romantic 138–139
Chekhov, A. 85
chick flicks 8, 107
Christianity 18, 23
cinema 39, 44, 57 *see also* film; romantic films; historical materialist approach to 43; *vs.* 'real life' 8; sociological approaches to 55
cinema-going 43; practice of 43–44
cinematic representations 6
cinematographic verisimilitude 56
circuit of culture 58
class 7, 41, 116; endogamy 10; intersection of 9
classed love 155–156
classic masculinity 139, 141
coherence 17
Colombia 1; civil conflict 1; companies of 1; massacres 1; passion of 1
comedies: of remarriage 64; resilience of 8

commercial cinema, elements in 8 *see also* cinema
commodification of romance 83–87
commodified reality 153–154
commoditisation 151
companionate love/liking 18
compulsory monogamy 92–93
conflict: anthropology of 1; resolution 137
confluent love 133–134
Connell, R. W. 140, 142, 146, 158
connotation 6, 23, 58, 89, 93
consumer capitalism 113
consumerism 3, 61, 84; forms of 154
Consuming the Romantic Utopia: Love and the Cultural Contradictions of Capitalism (Illouz) 7, 34
contemporary dating, features of 85
contemporary intimacy 98, 145
contemporary relationships 10, 30, 34, 110, 114–115, 135–138, 156
contemporary romance: comedies 128–129; films 106, 151; ideological regressiveness of 150; ingrained process of 84; love 121–122; sensibility 133; uncertainty of 158
counter-hegemony 7, 39–40
coupledom 29, 106, 129, 136
Cowie, E. 55
crime drama 56
cross-class romances 112, 156
cultural alienation 98
cultural competences 7, 34–35, 40, 57, 113, 124, 156
culture, American forms of 66
cynicism 128, 132, 143

dating 7, 34, 84, 112, 144, 153–155; apps 3; contemporary 85; online *see* online dating
delay gratification 25
Deleyto, C. 62, 107, 133
denotation 58
Derné, S. 42
desire 31–33, 54, 97; activation of 85; of association 94; heterosexual 157–158; for object 19, 29; physical 62; privatisation of 31–32; sexual 99; transformation and 85
devotion 27, 36, 115
dialogical intimacy 89
Diamond, E. 41
disbelief 118, 139, 143; suspension of 118, 155–156

discipline's history 57
distance 7, 22, 31–32, 91, 93, 107, 124, 150
Doane, M. A. 53–54
domestic-outer spaces 124
domination 20, 26, 39, 141
drama *see also* melodrama: resilience of 8; romantic 59, 109, 124; sentimental 59
Dröge, K. 83, 154–155
druidic beliefs 30
Dyer, R. 64

eBay 154
The Ecological Approach to Visual Perception (Gibson) 90
economic liberalism 23
economic rationality 132
economic survival 156
economy of attention 84, 154
effects theory tradition 57
'effects' tradition 9
egocentric attitudes 21
Elsaesser, T. 8, 60
emotions/emotional: bonds 151; intersection of 9; labour 110, 122, 153, 156; overwhelming of 67; realism 40, 72, 155–156
empirical realism 8, 40
encoding/decoding model 57–58
Engels, F. 37
episodic sexuality 9
eros 18–22, 33, 35–36; expressions of 19–20; importance of 20
escapism 7, 43, 64, 108
ethnographies of audience 58
Evans, P. 107, 133

false consciousness 37–38, 55, 65
fantasy 106; notions of 64; realm of 107
Faris, A. 96
female 54; characters 144; cinema-going 43; purity 96–99; sexuality 61, 98, 153–154; subjectivity, problem of 60–61
feminine/feminism 128, 144–145; fixation of 144–145; genre 64; literary 65; masculinity 9, 158; struggles of 97
film 7; accretion and elimination of 4; audiences 8–10; contemporary romantic practices 7; as 'dispersible text' 69; elements in 8; emotional realism of 119; festival 72–73; gender roles in 9; gross misreading of 141; ideology,

mystification of 42; language of 4; narrative and personal investment in 150; 'reality effect' of 119; romantic love in 7–8; symbolic elements in 150; textual analysis of 4; theory 54
Fisher, H. 94
Fiske, J. 69
(500) Days of Summer 4, 6, 9, 127–129, 134, 149, 157–158
focus groups 5, 11, 68, 77, 83, 128
Foucault, M. 57
Freud, S. 19, 25
friendship 62–63, 137, 157; female 108; male 63; romances 61; same-sex 63
Fromm, E. 20–22
frustration 26, 84, 87, 89, 99–100, 106, 114, 120–121, 152

game, classed rules of 120–125
gender 7, 35, 41 *see also* female; women; hegemonic ideologies 58; ideological naturalisation of 53; inequality 153; intersection of 9; relationship 43, 117
gender roles 29–30, 116; ideologies of 9; patriarchal ideology of 41
Gennep, A. van 40–41
genre 56; approaches to 56; characteristics of 59; combination of 56; features of 96; gender separation in 146; romantic 62
getaway romance, readings of 115
Giddens, A. 32–33, 35, 107, 133–134, 155; problem with pure relationship 33–34
Gledhill, C. 59–60, 117
globalisation 57; platonic love in 114–118
Gordon-Levitt, J. 85
Gottlieb, S. 22
Gramsci, A. 7, 39, 146
gratification 25
'Great Other' of transcendence 24
grief 137
Gripsrud, J. 53
Grossi, R. 29
group interviews 4–5, 111, 122

Hall, S. 57
Hardt, M. 24–26
Harlow, H. 17
harmony 17
hegemonic masculinity 141, 158
hegemony, characteristic of 39

Her (2013) 91, 127
heterogeneity 44
heterosexual/heterosexuality: desire, vitality of 157–158; ideas of 29; love 17; marriage 62; and monogamy 96–97; relationship 128, 158; romance 4; sensitivity 140
Hollywood 43, 60, 63, 69, 104–105, 116, 132, 136, 157; hegemonic discourse of 61
homophilia 63, 158
homophobia 63, 146, 158
human frailty 130
human groups, social/kinship construction of 94
Hutchby, I 90
hysteria 21, 60

identification 43; audiences 8–10; pleasures of 37
ideological resistance 65
ideological state apparatuses (ISAs) 38
ideology 40–44, 150; concept of 37; elaboration of 37; liminality and 40–44; role of 40; theories of 39–40
Iglesias-Prieto, N. 70
Illouz, E. 7, 27, 34–35, 42, 117, 123–124
illusion of reality 55, 57
imaginary love triangle 97
immanence *vs.* transcendence 28
incorporation/resistance paradigm 57–59
individual interviews 4–5
individualisation 31–32
individual subjectivities 90
industrialised rituals 41
institution dates 31
intensity 115
international cinema 2
interpellation 38
interpersonal associations 36
interpersonal interpenetrations 32
intersubjective subjectivity 20
intimacy 4, 6, 33, 88–89, 92, 153, 156, 159; codification of 32; contemporary 32–34, 98, 145; dialogical 89; discourse of 92, 110, 113; idea of 110; incursion of 146; individualised nature of 33; and relationships 82; transformation of 30
Irigaray, L. 29
ISAs *see* ideological state apparatuses (ISAs)

Johansson, S. 85–86
Johnson, P. 92–93

Jónasdóttir, A. 29
Jonze, S. 91
Juan, D. 36

Kaplan, E. A. 116
Kipnis, L. 159–160
Klesse, C. 93
Kristeva, J. 21
Krutnik, F. 8, 133
Kuhn, A. 43–44, 55, 64

Laplace, M. 60
Lasch, C. 23
Lash, S. 35
Lee, J. A. 18, 35–36
Lévi-Strauss, C. 35
LGBTQ romances 4
libidinal subjectivity 20
life: creation and preservation of 19–20; necessity of 20; *vs.* spirit 27–28
liminality 40–44; and liminoid 42
literary literature 18
literary traditions 2
literature: literary 18; on melodrama 59; religious 18
Livingstone, S. 66
logos 8, 20
longevity 82, 115
love 6, 81–83, 129–130, 134, 144–145, 159; ambivalence of 36–37; in capitalist society 22; cautiously optimistic about 27; codification of 32; commodification of 10, 83–87; commoditisation of 154–155; conceptualisation of 24, 26, 29; constructions of 7; contemporary sociological approaches to 32–34; discourses of 19, 61, 156; elements of 21; figures of 153; in films 2; fractures of 135–136; hermeneutics of 17; heterosexist ideology of 29; hierarchy of 19, 26; ideological thought on 22; intersectional experience of 118, 156; intimate subject 87–90; invasion of 23; long-standing criticism of 155; Luhmann's view of 32; mature 21; narcissistic 21; normal ideology of 27; numbers and female purity 96–99; pessimistic outlook on 23; philosophy of 2–4; pleasure of 34; politics of 24–26; power of 23–24, 112; practice of 7; religious sublimation of 24; romantic affordances 90–96; schemes of 18; studio for 118–120; styles 17–18, 35;

triadic structure of 31; types of 21, 26, 35–36; vision of 19
Love as Passion: The Codification of Intimacy (Luhmann) 32
Love in the Western World (Rougemont) 30
Loving with a Vengeance: Mass-Produced Fantasies for Women (Modleski) 54
ludus 18, 35–36
Luhmann, N. 32

macho-masculinity 141
Madriz, E. 83
mania 18, 35–36
manic behaviour 114
Marcuse, H. 20, 22
marginalisation of female 145
marriage 144–145; attitudes towards 131–132; crisis of 64, 135, 157; free choice in 31; goal of 157; hegemonic desirability of 63; heterosexual relationships in 63; nature of 31; patriarchal ideology of 122; views on 31
married life, routine and duty of 33
Marxism 38–39
Marx, Karl 37
masculinity 82, 128, 140–147, 157–158; active 139; British 3; contestation of 10; definitions of 140; feminised 142; forms of 1; hegemonic position of 158; portrayal of 158; re-evaluation of 62; representation of 156
masochism 140; nonphallic sexuality of 140
masochistic aesthetic 139
maternal love 17
mature love 21
Mayne, J. 53–54
media 64
melodrama 8, 56, 67, 128, 144; classic Hollywood 61; history of 9; literature on 59; popularity of 8; scholars on 8; straight 67; themes 60
memory, pain of 129
Metz, C. 38, 56
middle-class ethos 117
middle-class pathos 123
misogyny 158
modernity 128
Modleski, T. 54; model dichotomy of 54–55
monogamy 9, 29, 92, 95–96; compulsory 92–93
monolithic ideology 36
Moore, J. 87–88

Morin, E. 36
Morley, D. 58
motherhood 98, 116–117, 122
multi-directional relationship 72
Mulvey, L. 53
music/musician 3, 7–8, 105, 107, 112, 117, 119, 128, 137; financial instability of 7
Mussell, K. 55

Nakassis, C. 72
narcissism 21; love 21–22; primary/normal 21; rampant 23; secondary 21
narrative cinema 57
narrow love 23
Nationwide (Morley) 58
Neale, S. 8
negotiated cynics 66
negotiated romantics 66
Negri, A. 24–26
nervous romances 61, 132–133, 139
'new audience research' tradition 68–69
new romances 61
normal femininity, version of 27
'not-meant-to-work' romances 106–109

object 21
Once (Carney) 7, 9, 104, 118, 127, 155–157; platonic nature of romance 121–122; production and characteristics of 105–106; putative transgressive 124
online dating 9, 84–88, 154–155; landscape of 154; sites 83
online romantic activities 153–154
oppression 20
Ortega y Gasset, J. 42

Parameswaran, R. 83
parents 2
paternal love 17
pathos 8; middle-class 123
patriarchal demands 99
patriarchal ideology 27, 40, 64–65
patriarchal marriage, structures of 66
Pearce, L. 27
peer interaction 5
peer love 17
Plato 19–24
platonic love 19; in globalisation 114–118
Platonism 30
pleasure 7, 150; politics of 66–67
political control, forms of 39
politics of love 7
polyamorous relationships 94

polyamory 3, 92–93
polygamy, anthropological term of 94
popular culture 30; incursion of feminism into 62
pornography 85; romantic films and 87
post-classical romantic comedies 144
potentiality, recognition of 131
potential lovers 87
Potter, C. 36
Povinelli, E. 117
power distribution asymmetries 65
power relationships 83
pragma 18, 35–36
pragmatism 143
privatisation of desire 31–32
professional development 156
projective identification 36–37, 134
psychoanalysis 18, 31
pure relationship 33–34, 112, 114

queer theory, evolutionary biology to 9
queer, visibility of 129

race 41, 152–154
Radway, J. 27, 139
Rappert, B. 90
rationality of gratification 20
realism 81, 106–109, 150
realistic romances 108
reality effect 8
recycling 22
relationship 2, 4, 6, 62, 128–130, 134, 143, 153, 159; attitudes towards 131–132; caregiving within 30; commonality of 109; environment of 135; erosion of 130; expectations of 135; finitude 130; fractures of 135–136; gendered 109, 117, 127; labour 92; nature of 109; normative aspect of 135; pure 112; in romantic film 3, 137; rule of three in 97; through contemporary romantic practices 7; twoness of 29
religion/religious 35, 98, 120, 152, 154; literature 18; marriage 98
repression, reality principle of 20
respect 21
responsibility 21
Roland Barthes' concept 6
romance/romantic 81; academic studies of 55; actors, rationalisation of 90; affordances 9, 82, 90–96, 106, 108, 143, 154; agency 117; anxiety 157; behaviour 27; characters of 109–114, 138–139; de-sexualisation of 117; discourses of 109–114, 122; drama 109; endeavours, pressure for 90; ethos 120–121; experiences 111–112, 115–116, 123; films 8; genre 62; hegemonic script of 7; ideal and failed 65; idealisation of 143; identities 35–36, 94, 154; ideologies of 7; imagination 68; intention 124; liaisons, foundation for 10; narrative 104–105, 119; non-conduciveness for 123; practice 68; romanticisation of commodities 83–87; teleology of 156–157; time 42; working-class 114
romantic comedies 106–107, 140, 144, 146; Apatow-style of 145; bromance subgenre of 63; history of 61–62; melodramatic elements in 144; popularity of 61; re-affirmative character of 134; Rowe's analysis of shift in 145; traditional teleology of 129
romantic films 3, 60–61, 95, 138, 157; audiences of 2, 69; male characters in 138; relationships to 3; resilience of 8; teleology of 132–133; verisimilitude in 118
romantic love 9, 18, 22, 29, 32–33, 96, 112–113, 130, 133–135, 143, 153; ambiguity of 41; approaches to 18; cinematic representations of 159; commonplace in 152; critical engagement with 25; critiques of 27; cultural symbols and practices of 3; cultures of 98; descriptions 4; discourses of 10, 63, 84, 156, 159; elements of 32; environment of 135; failure of 130; in film and audiences 7–8; forms of 61; foundational myth of 30–32; fragile nature of 129; genre of 81; hegemonic commoditisation of 159; hierarchies of 28; history of 7; idealisation of 61, 141, 159; ideals and practices of 3; individualised nature of 33; interconnection between 127; Marxist feminist conceptualisation of 151; media narratives of 87; neoliberal logics on 155; outlook on 25; politics of 41; positioning of 37; reception and articulation of 68; representations of 3–4, 8, 72, 158–159; role of 28; thematic and discursive analysis of 5; theorisation and understanding of 67–68; triadic structure of 31; trope of 16
romantic relationships 18, 27, 33, 94–95, 111, 115, 132; egalitarian modes of 27; forms of 136; reality on 108; transformation of 30
Romeo and Juliet 157
Rougemont, Denis. de 30–32

Index

Roulston, K. 5
Rowe, K. 144
rural areas 120, 152, 159

same-sex friendship 63
same-sex relationships 3
scene 8
Screen theory 9, 53, 55
Seiter, E. 54–55
self: commoditisation of 154–155; hegemonic commoditisation of 159
self-abnegation 27
self-centred romanticism 121
self-commoditised love 34–35
self-conscious romances 61
self-development 33
self-love 21, 26
Sennett, R. 23
sex comedies 61
sexualities/sexual 35, 153; behaviour 27, 97; intercourse 85; orientation 96; partners 98; violence 153
Shohat, E. 42
Shumway, D. 3, 36, 41, 61, 63, 88, 146
singlehood 132, 137, 151–152
single lover 135
Snitow, A. B. 55, 64–65
social bond love 25
socialisation 17
social mobility 112, 114
society: dissolution of 31; principle of 20
socioeconomic context 104–105
Something Borrowed (Greenfield) 7
special relationship 134
spectatorship 38; female 54; modes of 53; monolithic view of 55
spirit, life *vs.* 27–28
spontaneous date 123
Stacey, J. 27, 43
Staiger, J. 43
Stam, R. 42
Star Gazing: Hollywood Cinema and Female Spectatorship (Stacey) 43
storge 18, 35–36
subject–object relationships 29

subject–subject relationships 29
suspension of disbelief 8

Tamil cinema 72
technology 6, 9, 81–83, 151; commodified love, commodified subject 83–87; intimate subject 87–90; numbers and female purity 96–99; romantic affordances 90–96
television, audiences of 67–68
telluric love 23
text–reader relationship 43
textual processes 53
Todorov, Tzvetan 56
traditional intellectuals 39
transcendence: 'Great Other' of 24; immanence *vs.* 28; level of 23
'transcending' genders 144
true intimacy 86; acknowledgement of 88
true love 23
Turner, Victor 40–41

uncertainty 10, 90; degree of 130
utopian thinking 37

verisimilitude 57, 108; lack of 119; notions of 64; in romantic film 118
viewing strategy 8–9
virtuous sex 93
visualisation 16
visual utopia 83
Voirol, O. 83, 154–155

Walkman, S. 58
Watts, A. 91
Western romance novels 83
Wilkinson, E. 26
Wombly, Theodore 91
women: films and melodrama to bromance 59–64; films, history of 9; love power 29; pornography for 64–65; ways of knowing 82–83
working-class romances 9, 114

youthful romanticism 124